Open Road's

Paris with Kids

by Valerie Gwinner

4th Revised Edition

Open Road Family Travel Guides

"Our family is similar to the authors: Franco-American, two kids (also boys) and a love of Paris. We thought we knew everything there was to know about Paris with kids, but this book taught us a wealth of new material, revealing an entire "new" city. If it could teach these old Paris hands a thing or two, just think what families new to Paris will learn. This book has a great mix of facts, fun, frivolity and fascination scattered throughout its pages, and is all you really need for a well-rounded trip to the City of Light. Buy it, pack it, and go!" – *Amazon.com review*

Open Road Publishing

Open Road's family travel guides cut to the chase. You don't need a huge travel encyclopedia – you need a *selective guide* to steer you right. If you're going on vacation for a few weeks or less, get a guide that brings you the *best* of any destination for the amount of time you *really* have for your trip!

Open Road – the guide you need for the trip you want.

Open Road Family Travel Guides
Right to the point
Uncluttered
Easy

Open Road Publishing
www.openroadguides.com

Text Copyright©2015 by Valerie Gwinner
- All Rights Reserved -
ISBN 13: 978-1-59360-200-0
Library of Congress Control No. 2015936434
Maps by Andy Herbach

About the Author
Valerie Gwinner is also the author of *Open Road's London with Kids*.

Acknowledgments
For their tips and moral support. my sincere thanks go to Kevin Reese and Mary Hall Surface, Brian and Deborah Howes, Mark Haskell and Elise Stork, Susan Campbell and Mark Pugliese, Charlie and Sue Calhoun, Victoria and Dale Pedrick, Karen Kuhlke and Suman Beros, Pam Roos, Zack Sorensen, Pernette Lezine, Camille and Fernand Beaucour – and to my mother, Anta Montet White.

For photo credits turn to page 215.

CONTENTS

Maps

Open Road's

PARIS WITH KIDS

1. INTRODUCTION

You're going to Paris? And taking the kids!!?

We heard this over and over when we first took our young children to Paris. For many people, a trip to Paris conjures images of beauty and romance, not strollers and diaper bags. It is a place for misty sunsets over the Seine, couples kissing under the chestnut trees, and lazy hours on café terraces.

Yes, Paris is all those things. However, what many people don't realize is that Paris is also the capital of one of the most kid-friendly nations in the world. France has prenatal care, parental leave, and child care policies that are the envy of most other industrialized countries. The country's education budget surpasses its budget for national defense. Very simply, children are a priority in France – and it shows. It shows in the quality and creativity of the local playgrounds. It shows in the fact that every major museum and monument in Paris caters to children with special activities and workshops. It shows in the care that goes into products that are

designed for children, whether it's books, clothing, or toys.

Even French food, a source of great national pride, caters to kids. Children in France are not just small people – they are gourmets-in-training. Thus you have cooking classes for kids at the Ritz Hotel, special children's menus in major restaurants, and jars of baby food

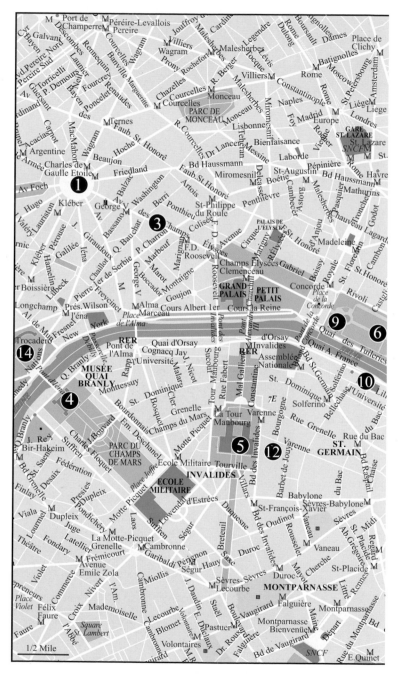

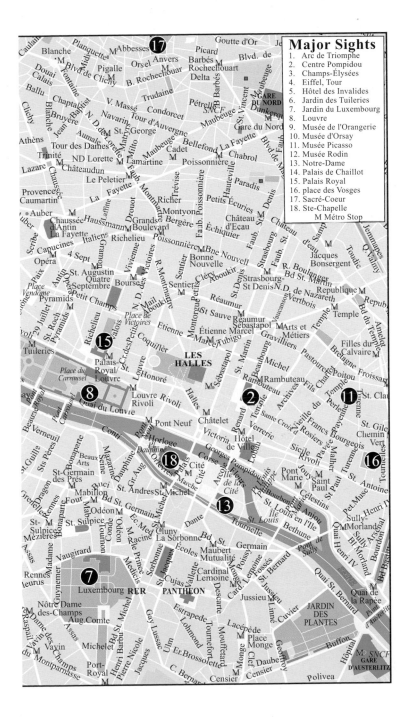

Major Sights
1. Arc de Triomphe
2. Centre Pompidou
3. Champs-Élysées
4. Eiffel, Tour
5. Hôtel des Invalides
6. Jardin des Tuileries
7. Jardin du Luxembourg
8. Louvre
9. Musée de l'Orangerie
10. Musée d'Orsay
11. Musée Picasso
12. Musée Rodin
13. Notre-Dame
14. Palais de Chaillot
15. Palais Royal
16. place des Vosges
17. Sacré-Coeur
18. Ste-Chapelle
M Métro Stop

baby food at your local grocery store that feature choices such as sole meunière and canard à l'orange.

Paris offers a seemingly unlimited supply of activities and wonders for visitors of all ages – and many opportunities for reconciling the interests of adults and children. Admire Nôtre Dame Cathedral and have your kids hunt for their favorite gargoyles. Search for the Secret of the Sorcerer's Stone together through the historic Marais neighborhood. Enjoy the serene beauty of the Luxembourg gardens as your children play with miniature sailboats in the central fountain. Take the stairs down the Eiffel Tower and check out the view from the inside of the structure. Run a rat through a maze at the Palais de la Découverte science museum. Look for the Phantom's traces on a tour of the Paris Opera house. Go to the horse races in the Bois de Boulogne. Admire Monet's Water Lilies like the storybook character Linnea. View some of Paris' greatest buildings, bridges, and monuments from a bâteau mouche tour boat. Enjoy scoops of Berthillon ice cream on the Ile Saint Louis. Go on a candlelit tour of the Vaux le Vicomte Palace. Have lunch in a café under the chestnut trees of the Tuileries Park while your children go on a pony ride (see photo below). See a magic show at the Musée de la Magie. Take a family bike ride along the canals of the Versailles Palace gardens. Discover the underground labyrinth of Paris' Catacombs.

These are just some of the adventures that await you. Many more are described in the pages of this book. You'll also find kid-friendly strategies for visiting museums and monuments. There are recommendations for family-friendly hotels and restaurants, tips on where to enjoy a light meal or snack, as well as historical facts, legends, and anecdotes to bring the stories of Paris to life for kids and adults.

So what are you waiting for? Isn't it time you discovered Paris – with kids?

2. OVERVIEW

See It As a Great Adventure

Discovering a new place and culture with your children can be highly rewarding and supply family memories that last a lifetime. It's a chance to connect with each other without the distractions of home. It's also an opportunity to try new things that you might be embarrassed to do at home. For example, my first and only archery experience took place during a Medieval Festival in a French château. The boys talked me into it, and they were more than pleased when I managed to hit the bull's eye in front of a cheering crowd. If that's not reason enough to pack up the family bags, here are a few more:

• Children bring new perspectives to your travels. They see the world from a different angle. Kids point out details we might miss, such as how the Coca Cola tastes different, the sidewalks are wider, or that there are more mopeds and motorcycles than at home.

• Kids take you places you might otherwise skip, but secretly enjoy: for example, to the top floor of the Eiffel Tower, onto that old-fashioned carrousel, or into the Museum of Magic.

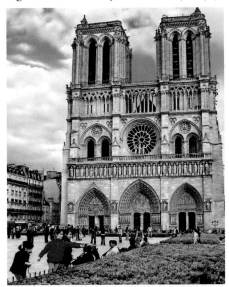

• Traveling with kids helps break down cultural barriers. It gives you something in common with other parents and brings out the kid-lovers in people who don't have children of their own.

• Traveling with children reminds us that it's okay to slow down. Enjoy the city at a human pace.

Take an afternoon nap. Have a leisurely café au lait while the kids quietly play in the hotel room. Spend some time watching the world go by from a park bench or café terrace. After all, you're on vacation.

Involve Your Kids

Children will be much more enthusiastic about traveling to Paris if you give them a role in the planning process – remember it's their trip, too. Even small kids can feel like they are part of the action if you include them in some background research. One of the best methods with young children is to introduce them to Paris ahead of time with books and videos that feature the city. It gives them a taste of what is ahead and things to look forward to. With small children, you can bring along the Madeleine books by Ludwig Bemelmans or Eloise in Paris by Kay Thompson and see how many places they recognize from the illustrations. In this guidebook we also highlight visits based on the story Linnea in Monet's Garden by Christina Bjork and Lena Anderson, the book/film of The Red Balloon by Albert Lamorisse, and the character Nicolas Flamel from the first Harry Potter volume.

If your children are older, encourage them to help plan your itinerary. You don't have to build your entire trip around their ideas, but you can give them a chance to pick their top choices. Cater to their interests. For example:

• Is your daughter a fashion slave? Take her to a (free) fashion show at the Galeries Lafayette Department Store. Follow up with a snack or meal in one of the store's many amazing eateries.
• Any Harry Potter fans in your group? Follow the footsteps of Nicolas Flamel, discoverer of the Sorceror's Stone
• Is your child a budding scientist? Spend a morning in the Cité des Sciences at La Villette. Take a break in the park's wonderful playgrounds, then embark on a canal boat tour for a unique ride through the locks.
• Do your kids like boats? Take them to the Maritime Museum to see full-sized historic ones, and then make your way to the Tuileries or Luxembourg Gardens, where you can rent miniature sailboats to float in the central fountains.

Balance Everyone's Desires

The secret to a successful family trip is to find ways to have something for everyone. If you build your whole trip around your children's desires, you will come home exhausted and frustrated. Similarly you can't expect a child to love Paris if he or she is made to sit through too many two-hour meals, wait for you to try on clothes in one store after another, or visit endless museums at a crawling pace. Paris is dotted with wonderful parks and playgrounds, pastry shops, and fun boutiques that spark kids' imaginations. It's easy to intersperse these with visits to museums, monuments, or other sights. Kids also love riding on a double-decker bus, taking a boat tour, or enjoying views from high places, so build these into your sightseeing plans.

Make Museums Fun

Few of us, kids or adults, can bear dragging ourselves through every room of a museum at a snail's pace. However, that doesn't mean museums can't be fun. Here are a few ideas:

• Go on a treasure hunt. You can let your kids choose some favorite post cards at the gift shop before your tour, and have them search for the objects they represent during the visit. You can also pick favorite themes, such as animals, dancers, or depictions of children, and hunt for these as you explore the museum.
• Pick up the free kids' booklets offered in most Parisian museums. They feature games and explanations. Although they are in French, kids can still enjoy the pictures, mazes, and other activities.
• Give your kids a lesson in navigation by handing them a copy of the museum's map (distributed for free at the entrance) and following their lead.
• Rent audioguides (available in English versions in many museums for a small fee) for your kids. They appeal to kids' natural love of gadgets and let them enjoy a private tour at their own pace.
• Cater to kids' interests. Paris has wonderful museums specializing in dolls, magic, science, fashion, ships, models, weapons and armor, animals, history, giant crystals, and more.
• Play "pick your favorite." Encourage your kids to choose which paintings, pieces of furniture, or objects they would put in their room if they could. Which armor would they wear if they were a knight? Which Greek god would they want to be? Which room would they want to sleep in if this was their mansion?
• Go for gore. Really! Kids are fascinated by tales of guillotines, monsters, martyrs, stranded sailors, and the like. You will find plenty of examples of these in paintings and historical objects in many Paris museums.
• Play a pretend round of Clue or another imaginary game. When visiting a museum that is housed in a mansion or palace (as many are), have your kids imagine in which room a crime would be committed, against whom, and with what weapon. Or have kids invent their own game based on favorite TV characters, video games, or collectors' cards.

• Surf online before you go. The major Parisian museums have websites that your kids can browse to pick out what they'd like to see.
• Take a break during your visit. Most Parisian museums have lovely cafés where you can refuel and rest weary feet.
• Divide and conquer. Split up. Let one adult have a few hours of culture while the rest of the group goes on a boat tour, plays in a park, or does some shopping.

The Demography & Geography of Paris

More than 2 million people live in the city of Paris, more densely populated than any other city in the developed world. For example, there are about twice as many people per square mile in Paris than in Tokyo, three times more than in London, and 2.5 times more than in New York.

Paris is divided into 20 city districts known as arrondissements. The first arrondissement is located in the center of the city, near Les Halles, and the numbers radiate out following the pattern of a snail shell. The 1st, 2nd, 3rd, and 4th arrondissements are on the Right Bank of the Seine River. The 5th, 6th, and 7th are on the Left Bank. The 8th, 9th, 10th, 11th, and 12th form a second tier of districts on the Right Bank. The 13th, 14th, and 15th make up a second tier on the Left Bank. Finally, the 16th, 17th, 18th, 19th, and 20th, constitute a third tier of arrondissements on the

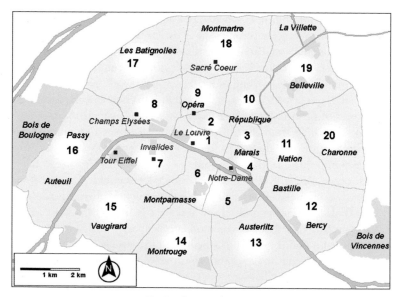

Paris Arrondissements

Right Bank. Mailing addresses for Paris will start with the number 75 for Paris. The last two digits of the postal code indicate the arrondissement. Thus 75005 indicates an address in the 5th arrondissement and 75016 is in the 16th arrondissement.

Here are some of the sights you'll find in each arrondissement:

1st: Les Halles, Louvre, Place Vendome, Tuileries

2nd: Opéra Garnier, Place des Victoires, Galerie Vivienne, Passage des Panoramas

3rd: Marais, including Pompidou Center, Musée Carnavalet, Musée Picasso, Musée des Arts et Metiers, Nicholas Flamel's House

4th: Nôtre Dame and Ile de la Cité, Ile Saint Louis, Marais, including Jewish neighborhood and Place des Vôsges

5th: Latin Quarter, including Boulevard Saint Michel, Sorbonne, Cluny Museum, Rue Mouffetard, Jardin des Plantes, Natural History Museums, Paris Mosque, Arènes de Lutèce (Roman Arena)

6th: Saint Germain neighborhood, Luxembourg Gardens, Saint Sulpice

7th: Invalides, Musée Rodin, Musée d'Orsay, Eiffel Tower

8th: Arc de Triomphe, Champs Elysées, Grand Palais, Palais de la Découverte, Parc Monceau, Place de la Concorde, Gare Saint Lazare, Rue du Faubourg Saint Honoré Luxury Shops.

9th: Grands Magazins (Haussman Department Stores), Passage Jouffroy, Passage Véro Dôdat

10th: Gard du Nord, Gare de l'Est, Canal Saint Martin

11th: Bastille neighborhood

12th: Saint Antoine neighborhood, Viaduct des Arts, Promenade Plantée, Gare de Lyon, Bercy neighborhood and gardens, Bois de Vincennes

13th: Les Gobelins, Butte aux Cailles, Chinatown, Gare d'Austerlitz

14th: Montparnasse neighborhood, Gare Montparnasse, Catacombs, Parc Montsouris, Rue d'Alésia discount clothing stores

15th: Parc André Citroën, Parc Georges Brassens, Aquaboulevard (Water Park)

16th: Trocadéro, Maritime Museum, Paris Aquarium, Museum of Monuments and Architecture, Balzac's House, Passy Cemetary, Musée de la Mode et du Costume (Fashion Museum), Musée Marmottan, Bois de Boulogne, Jardin d'Acclimatation

17th: Residential

18th: Montmartre neighborhood

19th: Parc de La Villette, Cité des Sciences (Science Museum), Parc des Buttes Chaumont

20th: Belleville neighborhood, Père Lachaise Cemetery

3. THE ISLANDS

Ile de la Cité

The Point Zéro, from which all distances to Paris are measured, is located on the Ile de la Cité. This is only fitting since this City Island (originally a cluster of smaller islands) is where the first inhabitants of Paris settled in about 250 BC. When the Romans took over in 50 BC, they expanded the city (then known as Lutetia) across the Seine River to the south, in the section now known as the Latin Quarter. But Ile de la Cité remained the political, judicial, and religious center of the city. It housed both the Temple of Jupiter, in honor of the most important of the Roman gods, and the Roman Governor's Palace.

During the medieval period, the Temple of Jupiter was replaced with a small Christian church and later with the great Nôtre Dame Cathedral. The Roman Governor's Palace was rebuilt as a Royal Palace. One wing, known as the Concièrgerie, was later turned into a prison. This is where Queen Marie Antoinette was held before she was guillotined.

NÔTRE DAME CATHEDRAL, *Place du Parvis de Nôtre Dame, on Ile de la Cité (Metro: Cité or Saint Michel-Nôtre Dame). Open daily, 8 am-6 pm. Entrance to the cathedral is free. The Tower visit is open daily 9 am to 6:30 pm (Apr-Sep) and 10 am to 5:30 pm (Oct-Mar). Entrance on the left as you face the cathedral. Adults: €7.50; Kids: free. To avoid long lines, plan on climbing up the towers when they first open or later in the afternoon, when crowds are thinner.* **Note***: As of January 2015, some parts of the tower visit are closed due to construction.*

Nôtre Dame Cathedral is truly the city's great lady, where some of Paris' most joyful or solemn moments have been celebrated. It was here that Napoleon crowned himself Emperor and that funeral services were held for Victor Hugo and Charles de Gaulle. Nôtre Dame was also the sight of joyous masses to celebrate the ends of both world wars.

Work on Nôtre Dame began in 1163 and took nearly 200 years to complete. The cathedral was built in the Gothic style, recognizable for its high walls, peaked arches, flamboyant decorations, and stained glass windows that seem to reach to the sky. Another telltale sign of a Gothic cathedral is the presence of flying buttresses, those elegant arcs that help carry the weight of the stone roof and walls.

Kids will enjoy yet another classic feature of Gothic architecture – the gargoyles. But here's something you should know. Real gargoyles have to be able to gurgle. True gargoyles are actually part of the roof's drainage system. When it rains, they collect water from the gutters and spew it out away from the building to protect the walls and windows from water damage. Those other monstrous sculptures, often depicted as gargoyles in movies and comics, are just decorative statues known as grotesques. See if your kids can spot the difference. Both serve a common purpose: to warn passers-by of the scary fate that awaits them if they lead a sinful life.

If you want to see the gargoyles and grotesques up close, you should climb the 386 steps to the top of the north tower. You'll get to seem them up close, and you'll enjoy one of the best views of Paris around. The visit takes you up the north tower, across the balconies and rooftops and down through the south tower. Before you descend, check out the enormous bell that hangs in the south tower. It is called Emmanuel (yes, big bells have names) and weighs 13 tons. It takes 8 people to ring the bell by hand. The Emmanuel bell rings a perfect F sharp. It was the first bell in the city to

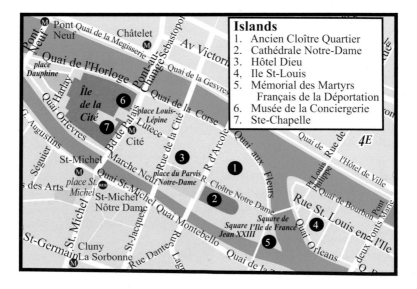

announce the end of World War I as well as the Liberation of Paris in World War II. Today it is only rung to celebrate big events or holidays.

The façade of Nôtre Dame has three entrances. The left doorway is dedicated to Mary, the mother of Jesus. The middle one represents the last judgment. The doorway on the right is dedicated to Saint Anne, the mother of Mary. Notice all the statues and sculptures. Did you know that, originally, they were all painted in bright colors (even the gargoyles)? Besides being decorations, these works served a practical function. In medieval times, most people were illiterate, but they did know the stories of the bible. They could thus "read" the illustrations and moral lessons depicted in the church's statues, carvings, and stained glass windows.

Ile de la Cité Highlights

- Find the Point Zero
- Hunt for gargoyles at Nôtre Dame Cathedral
- Go underground into the Crypte Archéologique
- Visit Marie Antoinette's prison cell and others at the Concièrgerie
- See the spectacular stained windows at the Sainte Chapelle
- Visit the Sunday Bird Market on the Place Louis Lepine
- Take a boat ride on a Bâteau Mouche
- See the Pont Neuf and Place Dauphine
- Spend a moment of contemplation at the Deportation Memorial

Inside Nôtre Dame there are spectacular stained glass windows, particularly the three round rose windows. The largest of these, above the front entrance, depicts Mary and the Infant Jesus flanked by two angels. The north rose window in the transept dates from the 13th century. It depicts the Virgin Mary surrounded by figures from the Old Testament. The south window, dating from the 14th century, depicts Christ surrounded by angels and saints. If you walk around the choir (the U-shaped area behind the altar), you can see 14th century wooden sculptures representing stories from the life of Jesus. Notice the organ. Built in 1730, it has nearly 8,000 pipes and 5 keyboards. There are free organ concerts on Sunday afternoons.

The cathedral can seat 6,000 people. It fills up for major holidays, funerals, or big events. On Christmas Eve, entrance is restricted to members of the parish and special guests.

Before we leave this magnificent cathedral, here's one more item of interest: More than 12 million people visit Nôtre Dame each year, but some of its most regular visitors are not people. They are birds, known as kestrels or sparrow hawks. Pairs of these birds nest in high perches above the gargoyles each year. Bird watchers gather behind the cathedral every June to watch the birds feed their newly-hatched chicks.

PARVIS DE NÔTRE DAME. The large esplanade in front of Nôtre Dame is known as the Parvis. If you look carefully on the pavement in front of the main entrance, you will find the brass marker that indicates the Point Zero. Here you can really say that you are in the center of Paris. It is the point from which all distances to the city are measured. You'll also notice lines on the pavement that delineate old streets and buildings. In medieval days, the Parvis was much smaller than it is today, and it was crowded with street vendors, musicians, jugglers, and even dancing bears. Wooden steps, like bleachers, have been erected on the Parvis, affording great views of the cathedral's façade.

Notice the statue of a man on a horse on the Parvis (toward the right as you face the cathedral)? It depicts Charlemagne, a great French king, who ultimately became Holy Roman Emperor in the year 800. He ruled over an area that stretched across France, Germany, Switzerland, Holland, Belgium, and most of Italy. Charlemagne had five wives, and encouraged trade, literature, and education even though he himself never learned to read or write.

The Parvis pavement also covers a wealth of Paris history that you can discover in the **CRYPTE ARCHEOLOGIQUE.** *Place du Parvis de Nôtre Dame (Metro: Cité) Open 10am-6pm. Closed Mondays. Adults: €6; Youth: €4.50; Kids under 14: free. Audioguides: €3.*

This is an interesting tour for any budding archeologist or explorer. The visit takes place underground, past ruins spanning 16 centuries.

SQUARE JEAN XXIII. This small park is located behind Nôtre Dame Cathedral. Here you can find plenty of shade, benches, and room for children to run. There are also water fountains to quench your thirst or clean off sticky fingers. It's a great place to stop for a snack. You can pick up food at one of the shops lining the cathedral (north side) or cross the pedestrian bridge to Ile Saint Louis where you can get some of the city's best ice cream cones.

MEMORIAL TO THE DEPORTATION. *Located across the small street from the Square Jean XXIII. Open 10am-5pm (winter), 10am-7pm (summer). Closed Mondays. Adults and Kids: Free. Note: Closed for repairs until May 2015.*

Touching in its simplicity, this memorial begins with a narrow staircase that takes you to a triangular courtyard. From there you enter a small chamber lit with hundreds of thousands of lights. These represent the men, women, and children of France deported to Nazi prison and concentration camps during World War II. Two small galleries hold urns that contain soil and ash from each of the concentration camps. Their names are inscribed on the walls. An eternal flame lights a tomb to the unknown deportee.

SAINTE CHAPELLE. *4, Boulevard du Palais. Metro: Cité. Open daily, 9:30am-6pm (Mar-Oct), 9:30am-5pm (Nov-Feb). Ticket sales stop 1/2 hour before closing time. Adults: €8.50; Kids under 18: free if accompanied by an adult. You can purchase a combined ticket for both the Sainte Chapelle and Concièrgerie. Adults: €12.50; Kids under 18: free. A free description of the stained glass windows is available in English. Audioguides are €4.50 and €3.50 for kids.*

Parent Tip: If you think that you will only be able to drag your child inside one church in Paris, the Sainte Chapelle is the one to see. The first view of the stained glass windows will surprise even the most reluctant visitor, especially on a sunny day. ❖

The Sainte Chapelle (Holy Chapel) was built in the 13th century by France's most zealously religious king, Louis IX (also known as Saint Louis). Saint Louis hired the same architect who had designed the plans for Nôtre Dame Cathedral. However, while it took 200 years to finish Notre Dame, the Sainte Chapelle was built in only seven years.

The Sainte Chapelle actually contains two parts: an upper chapel and a lower one. The lower chapel is more somber, but has a beautiful painted ceiling of golden fleur-de-lys against a royal blue background. It looks like a star-filled sky. The walls are also painted, as were those in most churches. On the floor are large engraved slabs of stone that cover tombs from the 14th and 15th centuries. Some children will enjoy their almost comic-book quality.

A small, spiral staircase leads to the upper chapel. This was the part reserved for the royal family and high officers. Unlike the lower chapel, the ceiling of this one seems to reach to the sky. The stained glass windows are spectacular. They are 15 meters (nearly 50 feet) high, and most contain their original 13th century glass. They are the oldest stained glass windows in Paris. The windows depict stories from the Old Testament and from the life of Jesus. The chronology progresses from left to right, and from bottom to top in each window.

CONCIERGERIE. *1, Quai de l'Horloge. Metro: Cité. Open daily, 9am-6pm. Adults: €8.50; Kids under 18: free if accompanied by an adult. You can purchase a combined ticket for both the Sainte Chapelle and Concièrgerie. Adults: €12.50; Kids under 18: free. Ticket sales stop ½ hour before closing.*
This was originally part of a royal palace, but it was turned into a prison in the 14th century. Poor prisoners were put in cells called paillasses that were dirty, crowded, and lined with hay. Those who could afford it paid rent for better prison cells with furniture and more privacy.

The Concièrgerie is especially famous for the many prisoners who were held here following the French Revolution. During the Reign of Terror from 1794 to 1795, the revolutionary tribunal condemned nearly 3,000 people to their deaths. Most of them spent at least some time here before losing their heads.

You can visit the Concièrgerie and tour the guard room, kitchen, and prison cells. Some of the cells have been rebuilt, as they were during the Revolution, complete with wax figures depicting guards and prisoners.

The visit begins with the guardroom, with its four large fireplaces. The pillars are decorated with sculptures of animals and people. Notice the giant slab of dark marble on one wall of the guardroom. This used to be a table top used for royal feasts. When the palace became a prison, this was the room where trials were held and prisoners condemned.

The kitchen is up a small stairway. It has several huge fireplaces for cooking food for as many as 3,000 people. The windows were originally just above the level of the river, so that supplies could be easily delivered by boat.

The next part of the visit takes you to the prisoners' galleries. There were separate sections reserved for men and women. You can see the courtyard with its fountain, where the female prisoners washed their laundry. There was a gate through which the women could speak to the male prisoners. You can also see the special cell reserved for

Queen Marie- Antoinette (Note: this is a re-creation of her original cell, which was later turned into a chapel). Upstairs you can visit other prison cells, including those reserved for the poor and the more upscale ones for people who had access to money or political influence. Famous Concièrgerie prisoners include:

- **Ravaillac**, a Catholic monk and religious extremist who murdered King Henri IV. He was executed.
- **Damiens**, who struck and lightly injured king Louis XV in 1757. He was tortured and executed.
- **Marquise de Brinvilliers**, who poisoned her father, brothers, and sister. She escaped but was ultimately caught, condemned, and beheaded.
- **Cartouche**, a popular, Robin Hood-like leader of a band of thieves. He died on the rack.
- **Jeanne de Valois**, a noblewoman who wrote false letters to persuade the Cardinal of Rohan to buy a diamond necklace for Queen Marie-Antoinette, which she kept for herself. She escaped from prison but later died in poverty in London.
- **Charlotte Corday**, who assassinated Jean-Paul Marat in his bathtub for being one of the leaders of the Terror. His death is depicted in a famous painting by David. She was guillotined.
- **Marie Antoinette**, married to King Louis XVI, born in Austria, and hated by her subjects. Her hair is said to have turned white overnight after her arrest by the revolutionaries. She was spared while they tried to negotiate a peace deal with warring Austria. It failed, and she was condemned to death. A faithful servant tried to help her escape, but she was caught and transferred to a more secure cell. She was guillotined in 1793.
- **Danton** and **Robespierre**, revolutionary leaders who sent many others to the guillotine, only to be later executed themselves for their excesses.

During the day, prisoners who had already been condemned to death by guillotine were allowed to wander around in the prison. Each evening, there would be an announcement declaring who would die the next day. Then a bell would ring and all the prisoners would return to their cells. Those who were condemned to die were sent to the Salle de la Toilette where they were searched and their valuables removed. Their collars were cut off, their hair was cut, and their neck was shaved to leave a clear target for the guillotine's blade

A small museum on the upper floor features artifacts from the history of the prison and some of its more well-known residents.

As you leave the Concièrgerie, notice the beautiful **CLOCK-TOWER** on the corner of the Quai de l'Horloge and Boulevard du Palais. It was completed in 1371 and has never stopped working. **PLACE LOUIS LEPINE MARKET**. *Metro: Cité.* There is a lovely flower market here Monday through Saturday. Then on Sundays, it is transformed into a lively pet market that features all sorts of colorful birds, as well as Guinea pigs, rabbits, and other small animals that will delight kids.

The imposing building you see on the east side of the Place Lepine is the Hôtel Dieu, Paris' oldest hospital. To the west of the Palais de Justice complex is a pretty triangular-shaped square called the Place Dauphine. It was built during the reign of King Henri IV in honor of his son (the Dauphin is the title of the king's heir). **PONT NEUF**. *On the western edge of the Ile de la Cité. Metro: Pont Neuf.*

Although its name means New Bridge, this is actually the oldest bridge in Paris. It was built from 1578 to 1604 and was the first bridge in Paris to be made of stone. If you look at the Pont Neuf from below, you can see that it is decorated with hundreds of grimacing faces. According to legend, the artist designed these faces as caricatures of famous men of the day. **BATEAUX VEDETTES DU PONT NEUF (TOUR BOATS)** *Square du Vert Galant. Down the steps on the Pont Neuf, behind the equestrian statue of King Henri IV. Boats leave every 30-45 minutes, 10am-10pm. Adults: €14. Kids age 4-12: €7. Kids under age 4: free. Note: Lower rates and specials are available if you book your tickets via Internet in advance.*

If you are jet-lagged, foot-sore, or just want a change of pace, this one-hour boat tour is a great way to see some of Paris' major sights and monuments. Kids enjoy the ride, and you'll see Nôtre Dame, the Eiffel Tower, and other attractions from a unique perspective. Tour guide explanations are in both English and French.

Ile Saint Louis

This small island in the middle of the Seine River is **one of the fanciest neighborhoods in Paris**. However, it wasn't always such a splendid spot. In the 17th century, the area was swampy and uninhabited. There were actually two separate islands. One was called the Ile Nôtre Dame, named for the cathedral. The other was called the Ile aux Vaches (Cow Island) – hardly a romantic beginning. In the 1660s, a building developer named Jean Christophe Marie got permission from King Louis XIII to drain and connect the islands. He then built elegant mansions that were bought up by wealthy financiers and magistrates. The island was named for King Louis IX, also known as Saint Louis.

The main street of this small island is filled with fun shops and lively restaurants. Sunbathers flock to the "shores" of the island on warm, summer days. Those in the know head to Ile Saint Louis for the ice cream. (See below.)

Ile Saint Louis Highlights

• Have some Berthillon ice cream!
• Stand on the pedestrian Pont Saint Louis bridge and watch the boats pass underneath

GLACES BERTHILLON. *#31, Rue Saint Louis en l'Ile. Metro: Pont Marie.*

The official vendor for Berthillon ice cream and sorbet is located at this address, though you can find stalls selling it all over the island. It is a treat not to be missed! They use only natural ingredients. The scoops are small, but loaded with flavor – ranging from dark chocolate to green apple, wild strawberry, and many wonderful choices in between.

4. LATIN QUARTER

The history of this neighborhood is seeped in its Latin roots. These roots stretch back through medieval days when great scholars and students walked its narrow streets speaking Latin. They reach back even further to the 1st century BC, when the Romans occupied Paris and built a great city in this area south of the Ile de la Cité. Today, the Quartier Latin still bustles with students and scholars. However, its rich assortment of museums, parks, markets, and shops also make it an ideal spot from which to discover some of the kid-friendly sides of Paris.

Roman Occupation of Paris

In the year 52 BC, Julius Caesar's Roman army defeated the Gauls (inhabitants of France) and captured their main city, **Lutetia** (today's Paris). When the Gauls saw that they were losing the battle, they set their city on fire so as to leave nothing for their enemies. The Romans rebuilt Lutetia, transforming it into a great Roman city, which served as a base for conquests further north. They constructed a forum, numerous aqueducts and public bath houses, an amphitheater, and an arena. They created a grid of paved roads. They built a Governor's Palace and judicial buildings. The Romans also erected many temples to their gods, including ones to Jupiter, Juno, Minerva, Mercury, Apollo, Bacchus, Hercules, Mars, Venus, Vulcan, and Ceres.

Several of the Latin Quarter's main avenues still follow the trace of old Roman roads, including the Boulevard Saint Michel, Rue des Ecoles, and Rue Monge. Many Roman vestiges were either reused subsequently to build defensive walls and buildings, or they remain buried under modern

Paris. However, you can still travel back in time to a gladiator battle in the Roman Arena or imagine a steam room in the old Roman bath house.

ARENES DE LUTECE. *Entrances from the Rue des Arènes, Rue de Navarre, and through a passageway in the Rue Monge (Metro: Place Monge or Jussieu). Open daily, 8am-sunset. Entrance is free.*

The Arènes de Lutèce were built by the Romans in the 1st century BC. They featured entertainment such as gladiator matches, chariot races, Christians thrown to the lions, and even naval battles. There were also mime and dance performances. Dramatic plays were performed at the Roman Theater, now gone, that was located near the Cluny Roman Baths (see later in this chapter).

The arena was built right into the side of a hill. There were 35 rows of seats that could hold as many as 17,000 spectators. It was used until the 3rd century A.D., at which time Paris was repeatedly invaded by Vikings, Goths, and Huns, and the Roman Empire began to crumble. The arena was abandoned, and many of the stones were used to build defensive walls and towers to protect the city.

For hundreds of years the Arènes de Lutèce were forgotten under rubble and new constructions. Then in 1869, workers widening the Rue Monge came upon some of the ruins of the old arena. At the time, the city was more interested in modernization than historical preservation, so a bus depot was built on top of them. In 1883, more of the ruins were discovered on the southern side of the arena. This time there was a great public outcry to save the site, including a letter to the President of the City Council from Victor Hugo (author of *Les Misérables* and *The Hunchback of Notre Dame*). The ruins of the arena were preserved and restored, although some parts remain buried under the Rue Monge and Rue de Navarre.

Today, people play much

Latin Quarter Highlights

• Have a mock gladiator battle in the Roman Arena (Arènes de Lutèce)
• Find the unicorns in the Cluny Museum
• Look for plaques to fallen heroes by the Place Saint Michel
• Play like princes and princesses in the Luxembourg Gardens
• Try some mint tea at the Paris Mosque
• Hunt for extinct and endangered animals at the Jardin des Plantes
• Shop for wild strawberries at the Rue Mouffetard market
• Buy a book at Shakespeare and Company
• Find a 400-year-old tree that's still alive!

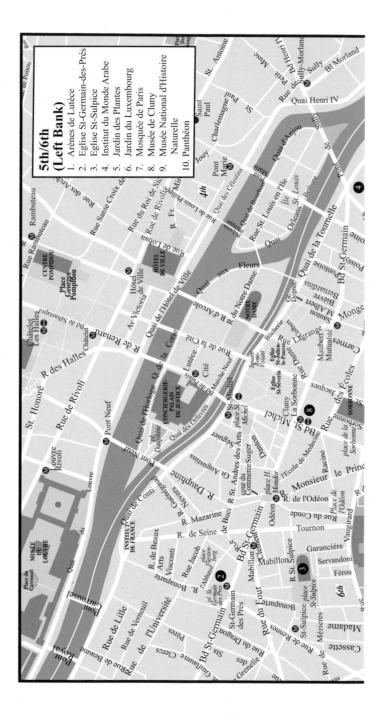

5th/6th (Left Bank)
1. Arènes de Lutèce
2. Eglise St-Germain-des-Prés
3. Eglise St-Sulpice
4. Institut du Monde Arabe
5. Jardin des Plantes
6. Jardin du Luxembourg
7. Mosquée de Paris
8. Musée de Cluny
9. Musée National d'Histoire Naturelle
10. Panthéon

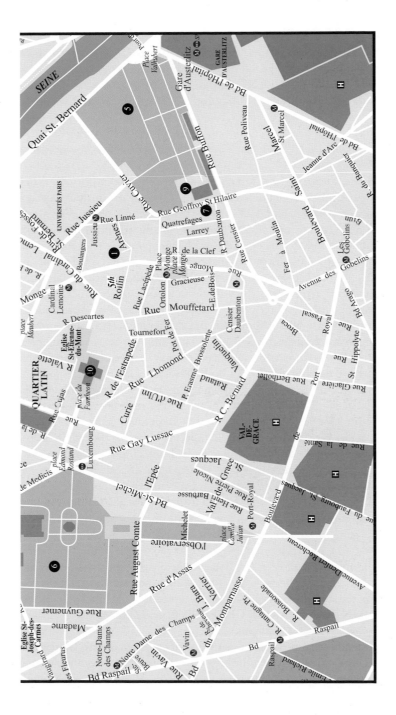

tamer games in the Arènes de Lutèce. It is a favorite spot for a round of boules, friendly soccer match, and children's games. There is a pretty little playground, just down the hill from the arena in the park.

THERMES DE CLUNY. *Located in the same building as the Musée National du Moyen Age (described below), 6, Place Paul Painlevé, just off the Boulevard Saint Michel. Metro: Cluny-La Sorbonne or Saint Michel. Open 9:15am-5:45pm (last entry tickets sold at 5:15). Closed Tues. Adults: €8.50 (includes audioguide); Kids: free. Free to everyone on the first Sunday of each month. Audioguide: €1.*

These Roman Baths were built in the 2nd and 3rd centuries AD. They included at least a dozen different rooms on two floors, including steam rooms, warm baths, and cool pools. There were also gymnasiums and rooms reserved for conversation. They were richly decorated with marble and bronze statues, painted murals, and elaborate mosaic floor tiles. There was a sophisticated water system that provided steam and filled the pools.

The Roman baths were free to the public. However, people didn't just go to the baths to get clean. They also went to socialize, conduct business, exercise, and visit the library. Special pools were reserved for women. Men often took part in wrestling matches or calisthenics before going into the bathing rooms. Businessmen would meet in the baths or in the surrounding gardens. There were masseuses and hairdressers. There were food and drink vendors and other boutiques. All in all, it was a very lively place.

As you visit the museum, you can still see the large **Frigidarium** (cold room) that had a pool with cool water, much like a modern swimming pool. The room has a high ceiling supported by beams and arches. At the base of the arches you can make out decorations representing the hulls of ships. They were originally decorated with mermaids and tritons (male mermaids) and filled with goods and weapons. Archeologists disagree about what the ship hulls stand for, but they may be a tribute to the importance of shipping in early Lutetia. The **Tepidarium** (warm room) and **Caldarium** (hot steam room) were to the west of the Frigidarium. They are now part of the outside gardens along the Boulevard St. Michel.

With the barbarian invasions of Paris in the middle of the 3rd century AD, the inhabitants of Paris fled to the fortified part of the city on the island of Ile de la Cité. The Thermes de Cluny were abandoned and fell into ruin. Some of the stones from the building were reused to build fortification walls.

MONTAGNE SAINTE GENEVIEVE. *Hill leading from Cluny and the Sorbonne up to the Pantheon.*

This hill is named for the patron saint of Paris, **Sainte Geneviève,** to whom people pray when the city is in trouble. Geneviève was young shepherdess, born in 422 in a village west of Paris. She was extremely pious, had religious visions, and is said to have started performing miracles at age 9 when she cured a blind girl by sprinkling water in her eyes. She saved villagers from illness and Parisians from starving. However, Geneviève's most famous moment came in the year 451 when Paris was threatened by Attila the Hun, who led his invaders from Germany through eastern France, killing and pillaging all the way. Word came that Attila was approaching Paris. The Parisians panicked and began to flee, but Geneviève gave them the courage to stay, convinced by a dream that their city would be spared. In the end, the Huns never reached Paris. They were defeated, and Geneviève was credited with having saved the city.

Geneviève could not save Paris from the Franks, however, who took over the city in 464. She ultimately befriended their king, Clovis and his wife, Clothilde, and persuaded them to become Christians. When Geneviève died in 512 at the age of 90, she was buried next to Clovis. Today her remains are in the Eglise Saint Etienne du Mont, which sits atop the Montagne Sainte Geneviève.

There is a statue of Sainte Geneviève on the Pont de la Tournelle (a bridge behind Notre Dame Cathedral).

EGLISE SAINT ETIENNE DU MONT. *Place Sainte Geneviève. Metro: Cardinal Lemoine. Open 10am-12pm, 4pm-7pm. Closed Mon.*

This church was built during the 1500s and 1600s and is named for Saint Stephen, who was stoned to death by an angry mob in 34 AD for preaching the teachings of Christ. He is the first Christian martyr, and you can see a statue of him, with a pile of rocks, by the church's entrance. The other statue depicts Sainte Geneviève. Inside there is a feature called a rood screen, a set of finely carved stone balconies and double spiral stairs, designed to separate the area reserved for the clergy from the more public part of the church. Though they used to be common, this is the only rood screen left in Paris. On the right, beyond the rood screen is a shrine with Geneviève's relics. Pilgrims still come and ask her for favors, or leave plaques of thanks for her miracles.

The Medieval Latin Quarter

In the 1100s, Paris became one of Europe's most important centers of learning. Many important scholars and students congregated in the neighborhood around the Montagne Sainte Geneviève.

Students came from all over Europe. There were so many of them that there was a serious student housing crunch. In the 1200s, many "colleges" began to form. These started out as places for students to live and study together, often under the direction of resident "masters." One of these was founded in 1253, by Robert Sorbon, a priest at Nôtre Dame Cathedral and confessor to King Saint Louis. It was built to house students, professors, and a library. It would soon become one of the most famous and powerful universities in the world, the Sorbonne.

CLUNY -MUSÉE NATIONAL DU MOYEN AGE, *in the same building as the Thermes de Cluny at 6, Place Paul Painleve, off Boulevard Saint Michel. Metro: Cluny-La Sorbonne or Saint Michel. Open 9:15am-5:45pm. Closed Tues. Closed Tues. Adults: €8.50 (includes audioguide); Kids under 18: free, but pay €1 for an audioguide. Free to everyone on the first Sunday of each month. Access to the Medieval Garden along the Boulevard Saint Germain is free. Audioguide: €1.*

The Cluny museum is a charming place to visit, and parents are surprised at how much their children enjoy it. The museum is not terribly big, but offers interesting glimpses at both Roman and medieval life. The visit takes you through beautiful examples of stained glass, gold work, jewelry, fabric, ivory carvings, and illuminated books. It takes you into the old Frigidarium of the Roman Baths building (see above). There are the 21 stone heads that were knocked off the statues of the biblical kings of Notre Dame Cathedral during the French Revolution. There is the tombstone from the grave of Nicholas Flamel. You may remember him from the first Harry Potter book as the discoverer of the Sorcerer's Stone. (Yes, he was a real person.) But the part that will most delight children is near the end of the

the museum visit. It features the famous Woman with a Unicorn tapestries. There are six of these tapestries, and they are magnificent. The first five depict the five senses: taste, touch, smell, hearing, and sight. The sixth one is called "My Only Desire" and its meaning is not entirely clear. Children delight in looking at the magical unicorn, and searching out all the different animals in each scene. One more note to Harry Potter fans. If they've seen the film version of the books, they may recognize these tapestries; their design decorates the Gryffindor Common Room.

The courtyard in front of the Cluny museum features a 15th century well, a sundial, and a facade decorated with gargoyles and other Gothic decorations.

Downhill from the museum is a nice medieval Garden that features medicinal and decorative plants of the period.

BOULEVARD SAINT MI-CHEL NEIGHBORHOOD. *Metro: Saint Michel.*

The Boulevard Saint Michel is one of the major thoroughfares of the Latin Quarter, and has been since Roman times when it was lined with Roman Baths, a Theater, and a Forum. Today, the boulevard bustles with college students and tourists. It is lined with lively cafés, fast-food places, clothing stores, shoe stores, pedestrian streets, and the big Gibert bookstores that have been around for over 100 years.

PLACE SAINT MICHEL AND QUARTIER DE LA HUCHETTE. *Side streets to the east of the Place Saint Michel.*

This neighborhood of cobbled pedestrian streets is filled with tourist shops and restaurants. The streets date back to Roman times, including the tiny Rue du Chat Qui Pêche (Street of the Fishing Cat), which is the smallest street in the city. If your party includes a high schooler who is studying French, he or she may enjoy seeing Ionesco's The Bald Soprano, which has been playing at the little Théâtre de la Huchette since the play was written in the 1950s.

If you cross the Rue Saint Jacques, you can admire the old medieval houses in the rue Galande.

SQUARE VIVIANI. *Between Eglise Saint Julien le Pauvre and the Seine. Metro: Maubert Mutualité or Saint Michel.*

If you've ever read the book, Linnea in Monet's Garden, you might recognize this lovely little park. It is just across the Seine River from Notre Dame Cathedral and across the street from the Hôtel Esmeralda, featured in Linnea's story. It was once the garden for the Eglise Saint Julien le Pauvre.

It also holds Paris' second oldest tree. Planted in 1681, the tree is a False Acacia, so old and gnarled that it leans on a stone crutch for support. The square offers a great view of Nôtre Dame Cathedral. This is a good place to take a break or enjoy a snack. Right around the corner to your left as you face the river is the famous English-language bookshop, Shakespeare and Company.

SHAKESPEARE AND COMPANY. *37, Rue de la Bûcherie, across the river from Nôtre Dame Cathedral (Metro: Saint Michel). Open daily. Note: This store does not accept any credit cards.*

Filled with expatriate Brits and Americans, this is one of the English-language bookshops of Paris where you can stock up on new and used books, for kids or adults. It has an interesting history that actually involves two bookshops:

The original Shakespeare and Company was located at 12, Rue de l'Odéon and run by a woman named Sylvia Beach. It was here that writers such as Ernest Hemingway, F. Scott Fitzgerald, James Joyce, and Gertrude Stein crossed paths. It was both an English-language bookshop and a lending library. During the German occupation of Paris in World War II, Beach refused to sell her last copy of James Joyce's Finnegan's Wake to a German officer. He threatened to confiscate all her books. She was forced to close the shop, and it never re-opened. During the Liberation of Paris, Ernest Hemingway, a war correspondent who was among the first Allied

troops to enter the city, made a point of dropping by Sylvia Beach's place to officially liberate it.

In 1951, George Whitman opened up his English bookshop, called Le Mistral, in a little street across the Seine from Nôtre Dame Cathedral. He also had a lending library on the second floor, and his shop became a meeting place for a new generation of English-language poets and writers. These included Americans, such as Alan Ginsberg, William

Burroughs, Henry Miller, and James Baldwin. Whitman installed cots in the library where struggling young writers could spend the night for free provided they read a book a day, worked an hour in the shop, and left a short autobiography and photo. They still do. When Sylvia Beach died in 1962, Whitman renamed his shop Shakespeare and Company to honor her. He also gave her name to his daughter. Whitman died in 2011 at the age of 98. The shop, now run by his daughter, Sylvia Beach Whitman, continues to extend a warm welcome to all book lovers, whether they are starving writers or not.

LUXEMBOURG GARDENS. *Located between the Boulevard Saint Michel, Rue de Vaugirard, and Rue d'Assas. Metro: Luxembourg or Nôtre Dame des Champs. Open sunrise to sunset. Entrance is free.*

The Luxembourg Palace and Gardens were built in the 17th century by Queen Marie de Médicis after the assassination of her husband King Henri IV. She bought the property from a Duke of Luxembourg, which is where it gets its name. The queen had the palace built to look like one in Florence, Italy where she had spent her childhood. However, Marie de Médicis did not get to enjoy her new palace for long. Her son, Louis XIII, banished her from France, and she was forced to live the rest of her life in Germany.

The palace served as a royal residence until the French Revolution when it was used as a prison. During the German Occupation of Paris in World War II, the palace was taken over as central headquarters for the German Luftwäffe (Air Force). Today it houses the French Senate.

In front of the palace is the **central fountain** of the Luxembourg Gardens (see photo on page 44). On weekends and holiday afternoons it is dotted with miniature sailboats that you can rent by the hour from a little stand. This is one of our boys' all-time favorite activities in Paris. It also provides great photo opportunities. Keep an eye on small children, however. The edges of the fountain slope downward, and I've seen more than one child slide into the water head first.

The central fountain is a favorite hangout for students and other Parisians relaxing in the green metal chairs that fill the park. It is a lovely spot to rest your feet and soak in the sun on a nice day. As you sit there, notice the statues of the queens of

France looking benevolently down at you from the surrounding terraces. Up the steps on the eastern side of the park there is a bandstand that offers free concerts in the summer, when the nearby outdoor café is also open.

Just east of the palace is the pretty, shady Médicis Fountain. Filled with goldfish, it presents an interesting optical illusion. Since the edges of the pool are on an incline, it looks like the water is slanted even though it is flat. The statue that adorns the fountain depicts a scene from the Greek myth of Acis and Galathea. Here is their story: Galatea was a water nymph. Acis was a fawn. They fell in love and became engaged. But the giant, one-eyed Cyclops, Polyphemus, wanted Galatea for himself. When he found the two lovers kissing in a cave, he threw a huge stone at Acis and crushed him. Galatea escaped into the water. Acis was turned into a river god. Polyphemus later had his eye poked out by Odysseus.

The western side of the park has public tennis courts, a place reserved for playing boules, chess tables, a puppet theater, a wooden merry-go-round, and old-fashioned two-person swings. This is also where you will find the Luxembourg's **amazing playground**. Although there is a small fee to enter, it is well worth it. (It's the only place I know in Paris where kids pay more than adults.) If you have small children you will want to go in with them. If they are a little older and more independent, you can do what many Parisian parents and nannies do: watch them from the metal chairs around the perimeter of the playground. The small building in the playground has a restroom and snack bar.

In the summer months there are also pony rides and little race cars for rent on the western side of the park. There is a beekeeping school (near the rue d'Assas entrance) with classes twice a week. You can buy the honey each October in the garden's Orangerie, which doubles as a small museum featuring temporary art exhibits. If you wander through the shady paths on the western side of the park, you may come across a small replica of the Statue of Liberty. It was one of the models for the big one in New York harbor, designed by French sculptor Auguste Bartholdi, with engineering help from Gustave Eiffel, of Eiffel Tower fame.

On the southeastern side of the park are the garden's greenhouses (not open to the public). There is also an orchard that is nearly 200 years old. The apples and pears from these trees are reserved for members of the Senate.

On the north side of the Luxembourg Gardens at #36 Rue de Vaugirard under the arcades, there is an inscription in the wall designating the official length of one meter. It is on a building that used to be the Agency for Weights and Measures and harkens back to the time (1795) when France adopted its first standardized system of measures: the metric system. The length of the meter, which was the baseline of the system, was calculated to be the equivalent of one-ten-millionth of the distance of the arc of the earth from the North Pole to the Equator. To help people get used to using meters, meter-stick measures such as this one were inscribed on the walls of buildings throughout the city.

PANTHEON, *Place du Panthéon. Metro: Luxembourg or Cardinal Lemoine. Open 10am-6:30pm (summer); 10am-6pm (winter). Adults: €7.50; Kids under 18: free.*

Initially designed as a church, the Pantheon is now a burial place for illustrious men and women; for example, Victor Hugo (author of Les Miserables and The Hunchback of Notre Dame), Louis Braille (who invented Braille writing for the blind), and Pierre and Marie Curie (who studied radioactivity). Paintings inside the Pantheon depict the life of Sainte Geneviève, death of Saint Denis, story of Joan of Arc, and crowning of Charlemagne.

Behind the Pantheon, you can take the Rue Clovis to the Rue Descartes. Notice half a block further down the Rue Clovis is **a remnant of the 12th century defensive wall** that used to protect Paris from invaders, such as the English King Richard the Lionheart. If you take the Rue Descartes to the Place de la Contrescarpe, you will enter the Mouffetard neighborhood, famous for its ancient market street, shops, and restaurants.

RUE MOUFFETARD, *between Place de la Contrescarpe and Avenue des Gobelins. Metro: Place Monge or Censier Daubenton.*

This charming street has been paved with stones ever since Roman times when it led all the way to Italy. The road used to go along the Bièvre River, which now runs underground as part of the Paris sewer system. For centuries, the Mouffetard area was dotted with farms and vineyards. In the 12th century, wealthy Parisians built their country villas around here. Over time the Rue Mouffetard was lined with narrow houses (many of which are still there), shops, tanneries, cloth dyers, and an open-air market.

The Mouffetard neighborhood (familiarly known as **La Mouf**) has been home to many famous residents. Medieval author, **Rabelais**, used to get drunk in a tavern called the Pomme de Pin (Pine Cone) on the Place de la Contrescarpe. Age of Enlightenment thinker **Denis Diderot** lived at #3, Rue de l'Estrapade, and **René Descartes** lived at #14, Rue Rollin. Sculptor **Auguste Rodin** was born at #3, Rue de l'Arbalète. **Ernest Hemingway** lived around the corner at #74 Rue du Cardinal-Lemoine and at #39, Rue Descartes. He described the neighborhood in his books, *The Snows of Kilimanjaro* and *A Moveable Feast*.

At #60, Rue Mouffetard, there is a small fountain called the **Fontaine du Pot de Fer** that dates back to Roman times. It was later connected to an aqueduct used by Queen Marie de Médicis to bring water to her Luxembourg Gardens and Palace.

The house at # 53, Rue Mouffetard is famous for its hidden treasure. On May 24, 1938, workers tearing down an old house found gold coins in the walls, stamped with the likeness of King Louis XV. There were 3,351 coins in all. They had been left there by a man named Louis Nivelle, who had been Louis XV's secretary. Nivelle disappeared mysteriously in 1757, but left a will that was found with the coins. In the will, Nivelle bequeathed the treasure to his daughter, who died in 1810. The discovery of the coins led to a 15-year legal battle between Nivelle's heirs and the people who uncovered the treasure. In the end, the gold was split between Nivelle's 84 descendants. However, they had to pay fees to the genealogists and the construction crew, as well as a big inheritance tax to the City of Paris.

RUE MOUFFETARD STREET MARKET. *Metro: Censier Daubenton or Place Monge. Open Tuesday-Saturday, 8am-1pm, 4pm-7pm and Sunday 8am-1pm. Closed Sunday afternoon and Monday.*

This market has been here for hundreds of years. Notice some of the old shop signs on the buildings. It is famous for its wide variety of fresh produce, meats, cheeses, and ethnic boutiques. Check out the wonderful bakeries and delicatessens with their specialties from France, Greece, Italy, and Asia. On weekends, French shoppers come in from the suburbs to enjoy the colors and tastes this market offers.

Parent Tip: Now that you've loaded up with food from the Rue Mouffetard, it's time to feed the budding scientist in every child with a visit to the nearby **Jardin des Plantes**. Here, children can run, have a picnic, ride a merry-go-round of extinct and endangered animals, get lost in a labyrinth, visit the zoo, and enjoy the wonderful **Natural History Museums**. ❖

JARDIN DES PLANTES (BOTANICAL GARDENS), *Located between the Rue Cuvier, Rue Geoffroy Saint Hilaire, Rue Buffon, and Seine River. Metro: Jussieu or Gare d'Austerlitz. Open sunrise to sunset. Museums open daily except Tues, 10am-6pm (Thurs. until 10pm). Greenhouses open daily 1pm-5pm. Menagerie (zoo) open daily 9am-5pm (summers until 6pm). Entrance to the park is free, though you do have to pay to enter the zoo, greenhouses, and museums.*

This park is a kid's haven. It contains a zoo, playground, labyrinth, and merry-go-round featuring extinct or endangered animals. There are huge greenhouses and botanical gardens. There is a paleontology museum, featuring skeletons of current and extinct animals; a gallery of evolution filled with real (stuffed) animals; a mineralogy museum with giant crystals; and a botanical museum.

The Jardin des Plantes began as a place where the royal botanists grew medicinal plants for the family of King Louis XIII. It was expanded during the reign of Louis XIV to accommodate plants brought back from expeditions to the New World and other foreign parts. The king's chief doctor headed the gardens. He oversaw the building of two greenhouses, including the Grande Serre (Large Greenhouse) that was designed to house France's first coffee tree. A 600-seat lecture hall was also added to promote the teaching of natural sciences and pharmacy.

Over time, many rare trees and plants were added to the park's collection. Some are still there today, including the oldest tree in Paris, planted in 1635. It is a False Acacia tree, and a twin to the one in the Square Viviani featured in Linnea in Monet's Garden. It is located in the Allée des Becquerels, near the Minerology Museum. The gardens also house a 150-year-old Ginkgo tree and a 250-year-old Chinese Sophora.

The park's **Labyrinth**, near the Rue Geoffroy Saint Hilaire side of the park, was built in 1640 on an artificial hill that had served as a trash pile. In the middle of the Labyrinth is a Cedar of Lebanon. This tree was secretly carried to Paris from London by botanist, Bernard de Jussieu in 1734. Along the route, the flower pot that held the small sapling broke. Legend has it that Jussieu carried the plant in his hat for most of the trip, catching a head cold as a result. The more reliable version of the story says that the pot broke only a few blocks from the park. Either way, the tree was safely delivered thanks to the botanist's hat.

MENAGERIE (ZOO). *Northwest corner of the Jardin des Plantes. Open daily except Tues. 9am-6pm (summer); 9am-5pm (winter). Closed Tues. Adults: €7; Kids ages 5-16: €5; Kids under 5: free. You can get a map at the entrance indicating where to find different animals.*

The Menagerie was created in 1793. It is the oldest public zoo in the world. Its first residents were animals that had been part of the royal menagerie at Versailles and were brought here after the French Revolution. They were joined by other animals that were confiscated from carnivals and street performers. More animals were added in 1795, including France's first live elephants, stolen from a Dutch zoo after a successful French military campaign. The first giraffe arrived in 1826. It was a gift from the King of Egypt. The giraffe went by boat to Marseilles, then traveled slowly up to Paris to give people a chance to see it. It was such a hit that giraffe decorations on combs, umbrellas, and other items became all the rage.

In 1870, the Prussians laid siege to the city of Paris, ultimately forcing ruler Napoleon III to surrender. During the siege, the people of Paris were cut off from their food supplies and had to eat anything they could find. Even the zoo animals were killed, and their meat was sold to local restaurants.

Today, the zoo is home to some 800 animals. There are many large mammals, reptiles, and birds. There is also a "microzoo," where you can look at tiny creatures through a microscope.

GALERIE DE PALEONTOLOGIE. *Northeastern edge of the Jardins des Plantes (near the Seine entrance). Open 10am-5pm (weekdays); 10am-6pm (weekends). Closed Tues. Adults: €7; Kids ages 5-18: €5. Kids under 5: free.* **Note:** This museum is slated to be renovated, so catch it while you can.

This museum holds an impressive array of animal skeletons, including a mammoth and an entire blue whale. The upper floor features magnificent dinosaur skeletons and fossils. The building was first opened in 1898 and with its intricate ironwork decorations is itself well worth the visit.

GRANDE GALERIE DE L'EVOLUTION. *Southeastern side of the Jardin des Plantes, by Rue Geoffroy Saint Hilaire and Paris Mosque. Open 10am-6pm (until 10pm Thurs). Closed Tues. Adults: €7; Kids 4-18: €5; Kids under 4: free.*

This is a wonderful place to visit with kids. The building was renovated after being closed for decades and now offers exhibits of animals of all types. The great hall is quite spectacular, featuring a long caravan of mammals ranging from very large (elephants and giraffes) to smaller ones. The lower level has marine animals on exhibit. Birds are represented in flight along the upper floors, and there are monkeys climbing up the levels near the elevators. There is a fascinating room upstairs (level 2) featuring animals that are extinct or endangered. The top level has a rhinoceros that belonged to the royal menagerie of Louis XIV. It is the oldest animal in the museum.

GALERIE DE MINEROLOGIE. *Southern side of the Jardin des Plantes, near the Grande Galerie. Open 10am-5pm. Closed Tues. Adults: €6; Kids : €4.*

This museum was recently renovated and reopened in 2014. It is an interesting visit for anyone who really digs rocks and crystals. It features the world's greatest collection of giant crystals. There are jewels from the reigns of Louis XIII and Louis XIV. There are also meteorites from outer space. Unfortunately, this museum is in dire need of updating and is arranged like a dusty, private collection. It is not air conditioned, which can make it hard to tolerate if the weather is hot.

JARDIN ALPIN. Near the Menagerie. Entrance is free.

This small garden-within-a-garden features plants that would normally be found in mountains such as the Alps, Pyrenees, or Himalayas. They survive here thanks to careful placement and attention. It is a quiet place, rarely crowded, where kids can run happily through the alley ways and adults can get the impression of being in the fresh mountain air.

PARIS MOSQUE. *1, Place du Puits de l'Ermite. The restaurant, tearoom, and Turkish bath entrances are located at 39, Rue Geoffroy Saint Hilaire.*

Metro: Place Monge. The Mosque is open for visits daily except Fridays, from 9am-12pm, and 2pm-6pm. The restaurant is open daily, 10am-9pm.

The Paris Mosque was built from 1922 to 1926 as a gesture of thanks to the North African troops who fought alongside the French during World War I. It was designed to look like the mosque in the Moroccan city of Fez. Four hundred fifty artisans and technicians from Morocco, Algeria, and Tunisia worked on the building. It is beautifully decorated with mosaics, intricate wood carvings, fine rugs, and shady gardens. The minaret tower is 33 meters (109 feet) high.

Across from the entrance to the Jardin des Plantes is the entrance to the Mosque's **restaurant and tearoom**. You can enjoy tea and snacks inside or in the outdoor gardens, which are decorated with blue and white tiles, shady trees, and a fountain. The restaurant offers couscous and other North African culinary specialties eaten on huge brass tray tables. It's a taste of the exotic in the middle of Paris.

OPEN-AIR SCULPTURE GARDEN. *On the Seine, along the Quai Saint Bernard. Metro: Jussieu or Gare d'Austerlitz. Open daily, sunrise to sunset. Entrance is free.*

This spot combines a park, art, and nice views of the Seine River. The sculpture garden runs along the river from the Jardin des Plantes to the Institut du Monde Arabe. It is filled with works by modern artists such as Joan Arp, Constantine Brancusi, and Cesar – who sometimes appeal more to children than to adults. There are also paths for roller blading, ping-pong tables, and a playground. Sometimes after a particularly wet winter, the park becomes flooded by the rising waters of the Seine. Then some of the sculptures end up partially submerged.

INSTITUT DU MONDE ARABE. *1, Rue des Fossés-Saint-Bernard. Metro: Jussieu, or Cardinal Lemoine. Access to the building is free. The museum is open, 10am-6pm, Closed Mon. Adults and Children 12 and up: €9. Children under 12: free. There are often special exhibits with separate entrances and entrance fees.*

This Institute celebrates Arab culture and heritage with a museum, films, concerts, dance performances, and food. The museum has a permanent collection but is especially interesting for its temporary exhibits. The **top floor restaurant** offers yummy food for lunch or tea, along with great views of the Seine and Paris. There is a gift shop on the ground level. Note the buildilng's windows. They are designed to look like Arab mosaics. But they serve a practical purpose, too. Like the lens of a camera or the pupil of your eye, the openings are designed to widen or narrow automatically depending on how bright the light is outdoors.

CLAUDE NATURE SHOP. *32, Boulevard Saint Germain. Open 11am-7pm. Closed Sun. Metro: Maubert Mutualité.*

This little shop appeals to bug lovers of all ages. It sells collectors' quality butterflies and other exotic bugs. It's worth a look even if you are not buying.

MAGIC SHOW - METAMORPHOSIS. *On a houseboat across from 55, Quai de la Tournelle (Apr-Sep), Metro: Maubert Mutualité. Sunday Brunch at 12:30pm and plus magic show at 3 pm. Adults: €38 for brunch and show, €16 for show and snack. Kids: €32 for brunch and show, €6 for show and snack. Note: from Oct to Mar this boat moves upstream to by 7, Quai Malaquais across from the Pont des Arts, Metro: Pont Neuf or Saint Germain des Près.*

This houseboat offers floating magic shows. Special family-friendly shows are presented on Sunday afternoons. Other performances are presented Tuesday-Saturday at 9:30 pm.

GARE D'AUSTERLITZ. *Along the Boulevard de l'Hôpital by the Quai d'Austerlitz.*

This train station is named for one of Napoleon Bonaparte's successful battles against the Austrians and Russians. It is where you come to catch trains to or from southwestern France, Spain, or Portugal. You can catch up on some of your correspondences at the station restaurant. The menu is printed on a postcard.

5. SAINT GERMAIN

Saint Germain des Près is home to Paris' first official café, established in 1686. It is famous for attracting the intellectual crowd and fancy fashion designers. There are also plenty of treats for children, too, in the side streets of Saint Germain. These range from the magnificently restored **Musée d'Orsay** (formerly a train station) to the mysteries of a summer solstice at the **Place Saint Sulpice**.

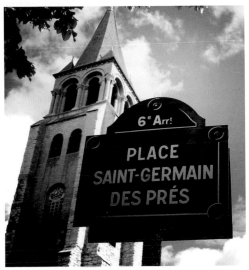

ÉGLISE SAINT GERMAIN DES PRÈS, *Place Saint Germain des Près. Metro: Saint Germain des Près. Entrance is free.*

This is the oldest church in Paris. It was built in 543, by the Merovingian king, Childebert, who was feeling guilty for having murdered so many relatives and rivals to get to the throne. The church has had to withstand many attacks from invading Vikings and others. It was originally fortified, complete with watchtowers and a moat. The bell tower (still standing) was built in the year 1,000 AD. It was part of the defensive walls and is the oldest bell tower in Paris. Much of the church you see today dates from the 11th and 12th centuries and is a good example of the Romanesque architectural style. In the late 1600s, the Église Saint Germain des Près was turned into a prison. With the Revolution of 1789, it was changed into a saltpeter factory (used to make gunpowder). After the Revolution, the church resumed its religious role.

Next to the church, along the Boulevard Saint Germain, there is a little park with a small playground called the **Square Boucicault**. It is named for Aristide Boucicaut, the man who invented the first department

Saint Germain Highlights

• Check out the 1000 year old church tower
• Find the portrait of Benjamin Franklin in the Cour du Commerce Saint André
• Look for the brass Paris Meridian line in the Eglise Saint Sulpice
• Find the polar bear sculpture and bedroom furniture by Macintosh at the Musée d'Orsay
• Check out the animals at Deyrolles, Paris' finest taxidermist shop
• Go for a Canal Boat Ride

store, the nearby Bon Marché.

RUE DE BUCI. *Just east of the Eglise Saint Germain des Près.*

This street is lined with wonderful bakeries, food shops, and cafés. It is a good spot to take a break and watch the fashionable Saint Germain crowd go by.

RUE SAINT ANDRE DES ARTS. *Just east of the Rue de Buci, Metro: Odéon.*

This bustling street is lined with shops, small restaurants, and an artsy movie theatre. It is a fun way to get from the Rue de Buci to the Place Saint Michel. You can also take an interesting detour into the **Cour du Commerce Saint André** (heading east, on the right, shortly after you enter the street). This cobbled lane has welcomed pedestrians to its shops and restaurants for hundreds of years. It leads to the Carrefour de l'Odéon. On the right, you will see the Paris' oldest café, the Café Procope. Notice the portraits in the window. There's one you should recognize from American history books: Benjamin Franklin.

ÉGLISE SAINT SULPICE, *Place Saint Sulpice. Metro: Mabillon or Saint Sulpice. Open daily, 8am-7:30pm. Entrance is free.*

The outside of this church is odd and slightly out of proportion. That's because it was built and rebuilt over the centuries and combines a mish-mash of different architectural styles. The tower on the right was never completed.

The inside of Saint Sulpice is more interesting, especially if you are traveling with any fans of Dan Brown's *The DaVinci Code.* One of the scenes in that story takes place here in Saint Sulpice and has to do with a clue connected to the brass line, which you can see on the floor of the church leading to a white marble obelisk. The line and obelisk are part of a **gnomon**, a sort of sundial that indicates days of the year, instead of hours of the day. Here's how it works: If you look up at the stained glass windows above the meridian line, you can make out a circular hole in one of the windowpanes. On the stroke of noon, the light from the sun (provided it isn't cloudy) goes through the round hole in the window and lands on a point along the brass line. That point indicates the day's date. There is a special marble plaque indicating the spot where the light hits on the day of the Summer Solstice (June 21). Small brass plaques mark the Spring and Fall Equinoxes. On the day of the Winter Solstice (December 21) the sunlight hits a spot on the obelisk decorated with the Zodiac symbol, Capricorn. A Sagittarius symbol marks the date for November 21, and Aquarius marks the spot for January 21.

A small chapel (called Chapelle des Anges) on the right as you enter the Eglise Saint Sulpice features three famous paintings by Eugène Delacroix. One depicts Saint Michael fighting the Devil. Another depicts the story of Heliodorus, ordered by the king of Syria to steal the treasure from a Temple, but chased away by three angels (one on a horse). The third painting shows Jacob wrestling with an angel as he is being tested by God.

In another side chapel, there is also a small organ that once belonged to Queen Marie-Antoinette, and on which a young Mozart performed. The church's main organ is one of the biggest in the world.

MARCHÉ DE SAINT GERMAIN DES PRÈS. *12, Rue Lobineau. Metro: Mabillon. Open 10am-7:30pm. Closed Sun.*

This covered market once housed the Saint Germain Fair, then food stalls. Today, it has been transformed into a shopping mall with plenty of stores and restaurants.

MUSÉE D'ORSAY. *1, Rue de la Légion d'Honneur (formerly Rue de Bellechasse). Metro: Solférino or Musée d'Orsay. Open 9:30am 6 pm, later on Thurs. Closed Mon. Adults: €11; Kids under 18: free. Fees are reduced after 4:30pm (except Thurs) and after 6 pm Thurs. Free to all every first Sun. of the month. Combined Adult ticket for Musée d'Orsay and Musee the l'Orangerie (in the Tuileries): €16. Audioguide rental: €5. The Musee d'Orsay for Families, offering nine themed tours is available on touchscreen tablets that can be rented for €5. Ask for free children or family guides at the entrance. Wheelchairs and strollers available free of charge.*

Note: To avoid long lines, you can purchase tickets in advance at FNAC stores or online: www.musee-orsay. fr/en/visit/admission/ ticket-purchase.html Enter through Entrace C (Reserved Entrance).

This magnificent museum has something for (almost) everyone – Impressionist paintings and sculptures, cool furniture, giant clocks, models of buildings, and more – and it is located in the very impressive setting of a former train station, known as the Gare d'Orsay.

The Gare d'Orsay was one of the first train stations in Paris built for electric trains. It was very modern for its time, with electric elevators and more metal than was used in the construction of the Eiffel Tower. It was also very elegant and even contained a fancy hotel. For decades, the Gare d'Orsay was Paris' departure point for nearly 200 trains a day servicing southwestern France. However, as trains became longer, the station became to be too short to accommodate them. By 1939, the Gare d'Orsay was no longer servicing passenger trains. During World War II, the station was used as a center for sending care packages to war prisoners. When the war was over, it became a triage center for returning prisoners. It remained empty and out of use for decades, until it was refurbished and reopened to the public as a museum in 1986.

Today the museum features a magnificent collection of art and architecture dating from 1850 to 1915. You still get a feel for the beauty of the original train station as you walk in the central exhibition hall with its soaring ceiling. Look at the giant clocks. They may remind you of the movie, Hugo, about a boy who lives secretly in a Parisian train station rewinding the clocks.

The ground floor contains grand statues from the 19th century. Smaller exhibit halls on each side feature works by Ingres, Delacroix, Millet, Daumier, and Courbet. Toward the back of the main floor is an interesting wooden model of the Paris Opera and small scenes from famous operas. The upper levels feature exhibit rooms that take you through late 19th and early 20th century painting. These range from a large white statue of a polar bear (generally a big a hit with young children) to works by Dégas, Cézanne, Renoir, Manet, Monet, Van Gogh, and Toulouse Lautrec.

The exhibit spaces in the back of the museum feature beautiful examples of Art Nouveau and Arts and Crafts style furniture and decorative arts. Keep going up the steps, they cover several floors. Believe it or not, many children really enjoy this section. It doesn't take much for them to imagine what it would be like to live with such cool furniture.

The museum offers several beautiful eateries, ranging from the Café de l'Ours, near the white polar bear statue, to the Art Nouveau-inspired Café Campana by the Impressionist galleries, to the fancy first floor restaurant (take a peek even if you don't want to stay for a meal).

Near the Musée d'Orsay, at 56, Rue Jacob note the plaque on the former Hotel York mansion. This is the spot where Benjamin Franklin, John Jay, John Adams, and representatives from Britain and France signed the Paris Peace Treaty of September 3, 1783. It was this treaty that officially recognized American Independence from Britain.

BERGES DE SEINE (RIVER WALK). *Along the right bank of the Seine between the Musée d'Orsay and Pont de l'Alma. Metro: Musée d'Orsay, Assemblée Nationale, Invalides, or Pont de l'Alma.*

This river walk was recently inaugurated along a 2.3 kilometer (1.4 mile) stretch free of motorized vehicles. There are play spaces for kids, cafés, free fitness classes, floating gardens, and teepees and shipping containers that people can rent for private parties.

DEYROLLE, *46, Rue du Bac. Metro: Bac. Open 10am-7pm, but with a break for lunch, 1pm-2pm. Closed Sun.*

This surprising store is Paris' last taxidermy shop. It has animals ranging in size from insects to grizzly bears. There are also drawers filled with fossils and minerals. You will feel like you've walked into a natural history museum, except that you can actually purchase the displays. The shop adheres to strict rules regarding endangered species. The large animals come from zoos and farms where they died of natural causes. In 2008, a fire on the first floor destroyed all of the entomology collections and many of the taxidermy animals. Fourteen fire engines and 55 firefighters were needed to put out the blaze. It has since been fully restored.

AU BON MARCHÉ DEPARTMENT STORE. *24, Rue de Sèvres (Metro: Sèvres-Babylone), Open 10am-8pm (9pm closing Thurs-Fri). Closed Sundays.*

This is the world's first department store. When it was launched in 1876 by Aristide Boucicaut it was an instant success. The original building was designed by Gustave Eiffel (of Eiffel Tower fame). **La Grande Épicerie**, on the ground floor, was recently renovated and offers gourmet foods from France and around the world. The pastry section alone is worth the visit.

PARIS CANAL BOAT RIDES. *By the Musée d'Orsay, on the Quai Anatole France. Metro: Solférino. Departs at 9:30 am, daily, from late March to early November. Arrives at La Villette at 12:30pm. Adults: €19; Kids 4-11: €12; Youth 12-25: €16; 2 Adults + 2 Children: €49.*

This is a 3-hour canal boat ride that takes you along the Seine, to the Paris Marina, up through the Saint Martin Canal, and to the Parc de La Villette. You get wonderful views of major Paris sights, pass through numerous locks, under lovely foot bridges, and through a long tunnel under the Place de la Bastille. It's a unique way to experience Paris. For children who enjoy boats, it's a delightful tour, though it may be too long for small tikes. Don't forget to bring snacks or a full picnic. When you get to the Parc de la Villette, you can enjoy its wonderful science museum, museum of music, and playgrounds.

6. MONTPARNASSE

The **Montparnasse** neighborhood gets its name from Greek mythology, where Mount Parnassus is home of the god Apollo and his muses. In the early 20th century it was a hangout for many artists, such as Picasso, Chagall, and Man Ray; writers such as Jean-Paul Sartre and Simone de Beauvoir, and composers such as Erik Satie and Igor Stravinsky. After World War I, the so-called "lost generation" of American writers also settled around Montparnasse. These included Ernest Hemingway, Gertrude Stein, Alice B. Toklas, F. Scott Fitzgerald, Henri Miller, Anais Nin, and Ezra Pound.

Much of the area's Bohemian charm has been erased either through urban renewal projects in the 1970s or because of rising property prices in the city. But the old streets and sights have not all disappeared. And the kid-friendly attractions of this neighborhood give you a chance to appreciate both the old and new aspects of this Mont-Parnassus, home of the Muses.

TOUR MONTPARNASSE. *Rue de l'Arrivée. Metro: Montparnasse-Bienvenue. Viewing galleries open daily, 9:30am 11:30pm (summer);9:30am-10:30pm (winter). Adults: €14; Youths 16-20: €11; Kids 7-15: €6.50; Kids under 7: free.*

Unlike many American cities, Paris does not have a skyline dotted with skyscrapers. But it does have the Tour Montparnasse. Completed in 1973, this is the tallest building in Europe. It has 59 stories. Many Parisians will tell you that the top of the Tour Montparnasse offers the best view in the city. Why? Because you can see everything but the tower itself, which they consider to be a terrible eyesore.

The view from the tower is spectacular. A 38-second elevator

Montparnasse Highlights

- Ride up to the top floor of the Tour Montparnasse
- Eat a crêpe
- Visit the masses of bones in the Catacombs
- Play in the Parc Montsouris
- Climb on rocks and rent a remote control boat at the Parc Georges Brassens
- Shop for discount fashions in the Rue d'Alésia

ride takes you up to an observation space on the 56th floor with a 360 degree view of the city. You can grab a bite at the 360 Café or go for a fancy meal at the Ciel de Paris restaurant.

Most of the Tour Montparnasse is filled with offices. There is a shopping mall on the ground floor and a large, public, indoor swimming center on the lower level (niveau – 1) with pools for water lovers of all ages. Note: opening hours vary according to the season and day of the week.

On the esplanade between the Tour Montparnasse and the Montparnasse Train Station there is an **old-fashioned carrousel** that runs just about every day of the year. In the winter the city installs a **skating rink** here as well.

GARE MONTPARNASSE. *Place Bienvenue. Metro: Montparnasse-Bienvenue.*

This train station serves destinations to the west and southwest of Paris. These include Chartres, the Loire Valley, Brittany, Aquitaine, and Spain. Outside, you may notice plenty of crêpe restaurants. These are holdovers from the late 19th and early 20th centuries, when many people from Brittany (where crêpes are king) emigrated to Paris and set up shop near the station. Above the station, on a rooftop covering the tracks, is a public park called the **Jardin Atlantique**, which has a playground and room to run. *Entrance is at 1, place des 5 Martyrs du Lycée Buffon.*

CATACOMBS. *Entrance is at 1, avenue du Colonel Henri Roi-Tanguy (Small building on the Place Denfert Rochereau). Metro: Denfert Rochereau. Open 10am-5pm. Closed Mondays. Ticket booth closes at 4pm. Adults: €8; Youths age 14-26: €4; Kids under age 14: free. Audioguides: €3. Note: This visit can be too scary for young or sensitive children and is not recommended for people with heart conditions or claustrophobia. Also beware that you will exit 2 kilometers south of where you entered, in the rue Remy Dumoncel. Take a left as you exit to get to Avenue René Coty, and another left on the avenue to return to Denfert Rochereau. The tunnels are a chilly 14 degrees C/57 degrees F, so bring an extra layer.*

The Catacombs are located in some of Paris' old rock quarry tunnels, which were dug under the city to supply the white stone used for buildings and cobbled streets. The tunnels were dug for hundreds of years until they made up a network that stretched nearly 200 miles.

In the 1780s, central Paris became so crowded that even the cemeteries began to overflow. The decision was made to transfer their contents (more than 6 million skeletons) into some of the abandoned quarry tunnels. These became the Paris Catacombs.

During the German Occupation of Paris in World War II, the Catacombs served as the headquarters for the French Resistance fighters.

Today, you can visit parts of the Catacombs and old quarries to see some of the millions of bones that were carefully transferred here and lined up along the walls and ceilings of the tunnels. Personally, I find it dank, dark, and creepy, but it's a big hit with many kids, especially fans of scary movies and the macabre.

PARC MONTSOURIS. *Between Boulevard Jourdan, Avenue Reuille, Rue Nansouty, and Rue Gazan. Metro: Porte d'Orléans or Cité Universitaire. Open sunrise to sunset. Entrance is free.*

This large park is located on the southern edge of Paris in what was once a small village, surrounded by windmill-covered hills. Here you will find pony rides, puppet shows, playgrounds, an area for roller blading, and summer concerts in the gazebo.

Nearby is the **Rue d'Alésia**, which features lots of clothing stores, including discounted designer goods.

PARC GEORGES BRASSENS. *Rue des Morillons. Metro: Convention. Open daily, dawn to dusk. Entrance is free.*

Two majestic bronze bulls guard the entrance to the park as a reminder that this was once the sight of one of Paris' slaughterhouses. Today, there are playgrounds, puppet shows, and a merry-go-round. There are beehives and a garden of scents. There are climbing walls made from stones recycled from old buildings.

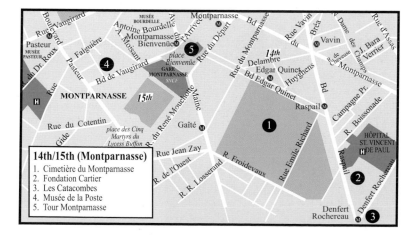

14th/15th (Montparnasse)
1. Cimetière du Montparnasse
2. Fondation Cartier
3. Les Catacombes
4. Musée de la Poste
5. Tour Montparnasse

7. EIFFEL TOWER

Once considered an eyesore by many Parisians, the Eiffel Tower is perhaps the most iconic symbol of Paris - and France! It really is a must-see, even if you don't have time to travel to the top.

EIFFEL TOWER. *On the Champs de Mars. Metro: Bir Hakeim. Open daily, 9 am-midnight (last elevator goes up at 11 pm). Stairs to levels one and two-Adults: €5; Youths 12-24: €4; Kids 4-11: €3, under 4: free. Elevator to levels 1 and 2 - Adults: €8.50; Youths 12-24: €7; Kids 4-11: €4, under 4: free. Elevator to level 3 - Adults: €14.50; Youths 12-24: €13; Kids 4-11: €10; under 4: free. Ticket offices for the elevator ride are in the north and east pillars, and you can purchase tickets to take the stairs in the south pillar. You can download a guided tour on your phone (www.tour-eiffel.fr/en/pre*

paring your-visit/buying-your-tickets.html). The tower's website has a special section for kids, with a terrific downloadable booklet in English and French full of fun facts, games, and more (www.tour-eiffel.fr/en/childrens-tower.html).

Parent tip: To avoid long ticket lines during high tourist seasons buy tickets on line (ticket.toureiffel.fr/index-css5-sete-pg1-lgen.html) or visit the tower early in the morning or in the evening. Caught midday in a long line? Don't worry. It's better organized than it looks, and the lines actually move fairly quickly. If your family is active and adventuresome, the line to walk up the stairs is usually much shorter than the one for the elevators. ❖

Kids love the Eiffel Tower, and who can blame them? It's big, it's cool, and seen from up close it's surprisingly beautiful. Here's how it works. The Eiffel Tower has three levels. You can take the elevator or walk up the stairs as far as level 2. You must ride a special elevator to reach level 3. If you walk up, you can purchase tickets for the top level at the ticket office on level 2. One option is to ride the elevator up and take the stairs down from level 1 or 2. This offers a unique view of the inner structure of the tower, and you can take a break by reading some of the

Eiffel Tower Highlights

- Ride the elevators to the top of the Eiffel Tower
- Take the stairs down at least one level to see the tower from the inside
- Peer at the ground from the glass floor of the tower's first level
- Go on a family-friendly bike or Segway tour
- Go on a boat tour down the Seine
- Look for the Statue of Liberty on the tip of the small Swan Island in the Seine

historical interest markers along the way. However, this route is not recommended for very small children or for people with vertigo. The Eiffel Tower was built to celebrate the 1889 Paris International Exhibition, and the 100th anniversary of the French Revolution. It was designed by **Gustave Eiffel**, an architect/engineer who also designed the interior support skeleton for the Statue of Liberty. Although it is the city's most popular landmark today, many people hated the tower when it was first built. A group of leading artists, writers, and politicians sent an editorial to a major newspaper decrying the project, saying that the tower design looked like a gigantic factory chimney.

Construction of the Eiffel Tower took two years. The day it was finished, on March 31, 1889, Gustave Eiffel climbed up the 1,710 steps to the top and raised a French flag from it. Until the Chrysler Tower was built in New York City (1930), the Eiffel Tower was the tallest building in the world.

Originally, each level of the Eiffel Tower was painted a different color, ranging from dark bronze at the bottom to a golden yellow on top. The colors have varied from lighter to darker over the years. The tower is repainted every 7 years. It takes 25 painters, 40 tons of paint, and nearly a year to finish the job.

In 1909, there was talk of tearing down the Eiffel Tower. Then it was discovered to be an ideal spot for a radio-telegraph center. During World War I, the tower housed a military spy center that tracked down enemy agents. The most famous of them was a woman known as Mata Hari, accused of spying for Germany. Ironically, Mata Hari was a familiar face at the Eiffel Tower. Prior to the war, she had been a dancer in the tower's first floor restaurant. After the Liberation of Paris in World War II, there was a nightclub on the Eiffel Tower, where American soldiers were welcomed free of charge.

Today, the Eiffel Tower is used by numerous TV and radio stations to emit their signals. It also holds a weather station and devices to measure the city's air quality.

The Eiffel Tower is 320 meters (984 feet) tall. In hot weather it can increase in height by as much as 6 inches due to the expansion of the metal. The Eiffel Tower contains 15,000 pieces of metal and 2.5 million metal rivets. It weighs 9 million kilos (7,000 tons). On a clear day, you can see as far as the Chartres Cathedral (more than 50 miles away) from the top level. On a stormy day, there's a good chance the tower will be struck by lightening. It averages 50 lightening strikes each year.

Lots of people have tried various stunts from the Eiffel Tower, ranging from the catastrophic (e.g., unsuccessful attempts to parachute from the tower or fly an airplane through it) to the funny (e.g., coaxing an elephant up the stairs to the first level) and the daring (e.g., bungee jumping off the second level or walking a tightrope wire from the tower to the Trocadero, across the river).

Level 1 has been rebuilt to include a glass floor overlooking the ground from the center of the tower, an interactive museum, and a restaurant called 58 Tour Eiffel, which offers fancy picnic lunches (from €21) and expensive, trendy dinner service. Level 2 has a buffet-style snack bar, the very upscale Jules Vernes restaurant, and the official Eiffel Tower gift shop. Level 3 has a reconstruction of Gustave Eiffel's office.

CHAMPS DE MARS. *Metro: Bir Hakeim or Ecole Militaire. RER: Champs de Mars. Open day and night.*

This park is named for the Roman god of war, Mars, and it marks the spot where the Gauls (early Celtic settlers of Paris) were defeated by Roman invaders in 50 BC. It has been used as a practice field for the nearby Military Academy and the sight of some of the world's first hot air balloon rides. Now it is a quiet park, a favorite spot for skate boarders and roller bladders.

FAT TIRES' BIKE AND SEGWAY TOURS. *Located 3 blocks from the Eiffel Tower at 24, Rue Edgar Faure, Metro: Dupleix. Phone: 01-56-58-10-54. North America Toll-Free: +1 866 614 6218 Website: http://paris. fattirebiketours.com/*

This company is American owned and offers English-language tours of Paris via bicycle or Segway. Their "Skip the Line" tours include visits to major monuments, with a priority entrance. They also have tours in Versaille and Monet's House in Giverny. The tours are designed to be fun and not grueling. They stay on flat parts and avoid traffic. It's a great way to see the city. The tours are also very family-friendly, but you should contact them in advance to reserve child bikes, seats, or trailers.

BATEAUX PARISIENS TOUR BOATS. *Port de la Bourdonnais, at the foot of the Eiffel Tower, Metro:Bir Hakeim. Daily departures every 30 minutes, 10am- 11pm. Price: Adults €13; Kids 3-12 €5; under 3: free. Kid-friendly cruises depart at 1:45 pm and 3:45 pm, Saturday and Sunday.* Try also **BATEAU VEDETTES DE PARIS TOUR BOATS.** *Port de Suffren (Metro: Bir Hakeim) Tours leave every 30 minutes, from 10 am to 9 pm. Adults: €13; Kids 4-11: €5; Kids under 4: free.* Tours with snacks or meals also offered for higher rates.

Kids love these boat cruises. It's a great way to see many of the major sights and monuments of Paris, especially if you are jet-lagged or foot sore. The vantage point is unique. The commentaries are in English and French. The regular tour lasts 60 minutes. See photo on next page.

STATUE OF LIBERTY. *On the tip of the Isle aux Signes (Swan Island), the island under the double-decker bridge called Pont de Bir Hakeim.* This is a miniature model of the Statue of Liberty that stands in New York harbor. It is a reminder that the statue was a gift from France to the United States and that it was designed by the French sculptor Auguste Bartholdi. Gustave Eiffel (of Eiffel Tower fame) designed the inside support structure for it. The full-size Statue of Liberty arrived in New York in 1885, dismantled into pieces that filled 214 packing crates. It was officially inaugurated on October 28, 1886. At the time, the Statue of Liberty was the tallest (305 feet) building in New York City. The best place from which to see the Paris version of the statue is from a tour boat. You can also see another version in the Luxembourg Gardens, one in the Museum of Arts and Industry in the Marais neighborhood, or a full-size replica of the statue's torch by the Pont de l'Alma.

PARIS SEWER TOUR AND MUSEUM. *By the Pont de l'Alma, across from 93, Quai d'Orsay. Metro: Alma-Marceau. Open 11am-5pm (May-Sept), 11am-4pm (Oct-Apr). Closed Thur and Fri, and 2 weeks in January. Last entry tickets are sold one hour before closing time. Closed during heavy rains. Adults: €4.20; Kids 6-16: €3.40; under 6: free.*

This is the kind of unusual visit that kids (and many adults) really enjoy and remember. Okay, you do have to get used to the smell, but it's not as bad as you might expect. The sewer tunnels cover about 1,400 miles. They run directly under every Paris street, with wider tunnels for broader avenues. Each tunnel is named for the street above it, so that anyone with a road map of Paris can find his or her way. More than 300 sewer workers, engineers, and other specialized staff maintain this vast and critically important system.

8. LES INVALIDES

The Invalides complex was built in 1670 by King Louis XIV as a home for wounded war veterans, and the buildings along the eastern side still fill that function. The rest has been transformed into a museum and the final resting place for Napoleon Bonaparte.

NAPOLEON'S TOMB IN THE EGLISE DU DOME. *Invalides complex. 129, Rue de Grenelle. Métro: Invalides, Latour-Maubourg, or Varenne. Open 10am-5pm (winter), 10am-6pm (summer). Adults: €9.50; Kids under 18: free. Combined ticket for the tomb, Musée de l'Armée, and Musée des Plans Reliefs.*

The large, golden-domed church in the middle of the Invalides complex was built during the reign of Louis XIV. It was restored in the 1980s, when more than 500,000 pieces of gold leaf were used to bring back the dome's golden luster. The four statues decorating the top of the Dôme represent Hope, Charity, Spirituality, and Religion.

Two of the Invalides' architects, Liberal Bruant and Jules Hardouin Mansart, are buried in the church. So is Marshall Foch, who commanded the allied French, British, and American troops at the end of World War I. But the most famous tomb in the church belongs to Napoleon I.

Who was Napoleon I? Napoleon Bonaparte was born on the island of Corsica. After leading successful military campaigns in Italy, he was elected First Consul of the Republic in 1799. Napoleon established a new constitution for France, a new code of laws, a national education system,

and reformed the judicial system. He created the nation's leading universities and Academies of Art, Science, Literature, and Engineering. In 1802, Napoleon was elected Consul for life, and in 1804 declared himself Emperor. He conquered most of Europe, except Britain, but in 1805, he began to suffer military defeats. In 1812, he lost four-fifths of his men in the frozen Russian winter. In 1814, he was forced from power and sent into exile on the Italian island of Elba. Napoleon returned to power in 1815, only to be forced from power once again after his military defeat at Waterloo. He was exiled to Saint Helena, an island in the south Atlantic, where he died.

In 1840, Napoleon's remains were returned to the Invalides with great pomp and circumstance. The remains are contained inside **an enormous granite sarcophagus**. It was a gift from Tsar Nicholas I of Russia, which is ironic since it was Napoleon's unsuccessful attempt to take over Russia that began his downfall. Within the sarcophagus there are 6 coffins, nestled one inside the other like Russian dolls. They are made of iron, wood, lead, lead, ebony, and oak.

Side chapels in the Eglise du Dôme contain the remains of Napoleon's brothers, Joseph and Jerome, and his son, Napoleon II. The adjacent **Saint Louis church** contains a collection of flags that were captured from the enemy during Napoleon's many military campaigns.

MUSÉE DE L'ARMEE (MILITARY MUSEUM). *In the Invalides complex. 129, Rue de Grenelle Métro: Invalides, Latour-Maubourg, or Varenne. Open daily 10am-5pm (winter), 10am-6pm (summer). Combined ticket for tomb, Musée de l'Armée, and Musée des Plans Reliefs. Adults: €9.50; Kids under 18: free.*

This Military Museum features exhibits ranging from prehistoric battles to 20th Century World Wars. It is quite interesting, even if you are not a military history buff. The ground floor is filled with suits of armor. The upper floors feature exhibits on the Napoleonic wars, including a display of Napoleon's horse, Vizir. There is a section dedicated to World War I, with lots of (fairly boring) maps and uniforms – the most touching is one from a man in the trenches that is caked with mud.

However, the best part of the museum is newer section dedicated to World War II. Both children and adults will be moved by its exhibits

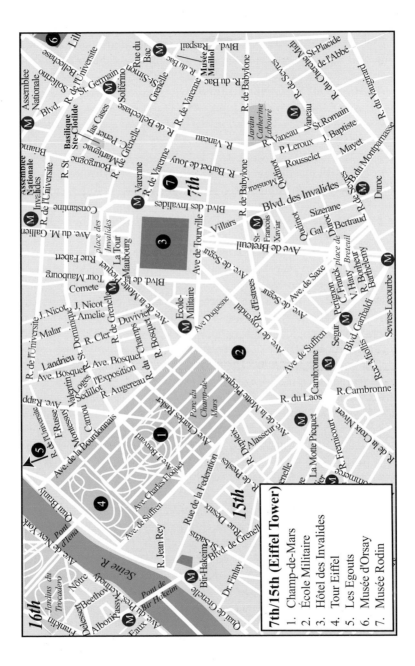

7th/15th (Eiffel Tower)
1. Champ-de-Mars
2. École Militaire
3. Hôtel des Invalides
4. Tour Eiffel
5. Les Egouts
6. Musée d'Orsay
7. Musée Rodin

(conveniently labeled in both English and French). The rooms not only show artifacts and films about the fighting and military strategy. They also offer glimpses into the war's effect on ordinary people, including children. The exhibit is organized chronologically and gives a good view of just how many countries and people were affected by WWII.

MUSÉE DES PLANS RELIEFS. *In the Invalides complex. 129, Rue de Grenelle. Métro: Invalides, Latour-Maubourg, or Varenne. Open daily 10am-5pm (winter), 10am-6pm (summer). Combined ticket for tomb, Musée de l'Armée, and Musée des Plans Reliefs. Adults: €9.50; Kids under 18: free.*

This small museum is on an upper floor of the Invalides complex. It presents a collection of made-to-scale wooden models of fortresses, ports, and towns across France. They were prepared for King Louis XIV as part of his strategic defense plans. They were so important that their existence was kept secret for many years.

Parent Tip: There is a recently renovated café in the Invalides. But if you are visiting on a nice day, you may want to head instead to the nearby Musée Rodin gardens for lunch or a snack. Entry for the gardens is only €2 for adults and free for kids under 18. There you can enjoy your food in a quiet garden with famous sculptures and plenty of room for kids to move around. ❖

MUSÉE RODIN. *77, Rue de Varenne (Metro: Varenne), not far from the Invalides. Open Tues-Sun, 9:30 am - 5:45 pm (April-September) and 9:30 am - 4:45 pm (October-March). Closed Mondays. There is a nice, outdoor café, open during spring and summer. Adults: €6 for museum and gardens or €2 for just the gardens; Kids under 18: free; Family ticket for 2 Adults + 2 Kids: €10. Free to all on the first Sunday of each month. Special family visit audioguide: €3 for the first + €1.50 for each additional one.*

The recently renovated museum has collections of drawings and sculptures by Rodin, his pal Vincent Van Gogh, and his girlfriend and artistic partner Camille Claudel. It also features excellent temporary exhibits. It is located in the house where Rodin lived and worked.

The gardens alone are worth a visit, and they offer many of Rodin's most famous works. There's room to run and an excellent café. Just remind your kids not to touch the sculptures.

Some of the major sculptures you'll see in the garden include:

The Gate to Hell: This elaborate, bronze doorway is based on the Inferno, a long poem by the Italian writer, Dante. It depicts characters from the poem including Ugolino – a crawling man imprisoned for treason and forced to starve to death with his children and grandchildren; Paolo and

Francesca – caught in the act of kissing and killed by Francesca's husband; Adam and Eve – banned from Paradise; and other tortured souls trying to climb their way out of the deepest depths of Hell. Rodin worked on this piece for 20 years. It was commissioned to decorate a Museum of Decorative Arts that was never built (on the site that now houses the Musée d'Orsay).

The Thinker: This seated man with his head on one hand is one of Rodin's most famous sculptures. He originally designed it as a small statue for his Gate to Hell, and later turned it into a large piece. It is a portrait of Dante. See photo below.

The Kiss: Rodin's most popular sculpture was originally a small part of the Gate to Hell. It depicts the two lovers, Paolo and Francesca, shortly before they are discovered and stabbed by her husband.

The Burghers of Calais: This group of six figures commemorates a real story from 1347. Calais, a town on the northern coast of France, had been under siege by the English for nearly a year. To save the town from starvation, the six leading men in the town offered their lives to the English king, Edward III, in exchange for the safety of their townsfolk. The English king accepted, but his wife, Queen Phillippa, was so moved by the burghers' sacrifice that she talked the king into sparing their lives.

Statue of Honoré de Balzac: Rodin's portrait of the famous French author/playwright was commissioned by the Society of Literary Men, led by author Emile Zola. In the end, however, the statue became tangled in larger artistic and political controversies, so the Literary Society refused to accept it.

Here's a tip if your kids think the sculptures are boring. Rodin used the same model (a poor, ragged man who hauled coal for a living) for several of his sculptures, including John the Baptist, one of the Burghers of Calais, one of the damned souls of the Gate of Hell, and the Man with a Broken Nose. Ask your kids if they can find him.

MUSÉE DU QUAI BRANLY (ETHNOGRAPHY MUSEUM). *37, Quai Branly.(Metro: Iena, or Pont de l'Alma) Open 11am-7pm (until 9pm Thurs,Fri,Sat). Closed Monday. Adults: €9; Kids under 18: free. Additional fees apply for special exhibits. Free to everyone on the first Sunday of each month. Audioguide: €5. You can download a short guidebook in English. (www.quaibranly.fr/fileadmin/user_upload/musee_pratique/venir_au_musee/mqb_guide_exploration_GB.pdf)*

If you or your kids are fascinated by exotic objects from different cultures, this museum has wonderful ones, such as African drums, North American totem poles, masks from Pacific Islands, Asian costumes, and more.

If your group is not up for the museum, they may still enjoy the outside of this building. It has jungle-like plants growing on the walls and gardens with ponds, plants, and walkways. There's a nice café in the garden offering breakfast, light lunch, snacks, and a children's menu. It's a great place to stop if you are walking from the Eiffel Tower to the Invalides.

9. LOUVRE

And now let's cxross over to the **Right Bank**!

The **Louvre** and **Tuileries gardens** can be very intimidating. The sheer size of the place (the Louvre is the biggest museum in the world) can be a real turnoff for children. The formal layout of the buildings and gardens can feel cold and hostile. Yet, there is much here to delight even the most flat-footed museum goers. All it takes is a little planning, and knowledge of a few fun facts and good tips.

LOUVRE MUSEUM. *99, Rue de Rivoli and 34-36, Quai du Louvre. Metro: Louvre or Palais Royal. Open 9am-6pm (until 9:45pm Wed, Fri). Closed Tues. Adults: €12; Kids under 18: free. Special exhibits are extra. Reduced rates apply after 3pm (6pm Wed,Fri), and entrance is free on the first Sunday of each month. Audioguides with 3-D images: Adults: €5; Kids: €3. Or download the audioguide app (http://www.louvre.fr/en/louvre-audio-guide-app). Free strollers and wheelchairs are available from the information desk under the Pyramid. Hang on to your entry tickets and you will be able to enter and exit the museum all day. Check out the museum's website for a fun set of stories and anecdotes about the Louvre in English specially made for kids: www.louvre.fr/en/tales-of-the-museum.*

Parent tip: Lines to enter the glass pyramid at the Louvre entrance can be very long and hot in the summer. It's a little faster if you enter through the shopping mall, from the steps leading underground by the Arc du Carrousel or via the metro entrance. However, even this method leads to long security and ticket lines inside. The **quickest way to enter the Louvre** and avoid lines is to use the little-known **Porte des Lions entrance**. This is in the Southwest

Louvre Highlights

• Go on a treasure hunt for your favorite Louvre masterpieces
• Visit the old moat and walls of the medieval Louvre
• Check out the underground shopping mall and US-style food court in the Grand Louvre
• Have lunch on the Louvre's open-air terrace or in an open-air café in the Tuileries
• Stand in the alignment of the Louvre pyramid and Concorde obelisk and check out the views
• Rent a toy sailboat at the central fountain in the Tuileries
• Try out the Ferris wheel and other rides in the Fête des Tuileries
• Admire elegant fashions through the ages at the Musée de la Mode
• Play in the Palais Royal gardens and look for its cannon
• See Monet's water lilies in the Orangerie Museum
• Look at the pet stores along Quai de la Mégisserie
• Draw a picture from the Pont des Arts.

wing of the Louvre, along the Seine, nearly level with the Arch du Carrousel. Look for the (female) lions on either side of the entrance. To avoid crowds inside, you may want to consider visiting the museum in the late afternoon between 4 and 6pm or on Wednesday or Thursday evenings when it's open until 9:45 pm. ❖

The Louvre's history stretches back more than 800 years. It was first a fort, then a fortified castle, a luxurious palace, and finally a world-famous museum. The first Louvre was built in 1200 by King Philippe Auguste. It consisted of a large, fortified tower built along the city walls at their most vulnerable point: the city's western edge. The purpose of this fort was to help protect Paris from the invading English Plantagenets, led by Richard the Lionheart. The early Louvre fortress also was used as a prison, an arsenal to store weapons, and place to safeguard royal treasures.

In 1360, King Charles V transformed the Louvre into a fortified castle with turrets and protective walls. It was occupied by the English for 16 years during France's 100 years war with England. In the 1500s, King François I rebuilt the Louvre as a Renaissance Palace. His son, Henri II expanded it further, and Henri's wife, Catherine de Médicis added the Tuileries Palace (later destroyed). King Henri IV added the long galleries along the Seine.

In the 1670s, King Louis XIV moved his royal court to Versailles and abandoned the Louvre. In his absence, numerous artists, writers, philosophers, and men of science moved in. Part of the building was made into a museum to show off the royal art collections. Many of the artists living in

the Louvre also ex-
hibited their works
in the arcades along
the ground level at
a Fair known as the
Foire aux Croutes.
(Croute means a
crust of bread and
is slang for crummy
art).

In 1789, King
Louis XVI was for-
ced by the revolutionaries to leave the Palace of Versailles and move back
to the Louvre. He tried to escape Paris in 1791 with his family, but they
were caught and imprisoned. From 1792 to 1793, a guillotine was set up
in the middle of the Place du Carrousel. The king was beheaded, and a
new museum was officially inaugurated in the Louvre. When Napoleon I
came to power, he moved into the Louvre and undertook further expan-
sions and renovations. He also kicked out the last of the artists still living
in the building, but added many works of art to the museum's collection
from pieces collected during his many military campaigns. Napoleon III
also expanded the Louvre with lavish rooms that you can still visit today
in the northern wing of the building.

In 1980, French President François Mitterand launched a huge project to renovate and expand the Louvre. Architect I.M. Pei designed the
glass pyramid (cleaned regularly by window washers using mountain
climbing gear) and underground galleries. The exhibit halls were renovated, and excavations on the eastern side uncovered remnants of the early
medieval fortress that was once the original Louvre building. They are now
part of the medieval Louvre visit.

Highlights: The Louvre is a huge museum. A good place to start is
with the museum map, available where you buy tickets It will help you
find some of the most famous pieces. Here is a quick tour:

Mesopotamia (Richelieu Wing, ground floor): There are two im-
mense bulls with human heads that once guarded the Palace of Sargon,
built in 720 BC. Notice that from the front they have two feet, from the
side they have four, and if you look from an angle there are five!

Persia (Sully Wing, ground floor): Check out the magnificent tile
friezes. One depicts archers and the other a griffin. They are from the
palace of the great Persian King Darius, defeated by Alexander the Great

in the 5th century BC. Darius' palace also had 72 columns, 21 meters (70 feet) high, topped with two bulls. Two are displayed. Imagine how a whole palace full would have looked.

Egypt (Sully Wing, ground and first floors): The Egyptian galleries take you through different aspects of ancient Egyptian life like food, music, and religion. There are lots of mummies and sarcophagi, even mummies of animals. There are also many small objects from daily life. You will see many statues of Egyptian gods and pharaohs.

Ancient Greece (Sully Wing, ground floor, lower level, and first floor): There are wonderful Greek sculptures and vases. The most famous statues are the Venus de Milo, still beautiful even though she's missing her arms, and the dramatic Victory of Samothrace. This statue has lost her head, has wings for arms, and has folds in her clothing that seem to be moving in spite of being made of stone. It was built to celebrate a Greek victory on the island of Rhodes and originally stood on a great rock overlooking the sea.

Ancient Rome (Denon Wing, ground floor): You'll see Roman mosaics and remarkable paintings saved from the walls of villas around Pompeii. They were buried in the ash of the Mount Vesuvius volcano when it erupted suddenly in 79 AD. There are also lovely funeral sculptures.

Medieval period (Sully Wing, lower level): The most fascinating section is the underground exhibit of the medieval Louvre itself, discovered in the 1990s during the museum's renovation. It shows the foundations of the castle, moat, and protective walls built by King Philippe Auguste in 1200. You'll also see a collection of objects that were found during the archeological excavation of the fortress, including a gold helmet belonging to King Charles VI that was thrown into a well by robbers.

Renaissance (Denon Wing, first floor and Richelieu Wing, first floor): The most famous work in this section is Leonardo da Vinci's *Mona Lisa*. There are also many other famous paintings by da Vinci, Raphael, Michelangelo, Donatello, Boticelli, Bellini, and Titian. Don't miss the funny portraits of the four seasons by Giuseppe Archimbaldo (gallery 5). The faces are composed of seasonal fruits and vegetables.

19th century paintings (Denon Wing, first floor and Sully Wing 2nd floor): There are several huge paintings that often captivate children here. Look for the paintings of Napoleon I by Jacques Louis David, including the one in which he is crowning his wife, Josephine. Another classic favorite is the Raft of the Medusa by Gericault. It is based on a true story of a shipwreck that left 150 men drifting on a raft for 13 days. Only 15 survived starvation, madness, and cannibalism. Notice, too, Eugene

Delacroix's painting of Liberty Guiding the People. It has become a symbol of France. The painting does not actually depict the 1789 Revolution, but rather another popular rebellion in 1830.

Napoleon III's apartments (Richelieu Wing, first floor): These are preserved to reflect the rich gold and red velvet decor of this period. Here you really get a sense for what the Louvre was like as a palace.

TUILERIES GARDENS. *Between Rue de Rivoli and Seine River. Metro: Tuileries, Louvre, or Place de la Concorde. Open daily, sunrise to sunset. Entrance: Free.*

Stretched between the Louvre Museum and the Place de la Concorde is the very pretty esplanade of the Tuileries Gardens. If you stroll along the middle lane of the gardens you can see the Glass Pyramid of the Louvre through the Arc du Carrousel in one direction. Then turn and look at the Obelisk in the Place de la Concorde. Notice how it is aligned with the Champs Elysées, Arch de Triomphe, and beyond that the Grande Arche de la Defense 10 kilometers (6 miles) away. The photo opportunities abound.

The name for this garden comes from the French word for roof tiles, tuiles. Before the area became part of the Louvre Palace domain, it housed a roof tile factory, a tuilerie. In the late 1500s, Queen Catherine de Médicis built herself a residence called Tuileries Palace. It was destroyed by fire in 1871, but used to stand in what is now the open section between the two longest wings of the Louvre.

The formal gardens were designed later by Louis XIV's favorite landscape architect, André Le Nôtre. He is also the one who designed the gardens at Versailles.

On the eastern edge of the Tuileries, standing like an entrance gate to the park, is the **Arc du Carrousel**. This triumphal arch was built in an imitation Roman style by Napoleon I to celebrate his military victories. You can see him on top, dressed as a Roman emperor. The golden horses pulling his chariot were stolen from Saint Mark's Cathedral in Venice, during one of Napoleon's Italian campaigns. It was an old tradition: the Venetians had stolen the horses centuries earlier from the city of Constantinople (Istanbul, Turkey).

The Tuileries Gardens are great place to relax after a walk through the Louvre or down the Champs Elysées. There are **playgrounds, pony rides**, and **miniature sailboats** for rent at the main fountain. There are also several good **cafés** in the park between the Louvre and the Place de la Concorde, where you can grab a meal or a snack on a nice day. If you are in Paris during the summer or winter holidays, check out the **Fête des Tuileries**. It includes fair rides and games for all ages. A ride up the central Ferris wheel offers one of the best views of Paris.

ORANGERIE DES TUILERIES. *Place de la Concorde, Jardin des Tuileries. Metro: Concorde. Open 9am-6pm. Closed Tues. Adults: €9; Kids: free. Special audioguide for kids: €5. Download the family visit app (https:// itunes.apple.com/fr/app/musee-lorangerie-for-families/id583307238?mt=8)*

If you are not up to facing the crowds in the more popular Musée d'Orsay across the river, the Orangerie is an excellent alternative. Housed in a former greenhouse, it has had a recent facelift. The museum is rarely crowded, not too big, and features beautiful Impressionist and modern paintings by artists such as Renoir, Cezanne, and Picasso. The most spectacular exhibit includes eight enormous water lily paintings by Claude Monet. They fill two rooms. You may recognize them from the book, Linnea in Monet's Garden.

JEU DE PAUME MUSEUM, *1, Place de la Concorde. Metro: Concorde. Open 11am-7pm, (until 9 on Tues). Closed Mon. Adults: €8.50; Kids: free.*

This museum features temporary exhibits of modern and contemporary art. It is housed in a former Jeu de Paume court of the Tuileries Palace. Jeu de Paume was an early form of tennis popular during the Renaissance.

MUSÉE DE LA PUBLICITÉ, MUSÉE DES ARTS DÉCORATIFS, MUSÉE DE LA MODE ET DU TEXTILE. *107, Rue de Rivoli. Metro: Palais Royal or Louvre. Open 11am-6pm. Closed Mon. One combined ticket allows access to all three of these museums. Adult: €11. Kids: Free.*

These museums are lodged in the northern wing of the Louvre. They are small and treat topics that appeal easily to children.

The Musée de la Mode features clothes fashions through the ages, from the Renaissance to Sci-Fi-looking futuristic styles.

The Musée de la Publicité has some wonderful old advertisement posters and TV ads.

The Musée des Arts Décoratifs features every day objects, such as toys, dishes, and furniture from the 13th century to today.

PALAIS ROYAL GARDENS. *Entrances to the gardens from the Place du Palais Royal, Place de Valois, Rue de Montpensier, and Rue de Beaujolais. Metro: Palais Royal. Open sunrise to sunset. Entrance is free.*

This former royal palace offers gardens where you can relax after a visit to the Louvre. There is plenty of room to run and play. You can also use the gardens as a starting point for a visit through some of Paris' shopping galleries and passages, starting with the **Galerie Colbert** and **Galerie Vivienne**, on the northern side. The courtyard is decorated with modern, black and white columns of different sizes. These were designed in 1986 by artist Daniel Buren and were widely despised when they were

first installed. Since then, they have become part of the landscape, and children are allowed to run among them or jump off of them. The arcades of the gardens are lined with cafés, restaurants, and fancy shops, including a lovely toy store and music box shop along the northern edge of the garden. The garden features fountains and tree-lined avenues. In the summer there are temporary sculpture exhibits, outdoor concerts, and plays.

Nestled in a flowerbed on the south side of the Palais Royal gardens is **a small cannon**. It was never used for defense purposes, but had another important role — as a timepiece. From 1786 to 1914, it would go off every day at noon, provided the weather was sunny. The canon sits on the line of the Paris Meridian. It was set up so that at midday the sun would pass through an eyepiece and warm up the fuse that shot off the canon. It was restored in 1990. Today this little cannon is set off each Saturday at noon by one of the park's guards.

On the western edge you will see one of Paris' most illustrious theaters, the **Comédie Francaise**. The famous French playwright, Molière, performed here with his theater company. He even died in the theater after playing the leading role in his play, the Imaginary Invalid.

QUAI DE LA MÉGISSERIE. *Along the Seine, between the Pont Neuf and the Pont au Change bridges. Metro: Pont Neuf.*

The stretch of this road along the Seine River between the Pont Neuf and Place du Châtelet is filled with pet stores. Along with the usual array of puppies, kittens, fish, birds, and reptiles are more surprising pets, such as roosters, various types of pigeons, and enormous rabbits.

RUE SAINT HONORÉ. *Running parallel to the Rue de Rivoli.*

This road features an endless array of shops and boutiques. There is something for everyone, ranging from high fashion to Asian noodle restaurants, excellent pastry shops, and goofy souvenirs.

PONT DES ARTS. *Spanning the Seine River from the Louvre to the Saint Germain neighborhood. Metro: Pont Neuf or Louvre.*

The Pont des Arts was the city's first pedestrian bridge and was also the first to be made of iron. Half of it collapsed in 1979 after repeated damage from floods and boat accidents. It was rebuilt and reopened in 1984 and is now a favorite spot for artists and lovers. The views offer great photo opportunities. Or you can join the other painters who set up their sketchpads and easels to capture the scene. Maybe your budding artist will want to give it a try. The metal railings of the bridge are covered with padlocks representing love messages from the many romantics who pass by. The locks are periodically cut off to reduce weight on the bridge. See photo on next page.

10. LES HALLES

Author Emile Zola called **Les Halles** the "Belly of Paris." If other neighborhoods were the spiritual, intellectual, or fashion centers of the city, this was where the serious work of feeding the city took place. Les Halles was for centuries Paris' central wholesale marketplace – the realm of butchers and fishmongers.

Today the area has been transformed by modern art and urban renewal efforts. Entire areas have been turned into pedestrian zones, filled with shops, cafés, and art galleries. While you may argue about the architectural merits of these new constructions, your children will enjoy the car-free environment and street entertainment that await them in the belly of the beast that is Paris.

LES HALLES. *Metro: Les Halles.*

From the year 50 AD until 1969, Les Halles was Paris' central marketplace, and the neighborhood was filled with restaurants that offered hearty fare to the neighborhood's workers. In 1969, the wholesale food market, having outgrown this space, was moved to a suburb near Orly Airport. The beautiful glass and iron market buildings were torn down leaving an empty pit. In the 1980s, the hole was redeveloped as the **Forum des Halles**, featuring a large shopping center, movie theaters, and a metro station complex in three underground levels. It was never considered attractive, however, and in 2011 construction began to renovate the area once again with new buildings and green spaces.

The **Jardin Nelson Mandela** (Nelson Mandela Park) on the west side of Les Halles opened in 2013 (to be fully finished in 2016). It is ecofriendly and filled with playgrounds and kids' activities. A special adventure terrain section is reserved for kids ages 7-11 (see below).

TERRAIN D'AVENTURES (KIDS ADVENTURE TERRAIN). *Located in the Nelson Mandela Park, on the southwestern side of the Les Halles park complex, by the round building called Bourse du Commerce. Metro: Les Halles, Porte du Louvre exit. Opens at 10 am, closing times vary between 6-8 pm depending on the season. Closed on Mondays, and during lunch breaks (1-2pm) in July-August. During the school year, Tues, Thurs, Fri mornings may be taken up by school groups.*

This play area is reserved for kids ages 7-11 years, only. No adults. Kids can spend one hour in the park, running through rocks, canyons, playgrounds, megamachines, and more. The kids are monitored by trained staff. Don't worry if they can't understand French. They'll figure out plenty of ways to have fun. Their parents are encouraged to take a break. I recommend the cafés in the nearby Rue Montorgueil, to the right of the big Saint Eustache church.

On the northwestern side of Les Halles is the large Saint Eustache Church. In front is a large sculpture depicting a tilted head and hand by artist Henri de Miller. The contrast between its modern style and the gothic church behind it makes for interesting photo opportunities. To the left is a giant sundial. It's curved edges make it popular with roller bladers and skate boarders.

Les Halles Area Highlights

- Find the giant sculpture of a head tilted on its side
- Let your 7-11 years olds play in the Adventure Terrain of the Nelson Mandela Park, and take a break in a nearby café
- Pick out your lunch in the Montorgueil market street
- Watch the jugglers and other street performers in front of the Pompidou Center
- Check out the fun Stravinsky Fountain
- Look for gargoyles on the Eglise Saint Mérri
- Ride up the glass escalators in the Pompidou Center and visit the Modern Art Museum

RUE MONTORGUEIL MARKET DISTRICT. *North of Les Halles. Metro: Les Halles or Etienne Marcel. Open daily, except Mon.*

This pedestrian shopping street features an open-air market, food shops, restaurants, and cafés. It's an excellent place to take a break or pick up a snack. Children enjoy the old shop signs that line the streets. Don't miss the giant golden snail above the Escargot Restaurant. There's also a famous pastry shop, called Patisserie Stohrer at #51, which has been around since the days of Queen Marie Antoinette.

FASHION DISTRICT. *Between the Forum des Halles and the Place des Victoires, mainly along the Rue du Jour and Rue Etienne Marcel. Metro: Les Halles or Etienne Marcel.*

If your group includes a fashion slave, you may want to walk up the Rue du Jour and along the Rue Etienne Marcel to the Place des Victoires, where you'll find names like Kenzo, Cacharel, Maje, and Zadig et Voltaire.

POMPIDOU CENTER (ALSO KNOWN AS BEAUBOURG).
Rue Saint Martin and Place Georges Pompidou. Open daily except Tues,
11am-9pm. Metro: Rambuteau or Châtelet/Les Halles. The cost to ride the
escalators for the view is €3. Entrance fees vary for exhibits.

In the 1960s, the **Beaubourg** neighborhood of Paris was dirty and
dilapidated. President Georges Pompidou, a great fan of modern art,
launched a program to build a contemporary center for the arts and culture and revitalize the neighborhood. A team of Italian and British architects, Renzo Piano and Richard Rogers, scandalized many people by
putting together a multicolored, modern, monstrosity of a building, right
in the heart of historical Paris. Their idea was to turn the building inside-
out. All the parts that are usually hidden, such as water pipes and electrical

supply systems, were
not only exposed on
the outside but also
painted bright colors.
Each color has a role:
red is for transpor-
tation, yellow is for
electricity, blue is for
air-conditioning, and
green is for water.

Much of the Pom-
pidou Center's appeal
is outside. The wide plateau in front of the building features street performers of various types. On the south side of the Pompidou Center is
another esplanade, featuring the large, whimsical **Stravinsky Fountain**.
The fountain depicts scenes from Stravinsky's *Sacre du Printemps* (Rights
of Spring), *Oiseau de Feu* (Firebird), and *Ragtime*. The brightly colored
pieces are by an artist named Niki de Saint-Phalle, and the black ones
are by sculptor Jean Tinguely. They spin and spit water, to the delight of
children and adults alike. The whole area is car free, with much room for
children to run. There are also some excellent cafés for a snack or a meal.

MUSÉE NATIONAL D'ART MODERNE. *Entrance on level 4 of*
the Pompidou Center. Open daily except Tues, 11am-9pm. Purchase tickets
on the ground level. Adults: €11-13 depending on dates; Kids under 18:
free. Free to all on the first Sunday of each month. Audioguides (available in
English) are € 5 for adults and free for kids under 13.

This museum has an important collection of modern and contemporary art. The contemporary section (level 4) is filled with all sorts of

wild and wacky paintings and sculptures. There is a reconstructed shop covered with recycled bits turned into art. There are models of futuristic buildings designed in the mid-20th century. There are examples of Op-Art. It's a good reminder for children that art can be fun and does not need to be intimidating. The modern art collection (on level 5) has works by greats, such as Matisse, Leger, Picasso, Rouault, Delaunay, Kandinsky, and Calder. There is a whole section dedicated to Dada and Surrealism, including a reproduction of Andre Bretons' studio.

ÉGLISE SAINT MÉRRI. *76, Rue de la Verrerie. Metro: Châtelet.*

This large, flamboyant Gothic-style church is especially notable for its gargoyles. You can get a good view of them outside from the square with the Stravinsky Fountain. The church also has impressive 16th century stained glass windows and a 13th century bell (thought to be the oldest in Paris). The composer Saint-Saëns (who wrote the *Carnival of the Animals*) played the organ here. There are free concerts on weekends. See photo below.

11. MARAIS

This section of town was once covered with marshes (marais means marsh in French) running along the northern edge of the Seine River. Today, the **Marais** is a lively area, and a favorite among Parisians and tourists alike. The small, cobbled streets are full of colorful shops, fashion boutiques, and interesting eateries. There are numerous museums that appeal to kids' interests: toys (**Musée de la Poupée**); inventions (**Musée des Arts et Métiers**); history and gore (**Musée Carnavalet** and **Musée d'Art et d'Histoire Juive**); goofiness (**Musée Picasso**); and magic (**Musée de la Magie et de la Curiosité**).

PLACE DES VOSGES. *Métro: St-Paul or Bastille.*

This square (see photo below) originally housed a royal palace and gardens. In the late 1500s it was redone to include fancy apartment buildings. Author **Victor Hugo**, who wrote *Les Miserables* and *The Hunchback of Nôtre Dame*, lived in one, which has been turned into a small museum. Notice the buildings around the square. They seem to be made of red bricks, but if you look closely you'll see that they are actually made of stone that is covered with a thin layer of false bricks. The square has several

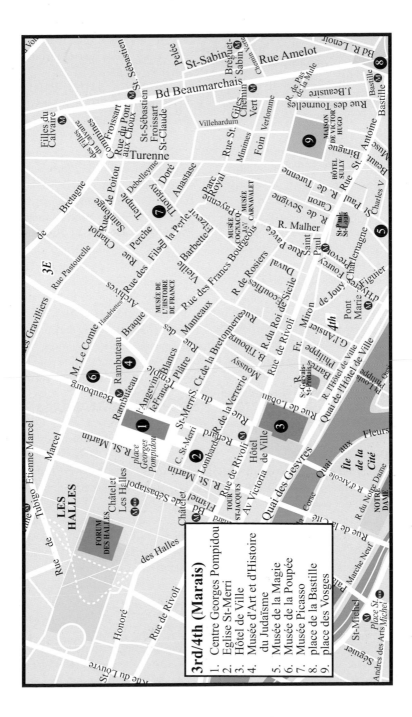

3rd/4th (Marais)
1. Centre Georges Pompidou
2. Eglise St-Merri
3. Hôtel de Ville
4. Musée d'Art et d'Histoire du Judaïsme
5. Musée de la Magie
6. Musée de la Poupée
7. Musée Picasso
8. place de la Bastille
9. place des Vosges

Marais Highlights

• Search for optical illusions and slights of hand at the Museum of Magic

• Pick out a Jewish pastry in the Rue des Rosiers

• Tour the Doll Museum

• Look for goofy animals at the Picasso Museum

• See models of Paris, the guillotine, and a ballroom fit for a queen at the Musée Carnavalet

• Follow the footsteps of Nicholas Flamel and search for the secret of the Sorcerer's Stone

• Admire the inventions at the Musée des Arts et Métiers

• Go ice-skating (in winter) in front of the Hôtel de Ville.

playground areas, and there are often street musicians performing under the arcades.

VILLAGE SAINT PAUL–THE SOUTHERN MARAIS. *Situated between Metro: Saint Paul and Metro: Pont Marie.*

This "village" used to contain a royal palace, gardens, and even a collection of wild animals. Today, it features a little park, called the **Jardins de Saint Paul** (through some archways off of the Rue Saint Paul, near the Seine) where you can see a fairly large section of the old fortress wall that used to protect the City of Paris in the late 1100s and early 1200s. There are even guard towers and plenty of open space to let children run free or enjoy a snack while parents look in on the windows of the antique boutiques that line the archways.

MUSÉE DE LA CURIOSITÉ ET DE LA MAGIE (MUSEUM OF MAGIC). *11, Rue Saint Paul (Metro: Pont Marie or Saint Paul). Open Wed, Sat, Sun, 2pm - 7pm. Adults: €9; Kids: €7. Combined ticket with the museum and automates is €12.*

Parent tip: Kids love this little museum. Beware, however, that its hours are quite limited. Without careful planning, you may end up facing a locked door and disappointed travel companions. ❖

This is great fun for anyone who enjoys a good magic show. The museum features optical illusion tricks, automates, and old-fashioned carnival games dating from 1800 to 1950. There are also live magic demonstrations, much of which you can understand even if you don't know a word of French. To round out the visit there is a shop full of magic tricks and paraphernalia.

HISTORIC JEWISH QUARTER. *Along the Rue des Rosiers and surrounding streets. Metro: Saint Paul or Hôtel de Ville.*

There have been Jews in Paris since Roman times, with periods when they were accepted and ones when they were expelled, or exterminated. Several parts of Paris have had Jewish neighborhoods, including the Latin

Quarter and Ile de la Cité. But the most long-lasting has been here in the Marais along the **rue des Rosiers and its side streets**. Jews first moved into this area in the 1200s. During WWII, most, including many small children, were rounded up and deported to nazi concentration camps. Numerous plaques and memorials mark their memory. Today, there are Jewish bookshops, bakeries, and restaurants, along with synagogues and prayer rooms. As the neighborhood has gentrified, some are being replaced with high-end and trendy fashion shops, though many of the original store facades remain.

In the narrow **Rue Pavée** – said to be the first paved road in Paris – at #10, there is a small synagogue with a beautiful façade. It is the work of the Art Nouveau architect Hector Guimard, famous for having designed Paris' original metro entrances.

MUSÉE D'ART ET D'HISTOIRE DU JUDAISME (MUSEUM OF JEWISH ART AND HISTORY). *71, Rue du Temple. Metro: Rambuteau or Hôtel de Ville. Open Sun-Fri, 11am to 6 pm and Sun 10 am to 6 pm. Closed Sat. Adults: €8 or €10 for the museum and special exhibits; Kids: free.*

This museum celebrates not only Jewish history and religion, but also the cultural and artistic contributions of Jews in Paris. The permanent collection features exhibits describing everyday life, religious festivals, the history of Jews in Paris, and the coming together of two traditions: Sephardim and Ashkenazi. There are paintings by Marc Chagall and Amadeo Modigliani. The museum is housed in a mansion built in the early 17th century. The gardens, which at one point had been designed by Louis

XVI's favorite landscaper, André LeNôtre, have now been redone and re-named to honor Anne Frank.

HÔTEL DE VILLE (PARIS CITY HALL). *Place de l'Hôtel de Ville. Metro: Hôtel de Ville. Free exhibits are often featured in the galleries on the back side of the building.*

This is Paris' City Hall. The building is very ornate and decorated with statues representing different French cities. The square in front of the Hôtel de Ville used to be the sight of public executions, lively markets, workers' strikes, and other festivities. Now it features exhibits, activities, and during winter months, an ice-skating rink (see photo on page 86). In late June, it is the starting and end point of the city's 5-mile **café servers' race**. Waiters and waitresses run through the streets of Paris in their work clothes (no running shoes) carrying a full tray of drinks. It's quite impressive!

CENTRAL MARAIS. *Metro: Saint Paul or Chemin Vert.*

A walk up the Rue Vieille du Temple, Rue Pavée, and along the Rue des Francs Bourgeois takes you past shops filled with funky gadgets, car-toon characters, or clothing by hip designers.

When you are ready for more sightseeing, you face the choice of three terrific museums:

MUSÉE CARNAVALET. *29, Rue de Sévigné. Métro: Saint-Paul or Chemin-Vert. Open Tues-Sun, 10am to 6 pm. Closed Mon. Entrance to the per-manent collections is free, but there is a fee for special exhibits. Audioguides: €5.*

The Musée Carnavalet is devoted to the history of Paris, from prehis-tory through the early 20th century. Although it may sound boring, you'll be surprised at how much of it can arouse your child's curiosity and imagi-nation. There are wooden canoes made by prehistoric fishermen and dis-covered along the Seine River. There is a room filled with old shopkeepers' signs. Have fun guessing what kind of trade they represented. There are models and maps of Paris through the ages. There's a set of locks from the Bastille prison (ask the guard to give you a demonstration), a portrait of Dr. Guillotin who designed the guillotine, and a chess set that King Louis XVI played in prison before his execution. There's the cradle in which Napoleon Bonaparte slept as a baby. There are replicas of a 16th century room, a room during the Revolution, and Marcel Proust's bedroom. There is a jewelry store and a ballroom from the Hotel Wendell, guaranteed to delight any fan of Cinderella. To finish the visit, the gift shop offers nice games, books, and souvenirs.

MUSÉE PICASSO. *Hôtel de Salé, 5, Rue de Thorigny. Metro: Saint Paul. Open Wed-Mon, 9:30am-5:30pm. Closed Tues.*

This museum finally re-opened in October 2014 after a massive, 5-year rennovation. There are new exhibit spaces, along with a remodeled garden, terrace, and café. All the works have been cleaned and reframed. The museum contains a huge collection of works by Pablo Picasso, whose long career lasted from 1894 to his death in 1973. Born in Malaga, Spain, Picasso spent much of his younger artistic life in Paris and later life in Provence. The pieces are organized chronologically, taking you through different periods of the artist's style: blue, rose, cubism, surrealism. There are also paintings by artists Matisse, Renoir, and Cézanne from Picasso's collection.

Young children may not get excited about the influence of African art on Picasso, his experiments with planes, or the fundamentals of cubism. But they do respond well to the humor and wackiness of many of the pieces – sometimes more than adults. Kids also enjoy hunting for depictions of children (e.g. Harlequin Boy, Girl Jumping Rope) and animals (e.g. crouching cat, bicycle goat). Don't be afraid to move at the pace of a short attention span. There's a lot to see and some of the best stuff is among his later works.

By the way, in case you are wondering why the mansion that houses the museum is called the **Hôtel de Salé** (Salty Hotel) it's because the original owner was in charge of collecting the royal tax on salt.

MUSÉE DE LA POUPÉE. *Located in the Impasse Berthaud, just off the Rue Beaubourg (Metro: Rambuteau). Open Tues-Sun, 1pm-6pm. Closed Mon. Adults: € 8; Youths 12-25: €6; Kids 3-11: €4. Kids under 3: free.*

This charming little museum is nestled in a lane, just half a block from the back of the Pompidou Center. It has a collection of dolls dating back to the mid-1800s and up through the 1960s. They are arranged with accessories and furniture to reflect the time period in which they were made. There are also two rooms devoted to temporary exhibits, often set up around fun themes like the history of the Barbie doll or plastic squeeze toys. The museum has a gift shop with doll accessories and dollhouse furniture. There is also a doll clinic that repairs valuable dolls and stuffed animals and can offer estimates of their age and value.

THE NORTHERN MARAIS – FOLLOWING THE FOOTSTEPS OF NICOLAS FLAMEL.

Do you have any **Harry Potter fans** in your midst? Do they remember how Harry, Hermione, and Ron searched the school library for clues about **Nicolas Flamel** during their first year at Hogwarts? Here's your chance to hunt him down yourself, and maybe discover the secrets of the Sorcerer's Stone.

Nicolas Flamel was a real person, born in Pontoise (town west of Paris) in 1330. He was a bookseller, who set up shop in Paris near the Place des Innocents (by Les Halles). It is said that one night, Flamel dreamt that an angel appeared to him with a mysterious book, saying that some day he would discover its secrets. A few days later, a stranger walked into Flamel's shop with the very book he had seen in his dream. It was about alchemy and supposedly held the secret to creating the sorcerer's stone, which could change ordinary metal into gold and guarantee eternal life. Flamel studied the book for years. Then in 1382, he claimed to have successfully turned mercury into gold. He did it again in 1386. Was it true? Who knows? What is certain is that Flamel did become a wealthy man. Though he and his wife continued to live modestly, they became generous benefactors, financing the building of 14 hospitals, 3 chapels, 7 churches, and several houses. Legend has it that Flamel also discovered the secret to eternal life. Records suggest that he died in 1417 though some will argue that he and his wife, Pernelle, are still alive today. His tombstone is on exhibit in the Cluny Museum.

For your Flamel tour, start at the **Tour Saint Jacques**, located just off the Place du Châtelet. This Gothic-style bell tower is all that remains of a church called Saint Jacques de la Boucherie. The church was built in 1523 for the butchers and tanners who worked in the nearby Les Halles (Paris' former central market). One of its most regular and generous patrons was Nicolas Flamel, who lived nearby. Most of the church was destroyed during the French Revolution, but the bell tower was saved.

The Tour St. Jacques was the starting point in Flamel's day for the religious pilgrimage to the church of Saint James the Apostle of Compostella in Spain.

Since 1891, the Tour Saint Jacques has served as a weather station for Paris. The tower holds meteorological instruments to measure the air quality, pollution levels, and other readings.

From the Tour Saint Jacques, if you head due north you will find a little pedestrian street (one block west of the larger pedestrian street, Rue Saint Martin). Look up at the street sign. This is the **Rue Nicolas Flamel**. Notice that the first cross street you meet is called the **Rue Pernelle**, named for Flamel's wife. They had an apartment near here, and their bookshop was only a few blocks away.

Here you may want to stray a bit from Nicolas Flamel to admire the Eglise Saint Mérri, visit the Stravinsky Fountain, check out the Pompidou Center, or visit the Doll Museum.

The trail of Nicolas Flamel resumes up the Rue Beaubourg (heading north). Take a right when you reach the old, narrow **Rue de Montmorency**. You have just stepped back into medieval times. Notice the house at #51. It was built in 1407 by Nicolas Flamel and is said to be the oldest house in Paris. He built it as one of his many charitable acts and as a place to house the poor. Tenants were given free room and board on the upper floors. In exchange they were asked to live an honest life and offer a prayer each day for Flamel and his wife. The ground floor of the building had shops that were rented out to help cover the costs of feeding and housing the tenants. Today, the ground floor features a restaurant called the Auberge Nicolas Flamel. It offers great food and friendly service, with several special "tasting" menus for dinner, and a more basic lunch menu, along with a kids menu.

MUSÉE DES ARTS ET MÉTIERS. *60, Rue Réaumur (Metro: Arts et Métiers). Open Tues-Sun, 10am-6pm (Thurs. until 9:30 pm). Closed Mon. Adults: €6.50; Kids are free. Special exhibits are extra. Free to all on Thursday evenings and on the first Sunday of each month. Audioguides: €5. The museum is handicap accessible and free to individuals accompanying persons with disabilities.*

This museum is a fun way to round out your Nicolas Flamel tour. It is just four blocks up the Rue Beaubourg from Flamel's house in the Rue Montmorency. The museum is chock full of scientific and artistic inventions, like the first calculator (1642), telegraph (1794), and automobile (1770). The exhibit rooms are airy and well done. There are numerous interactive computer stations to explore different sections. Much of the fun, however, comes from seeing models of early airplanes, drawbridges, and skyscrapers. There are early measuring tools, cameras, and bicycles. You'll see Volta's battery and Watt's steam engine. There's Edison's phonograph and Foucault's pendulum.

In the final room of the museum, a converted chapel, you'll see large-scale models of the Statue of Liberty (including a full-size replica of her thumb), the first autobus, early airplanes, and the Vulcain motor used in the French space shuttle, Ariane. Although this museum offers no direct links to the experiments of Nicolas Flamel, it's surely the kind of place he, as an inventor, would have enjoyed.

QUARTIER DU TEMPLE. *Around the Square du Temple. Metro: Arts et Métiers or Temple.*

This neighborhood is named for the **Templar Knights**, an order founded in 1169, whose headquarters were located here in a vast fortress. The Templars were both monks and knights, and they were famous for being highly skilled and disciplined fighters. They participated in the Crusades and guarded the king's troops. However, as their fame and fortune grew, they became seen as a threat to both the king and the church.

In 1307, they were declared to be heretics. Their leader was burnt at the stake, and members were hunted down and killed all over France. Later, the Templar fortress was turned into a prison, where King Louis XVI and Queen Marie-Antoinette were held for a time following the French Revolution. The king was beheaded within several months, and the queen was transferred to the Concièrgerie prison, from which she was eventually also condemned to the guillotine. The Templar fortress was torn down by Napoleon. All that remains today is the **Carreau du Temple square**, with its gardens and playground, and some markings on the pavement in front of the town hall to indicate where some of the towers once stood. Note at #18 rue Perrée, there is a building with a giant, five-story sundial on its façade.

MARCHE DES ENFANTS-ROUGES (COVERED MARKET). *Entrance is at 39, rue de Bretagne. Metro: Filles du Calvaire. Open 8:30am-1pm and 4pm-7:30pm, Tues-Sat; 8:30am-2pm, Sun. Closed Mondays.*

This market is named for the orphanage that once stood nearby, where the children wore red uniforms. It was renovated in the 1990s, and along with the food stalls has some very friendly eateries, popular with local families. There's one that only offers hamburgers and fries, which are excellent.

12. BASTILLE

In 1789, the storming of the **Bastille Prison** marked the launch of the French Revolution. Ever since, the neighborhood has maintained a reputation for feistiness. For many years, the Saint Antoine neighborhood east of the Bastille was home to woodworkers and craftsmen. Many of them made up the core of those ready to revolt against repressive governments, both in 1789 and during later rebellions.

During the 1980s-1990s, this area became home to artists, young designers, and cybernauts seeking less expensive living and retail space. It also welcomed the building of a new, modern opera house.

Today, the old mingles with the new around the Bastille. Small woodworking shops sit next door to new internet cafés. An old train route has been converted into suspended gardens. Houseboats still pass slowly through the locks of the city's canals, and a new park welcomes strollers to the canals' banks.

PLACE DE LA BASTILLE. *Metro: Bastille.*

The Bastille was originally a military fortress. It was built in the 1370s to protect the eastern edge of the city from invaders. The walls were 5 feet thick, and built to resist attack. Over time, they proved to be more useful at keeping people in than out, and the Bastille was transformed into a prison.

By the 1700s, most of the people shut inside the Bastille had been sent there by royal decree. Some were political prisoners. Others were there by request of their family members, who ap-

Bastille Area Highlights

- Hunt for traces of the old Bastille prison
- Walk, bike, or rollerblade above the crowds along the Promenade Plantée
- Watch a canal boat go through a lock, or take a ride on a canal boat and experience the locks for yourself
- Check out the exotic foods and spices at the Place d'Aligre Street Market
- Stroll along the Saint Martin Canal playing in the Arsenal

pealed to the king to lock away troublesome relatives; for example, someone who was spending too much money, causing embarrassment, or otherwise in the way.

By 1789, the Bastille was seen as a symbol of royal tyranny to many Parisians. So it was here on July 14 that they launched an attack on the prison. And thus started the French Revolution. The prisoners were freed and the building was set on fire. Eventually, some of the stones were recovered and used to build the Pont de la Concorde. One enterprising businessman gathered up stones and other remnants of the building to sell as souvenirs. He even carved some into miniature copies of the Bastille Prison. You can see examples of these at the Musée Carnavalet.

If you visit the Place de la Bastille today, you'll see an outline of the old prison on the pavement in the middle of the Place. A plaque at #4, Rue St. Antoine marks where the entrance was. The Bastille metro station (line 5) has an exposed fragment of the prison's foundation.

The tall column you can see today in the middle of the Place de la Bastille is called the **Colonne de Juillet** (July Column; see photo on previous page). The statue on top represents Liberty. But you might be surprised to learn that it does not commemorate the start of the French Revolution. Instead, it was erected to honor an uprising that took place in 1830, and later also commemorated a further one in 1848. Mexico City's Columna de la Independencia, built in 1910, is copied from this one.

During the first half of the 19th century, there was a large elephant made of wood and plaster in the center of the square. It was meant to be a model for a more glorious version celebrating Napoleon Bonaparte to be made of bronze. But Napoleon fell from power, the elegant elephant was never built, and the model moldered. It was eventually torn down in 1846.

PROMENADE PLANTÉE. *Access from numerous stairs and elevators along the Avenue Daumesnil and Rue du Sahel. Metro: Bastille, Gare de*

Lyon, Daumesnil, Bel-Air, or Porte Dorée. Open 8 am (9 am on Sat-Sun) to 5:30 pm (winter) and 9:30 pm (summer). Entrance is free.

The Promenade Plantée is a lovely elevated park planted along a 4.5 kilometer stretch of an old railroad line. It predates but is similar to the High Line in New York City. The promenade offers nice views, along with flower-lined paths and gardens. It is an excellent place for families, since there are no cars or streets to cross. In some sections the paths split into two: one is reserved for walkers and baby strollers, and the other for bikes and rollerbladers.

About midway along, the Promenade Plantée passes through a large park called the **Jardin de Reuilly**, which features wide green lawns, playgrounds, and a giant sundial. There is a public swimming pool, called the **Piscine de Reuilly** *(13, Rue Hénard, Metro: Montgallet).*

VIADUCT DES ARTS. *Under the Promenade Plantée, Along Boulevard Daumesnil. Metro: Bastille or Gare de Lyon.*

The area under the Promenade Plantée is called the Viaduct des Arts. It is made up of graceful, brick archways that have been converted into art studios, designer stores, craftsmen's workshops, computer stores, and cafés.

JARDIN DE L'ARSENAL. *Along the Arsenal Leisure Port of the Saint Martin Canal on the Boulevard de la Bastille side. Metro: Quai de la Rapée or Bastille.*

This park is situated along the Arsenal Port, where houseboats and other leisure craft stop or pass on their way through the canal locks and tunnel. The port is located on a spot that once held a moat for the Bastille Fortress, near its weapons arsenal. From the gardens, you can watch pleasure boats go by or enjoy the large playground and restaurant.

CANAUXRAMA (CANAL TOUR BOAT RIDES). *Near #50, Boulevard de la Bastille. Metro: Bastille. (Tel. 01.42.39.15.00). Daily departures at 9:45 am and 2:30 pm., Adults: €16; Kids 6-12: €8.50; Under 6: free.*

Canal tour boats leave from the Port de l'Arsenal for a 2.5 hour tour up the Canal Saint Martin through locks and rotating bridges to the Parc de la Villette, where you can go visit that park's spectacular playgrounds and Science Museum. There is a special sound and lights show early on as you go through the tunnel under the Place de la Bastille. The tour goes through traditional neighborhoods of Paris, with guided descriptions in English.

SAINT MARTIN CANAL. *Runs perpendicular to the Seine from Quai de la Rapée to La Villette. Metro: Quai de la Rapée, Bastille, République, Stalingrad, or Jaurès.*

Built between 1805 and 1825, the 4.5 kilometer canal connects the La Villette Basin to the Seine. It was originally designed to bring fresh water to the city from La Villette and for shipping barges carrying grain and other merchandise. Today, most of the boats are pleasure crafts. The canal contains nine locks, two rotating bridges, and a long tunnel that contains a light show. The open parts of the canal have become very popular with Parisians and visitors out for a stroll in this up-and-coming part of the city. Fans of the movie Amélie Poulain will recognize the arched pedestrian bridges, from which she skips rocks across the canal. If your kids are fascinated by graffiti and street art, they'll find plenty to satisfy their curiosity.

PARIS À VELO C'EST SYMPA, *22 rue Alphonse Baudin, Metro: St Sébastien-Froissart or Richard-Lenoir (up the Boulevard Richard Lenoir from Bastille). Open daily 9:30am-1pm, and 2pm-6pm (until 7pm Sat-Sun). Tel: 01 48 876 001, www.parisvelosympa.com/en/infos-pratiques.*

Paris is very bike-friendly, and here you can rent bicycles, including tandems, kids' bikes, and kid carriers, along with helmets, and other equipment for a cycling tour in Paris. They also provide guided bicycle tours. The Bastille neighborhood offers several excellent routes that keep you well away from traffic. The Promenade Plantée has special paths reserved for bikes and roller blades. There are also bike paths north of the Place de la Bastille along the Saint Martin Canal, and along the Seine River.

PLACE D'ALIGRE MARKET. *Place d'Aligre. Between Rue de Charenton and Rue du Faubourg Saint Antoine. Metro: Ledru Rollin. Open 9am-1pm, 4pm-7:30pm Tues-Sun. Closed Mon.*

This square contains both a covered market, originally constructed in 1777, and street vendors that spill onto the side streets. It features very interesting and exotic types of foods, including plenty of Caribbean and North African specialties. You also can find used clothes and flea market items.

GARE DE LYON. *Cour L. Armand. Metro: Gare de Lyon.*

This train station services routes going to the south of France, the Alps, and Italy. It was built in 1895, as part of the massive construction projects for the Paris Exhibition of 1900. The **large clock tower** (see photo below) is decorated with statues representing Paris and Marseilles. There are 40 murals inside the station representing many of the cities and towns along the routes served by the station.

13. BERCY

In the 1990s, **Bercy** was transformed from an area filled with empty wine warehouses to a family-friendly area of green and commercial spaces. During the construction, workers stumbled across several 7,000-year old dugout canoes. These once belonged to the people who fished and hunted along the marshy banks of the Seine during prehistoric times.

Modern Bercy has much to offer children. There is a great park filled with gardens, bridges, a maze, and play areas. Stores and restaurants round out the visit in a pedestrian section that makes you feel as though you have left the bustle of the city for a quieter village.

PARC DE BERCY. *Along the Seine in Eastern Paris, between Boulevard de Bercy and BercyExpo. Metro: Bercy or Cour Saint Emilion. Open 8am-8:30pm. Entrance is free. Note: Sections of the park may be closed due to construction in 2015.*

Bercy was formerly a huge wine depot, with easy access to transportation barges along the Seine. In the 19th century, when it flourished, Bercy was outside the Paris city limits and purview of its urban taxes. The neighborhood was very jolly, full of festivals and cafés along the river's edge.

Today, the Bercy Park is filled with wide expanses where children can run, explore, and discover. There are numerous gardens, including a vegetable patch tended by children, a vineyard, a botanical garden, a garden of scents, and a wonderful maze. There are ponds, large grassy areas, some very old trees, and small bridges. There are little buildings that house temporary exhibits or gardening workshops. The alleyways are named for famous wine regions.

Along a grassy expanse on raised terraces (not far from the pedestrian bridge across the Seine) are 21 sculptures called **Children of the World**. They are the creation of artist, Rachid Khimoune, and were erected in 2001 to honor children's rights. Each sculpture represents a different

Bercy Area Highlights

- Check out the sculptures of the Children of the World
- Go through the maze, see what's growing in the childrens' garden, and throw crumbs to the ducks in the Bercy Park
- Have a snack and enjoy the shops along the pedestrian zone of Bercy Village

country. They are made of bronze and dressed in recycled, urban materials such as sewer covers and tree grids. Originally, each sculpture had a name and indication of the country it represents, but many of the identifying plaques have disappeared, so you have to guess based on clues in the sculpture itself.

On the western side of the park is an odd looking, multi-sided structure with grass growing on the sides. This is the **Palais Omnisport de Bercy**, where various sports events and concerts are held. On the northern side of the Bercy Park, at 51, Rue de Bercy, is a remarkable building designed by architect Frank Gehry. It was originally built to house the American Center, which had moved from its old space in Montparnasse. For decades it had featured art exhibits, dance, and theater productions to promote Franco-American cultural exchanges. Unfortunately, the American Center went bankrupt shortly after moving to its new building. Now the building houses a **Museum of Cinema and Cinematheque** (movie theater), *open daily except Tues, 12pm-7pm. Closed Tues. Adults: €6; Kids: €3. Audioguides are free with purchase of entry tickets.*

On the eastern edge of the Bercy Park is a development called **Bercy Village**. It includes a pedestrian section filled with kid-friendly shops, restaurants, and cafés. *The shops are open 11am-9pm, Mon-Sat.* There is a large movie complex called **Ciné Cité** with 18 movie theaters. It often plays kid-friendly films, including American ones in English.

On the far side of the Bercy complex is a series of buildings called the **Pavillons de Bercy**. They contain fairground rides, games, automata shows, and carnival paraphernalia. But you can only visit them as part of a group. *53 avenue des Terroirs de France; call ahead to schedule a visit: 01 43 40 16 15.*

14. BOIS DE VINCENNES

The **Bois de Vincennes** borders the eastern edge of Paris. Like the Bois de Boulogne on Paris' western side, it is a remnant of the large ring of forests that once encircled the city. Formerly the domain of kings, the Bois de Vincennes is now a favorite among Parisian families, when they need a breath of fresh air. It features large woods, lakes, bike trails, a big zoo, a small farm, a castle, a museum, a tropical garden, terrific playgrounds, a horse racing track, and even a baseball field.

CHÂTEAU DE VINCENNES (CASTLE). *Entrance at La Tour du Village, 1, avenue de Paris. Metro: Château de Vincennes or RER Vincennes Station. Open daily 10am-5pm (winter), 10am-6pm (summer). Visits are by guided tours. Adults: €8.50; Kids: free. Audioguides: €4.50. Free to all on the first Sunday of each month.*

Here is your chance to see a real castle, complete with fortifications and a giant *donjon* tower. Vincennes Castle was originally constructed more than 800 years ago, and was used pretty much through the 19th century. Highlights include the donjon tower (or keep), 17th century palace rooms, the gothic Holy Chapel, and the walk around the defense walls.

VINCENNES ZOOLOGICAL PARK. *Entrance at the intersection of the Avenue Daumesnil and Route de la Ceinture du Lac. Metro: Porte Dorée, Saint-Mandé, or Château de Vincennes. Open daily, 10am-6pm, Mon-Fri;*

9:30am-7:30pm Sat-Sun (summer); 10am-5pm (winter). Adults: €22; Youths 12-25: €16,50; Kids 3-11: €14; Kids under 3: free.

This zoological park just reopened in April 2014 after extensive renovations meant to create much more natural environments for the animals. It is divided into different biozones representing

Bois de Vincennes Highlights

- Visit the Vincennes castle
- Go to the zoo
- Try out the playgrounds and fun rides in the Parc Floral
- Rent a rowboat and paddle around the lake
- Go to the Foire du Trone Fair

Patagonia, the Sahel, Europe, Amazonia, and Madagascar. Giant skylights help create the desired climatic conditions, and allow lots of birds, insects, amphibians, reptiles, and mammals to roam freely. Other habits contain large mammals and other zoo favorites.

On the way to the zoo from the Porte Dorée metro stop is a remarkable building called the **Palais de la Porte Dorée** (#293 Avenue Daumesnil). This Art Deco-style building was originally constructed for the Colonial Exhibition of 1931. It was intended to show off France's colonial influence and riches. The bas reliefs decorating the exterior are a tribute to a certain time and point of view, showing off the glory of France, depicted as a large front-facing figure, surrounded by images and people representing her colonies in Africa, Asia, and Oceania. It was converted to a permanent museum showcasing art and artifacts from those continents. These were transferred in 2003 to the Quai Branly Museum of Art and Civilization. The building now houses a **Museum of Immigration**. One holdover from the 1931 exhibition is an **aquarium**, featuring marine life from around the world, located in the building's lower level.

PARC FLORAL. *By the Esplanade du Château and Route de la Pyramide. Metro: Château de Vincennes. Then take bus # 112 or walk about 10 minutes. Open daily 9:30am-5pm (winter); until 8 pm (summer). Adults: €5.50; Kids 6-18: €2.75; Kids under 6: free. Ask for the map and the program to free "Pestacles" performances at the entrance. Note: Renovations of buildings may affect access to buildings or sections of the park.*

This park is a real treat for kids and families! When you first walk in you are greeted by several different gardens. There are flower gardens, pine gardens, and a garden of four seasons that blossoms all year. If you head towards the left, you come to a small museum that features exhibits on the ecosystems around Paris and a butterfly garden. If you keep going past the crêpe restaurant and big pond, you'll come to the children's section. It features wonderful playgrounds, complete with castles and climbing webs.

There also are some really fun activities, such as pedal-powered horse chariots, race cars, ropes courses, and a hilarious mini boat ride for babies, for which you will need to purchase tickets. They are organized according to age and size. Look at the horizontal bars at the entrance. They indicate the minimum and maximum heights for each ride.

The park features several eateries, ranging from light fare at the crêpe restaurant to a full (and still family-friendly) meal in the big restaurant by the pond.

There are two theaters in the park. One features a marionette show. The other has live performances and concerts.

If you enjoy miniature golf, don't miss the one in this park. Each hole features one or several of the major monuments of Paris. Can you get your ball through the Eiffel Tower or up the Montmartre hill? See if you can recognize all the sights. Hint: the course is laid out as if it were a big map of the city.

RENTING BICYCLES. Bikes are a great way to explore and enjoy this vast park. You can rent bicycles at the **Lac des Minimes** *(Tel. 01 30 59 68 38);* **Lac Daumesnil** (see photo below; *Tel 06 81 34 47 19)*; or the **Bicyclub** in the Parc Floral (Tel. 01 47 66 55 92).

FOIRE DU TRONE (FAIR). *In the Bois de Vincennes, near the Lac Daumesnil. Metro: Porte de Charenton. During the summer months.*

In the 9th century, monks used to hold a fair on this spot every year. Here we are, over 1,000 years later, and the tradition continues. The Foire du Trône is held every year, between Easter and the end of May. The fair is named for the thrown (trône) that once stood in the Place du Trône (now called Place de la Nation) in honor of the marriage of King Louis XIV and Marie-Therese. There are plenty of thrill rides, merry-go-rounds, carnival games, food, and other amusement park attractions.

15. CHAMPS ELYSEES & CONCORDE

The **Avenue des Champs Elysées** is one of the most famous avenues in the world. It was named for the Elysian Fields of Greek mythology, where heroes get to go after they die. Today, the Champs Elysées is more of a shopper's paradise. A popular old French tune describes it this way, "Whether it's sunny or rainy, midnight or midday, there's something for everyone on the Champs Elysées."

With its wide, tree-lined sidewalks, the Avenue des Champs Elysées also follows the perspective formed by the Louvre, Tuileries Gardens, Place de la Concorde and Arc de Triomphe. Great vistas and photo opportunities abound.

ARC DE TRIOMPHE. *Place Charles de Gaulle-Etoile. Access to the arch through the metro or underground passageway from the Champs Elysées. Do not attempt to cross the traffic circle. Metro: Charles de Gaulle/Etoile. Museum and viewing platform open daily, 9:30am-11pm (April-September); 10 am-10:30 pm (October-March). Adults: €9.50; Kids: free.*

The Arc de Triomphe graces the center of the Place Charles de Gaulle-Etoile and the top of the Champs Elysées hill. It is directly in line with the Louvre, Arch du Carrousel, and Concorde Obelisk to the east. To the west it is aligned with the modern, Grande Arche de la Défense. The perspective is one of the best in Paris.

Area Highlights

• Climb up to the top of the Arc de Triomphe
• Go shopping along the Champs Elysées
• See Paris' oldest puppet show
• Watch the rats go through their maze at the Palais de la Découverte
• Have your photo taken on the Pont Alexandre III
• Imagine living inside one of the statues on the Place de la Concorde

The Arc de Triomphe was built by Napoleon I to celebrate his military victories. It was meant to look like an ancient Roman triumphal arch, only bigger. Work on the project began in 1809. When Napoleon was ousted from power in 1814, the arch was still unfinished. It was finally completed in 1836. It is the biggest triumphal arc in the world.

Napoleon was not the first to think of building a monument on this hilly crossroad. Fifty years earlier, King Louis XV had plans drawn up for a monumental elephant to be built on this spot. It was meant to be as big as a palace with fancy rooms, staircases, and fountains that would pour out of the elephant's trunk. Too bad it was never built, but you can see drawings of it in the small museum inside the Arc.

For over a hundred years, the Arc de Triomphe has been one of the most recognizable monuments of Paris, and it has come to represent a symbol of patriotism and national glory. Great funeral and military parades have taken place in its shadows along the Champs Elysees. In 1920, the ashes of an unknown soldier killed in World War I were laid to rest under the Arc de Triomphe. A memorial flame was placed to mark the spot in 1923. It is re-lit every day at 6:30 pm.

The sides of the Arc de Triomphe are decorated with battle scenes. The most famous depicts a woman representing Liberty who is guiding the troops to victory. It is called La Marseillaise, which is the name of France's national anthem. There are also sculptures representing Peace and Triumph.

You can visit the inside of the arch and climb up the 284 steps to the top. The entrance is inside one of the legs of the arch. There is a small museum and a roof top terrace that offers terrific views of the city.

CHAMPS ELYSÉES. *Stretches from the Arc de Triomphe to the Place de la Concorde. Metro: Charles de Gaulle-Etoile, George V, Franklin Roosevelt, Champs Elysées-Clemenceau, or Concorde.*

In the early 16th century, Queen Marie de Médicis ordered that the marshy fields west of her Tuileries Palace be drained and transformed into

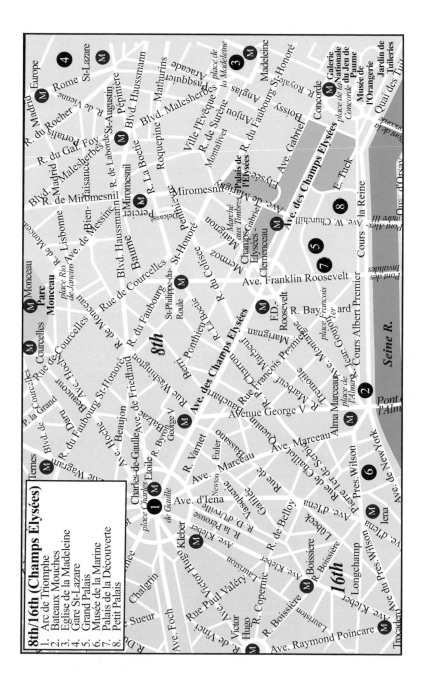

8th/16th (Champs Élysées)
1. Arc de Triomphe
2. Bateaux Mouches
3. Eglise de la Madeleine
4. Gare St-Lazare
5. Grand Palais
6. Musée de la Marine
7. Palais de la Découverte
8. Petit Palais

a tree-lined promenade. It was named the Cours de la Reine (Queen's Course). In 1667, King Louis XIV asked his favorite landscape architect, André Le Nôtre, to redesign the area. In 1709, the course was renamed Champs Elysées.

For many years, much of the Champs Elysées path was lined with houses, cafés, and cabarets. Cows grazed in nearby fields. In 1814-1815, invading Russian and Prussian troops camped out in the fields and gardens along the Champs Elysées, leaving the place a wreck. In the 1830s, the Champs Elysées started to undergo a massive facelift. Gardens were rebuilt. Sidewalks, fountains, and gas street lamps were added. Famous architects were hired to build fancy dance halls, theaters, circuses, restaurants, and mansions.

By 1900, the Champs Elysées had become Paris' most fashionable address. It was lined with luxury shops and cafés, and filled with elegant folks dressed in their finest clothes. The avenue's popularity was boosted even more with the completion of the first subway line in 1902. This line still runs directly under the Champs Elysées, from the Place de la Concorde to the Arc de Triomphe.

As you walk up and down either side of the Avenue des Champs Elysées, you will encounter a wide mix of shopping opportunities. There are occasional reminders that this avenue was once the heart of high fashion, with designer and high-end boutiques toting names like Louis Vuitton, Hugo Boss, Lancel, and Guerlain. There are gourmet eateries, like Fouquet's that continue to attract French movie stars, and the Elysées Palace that houses France's president. But you'll also see familiar chain stores, such as H&M, Abercrombie & Fitch, and the ubiquitous Mac-Do (as the French call McDonalds). There are several, large movie theaters, often featuring the latest Hollywood hits. To catch one in English, ask if it is in version originale. The version française will be dubbed in French.

Each year in July, the **Tour de France bicycle race** finishes on the Champs Elysées. You can try to join the crowds here, or opt for a less frantic perch along the race route, such as along the upper terraces of the Tuileries Gardens.

Below the Rond Point des Champs Elysées, where the avenue

intersects with Avenue Gabriel and Avenue Matignon, is the **oldest marionnette show in Paris** (on the left as you face the Place de la Concorde). The main character, Guignol, has been delighting audiences young and old on this spot since 1818. Shows take place daily during summer holidays (Wed, Sat, Sun during the school year) at 3pm, 4pm, and 5pm. Cost: €4.

Close by, at the lower end of the Champs Elysées, also on the left as you face the Place de la Concorde, is the Carée Marigny. This is where Paris' **stamp collectors** have been meeting to talk, buy, and sell their stamps for more than 125 years. Open every Thurs, Sat, and Sun, 7am-7pm.

PALAIS DE LA DECOUVERTE (SCIENCE MUSEUM). *On the western side of the Grand Palais, along the Avenue Franklin Roosevelt. Metro: Champs Elysées/Clemenceau. Open: Tues-Sat, 9:30 am-6 pm, Sun, 10 am-7 pm. Note: the ticket offices shut down 30 minutes before closing time. Closed Mon. Adults: €9; Kids and youths ages 6-25: €6; Kids under 6: free. Planetarium show: €3.*

The Palais de la Découverte (Palace of Discovery) started out as a temporary exhibit for the 1937 Universal Exposition in Paris. It featured the latest scientific discoveries and techniques. The exhibit was such a hit that it was made into a permanent science museum, with lots of hands-on experiments and demonstrations. However, some are hard to figure out if you don't read French. The Ecole des Rats is fun; watch rats push levers, open doors, and find their way through a maze to food. The static electricity exhibit will make your hair stand on end. You also can take a voyage into the center of a cell in the human biology section, or a virtual trip into space at the planetarium.

GRAND AND PETIT PALAIS. *Facing each other on the Avenue Winston Churchill by the Pont Alexander III (Metro: Champs Elysées-Clemenceau). The Petit Palais is open daily except Mon, 10am-5:40pm. Hours for the Grand Palais vary according to different temporary exhibits.*

The Grand and Petit Palais were both built of glass and metal for the Paris Exhibition of 1900. Today, the Petit Palais features French art from the Renaissance through the 19th century, including nice impressionist paintings. The Grand Palais is used for blockbuster temporary exhibits on everything from Ancient Egypt to contemporary cartoons. They both make an excellent backdrop for family photos.

PONT ALEXANDRE III. *Between the Invalides and the Grand Palais. Metro: Invalides or Champs Elysées-Clemenceau.*

Another great photo opportunity, this is Paris' most elaborately decorated bridge. It was started 1897 to commemorate a new alliance between

France and Russia and finished in time for the Paris Exposition of 1900. The first stone was laid by Czar Nicholas II of Russia, and the bridge is named for his father. On either side in the middle of the bridge are two statues representing the Seine and the Volga Rivers. At each end are statues of the mythical Greek winged horse Pegasus. They are covered in real gold leaf, as are many of the decorations on the bridge. The lamp posts were added in 1925. Their globes are made of hand-blown glass.

PLACE DE LA CONCORDE. *Metro: Concorde.*

This square was originally called Place Louis XV since it was started during his reign. Following the French Revolution, it was briefly renamed Place de la Revolution, and it was here that the guillotine was placed which was used to behead King Louis XVI, his wife, Marie Antoinette, and another 1,000 or so other unfortunates.

The tall **obelisk** in the center of the Place de la Concorde was a gift from Egypt to recognize the contributions of the French archaeologist Champollion, who was the first to decipher hieroglyphics. The obelisk was from the Temple of Ramses II in Luxor, where it was used to measure the sun's shadows. It dates from the 13th century BC. It took two years to transport the obelisk from Luxor to Paris. The obelisk still functions as a sundial. Look for the markings on the ground and see where the shadow of the monument's point hits them. That tells you what time it is.

There are **two large fountains** on the Place, representing river and maritime navigation. There are also eight large female statues. These represent some of France's main cities: Marseilles, Lyon, Lille, Strasbourg, Bordeaux, Nantes, Rouen, and Brest. In the late 1800s, people lived inside the bases of these statues. Note the small doors and windows.

PARC MONCEAU. *Along Boulevard de Courcelles. Metro: Monceau. Open daily 7am-10pm (summer), and 7am-8pm (winter).*

This park (see photo below) was developed in 1787, with lots of naturalistic features such as little rivers, water falls, woods, boulders, and artificial grottos. There are exotic touches such as a Chinese pagoda, an Egyptian pyramid, ruined Greek columns, and a Nomad's tent. There is a fine playground and plenty of room for kids to play. The Parc Monceau also is home to the biggest tree in all of Paris. It is an Oriental Sycamore, planted in 1853. At its widest, the tree's trunk measures more than 7 meters (23 feet) in circumference.

PARC CLICHY-BATIGNOLLES – MARTIN-LUTHER-KING. *147 rue Cardinet. Metro: Brochant. Open 8am-8:30pm, Mon-Fri, 9am-8:30pm Sat-Sun.*

This park, on land that was formerly a train depot, was opened in 2007. It is meant to celebrate three themes: sports, water, and the four seasons. It is built to be environmentally sustainable and offers places to play, relax, and run.

16. OPÉRA, GRANDS MAGASINS & GRANDS BOULEVARDS

This area is much more fun than you might think. In the neighborhoods surrounding the palace-like opera house are fabulous department stores and plenty of uniquely Parisian adventures along the Grands Boulevards.

PALAIS GARNIER OPERA HOUSE. *Place de l'Opéra (Métro: Opéra).*

Although the idea of taking children to the Opera House may strike you as absurd, we were surprised at how much our boys enjoyed taking a peek inside the building. To them it offered all the glitter and adventure of a real palace.

If your children like ballet, this is the place to see a performance or special demonstrations by dancers from the Opera's famous ballet school. Check the schedule here: *www.operadeparis.fr/en/calendrier.*

BRENTANO'S BOOKSTORE. *37, Avenue de l'Opéra. Métro: Opera or Pyramides. Closed Sun*

This is a good place to stop if you've run out of reading material. Brentano's is an American bookstore that has been around for over 100 years and has recently experienced a rebirth. Along with books in English for kids and adults, you'll find various gifts and souvenirs.

GRANDS MAGASINS–DEPARTMENT STORES.

Le Printemps, *64, Boulevard Haussmann. Métro: Havre-Caumartin or Auber. Open Mon-Sat, 9:30am-7pm (Thurs until 10pm), Closed Sun.*

Galeries Lafayette, *40, Boulevard Haussmann. Métro: Chaussee d'Antin. Open Mon-Sat, 9:30am-6:45pm, (Thurs until 9 pm), Closed Sun.*

Paris invented the first department store and still shows the rest of the world how to do them well. The Printemps and Galeries Lafayette chains have stores throughout the city and across France. But the Boulevard Haussman stores are the best. The buildings themselves are quite beautiful. There are elaborate, art-nouveau style skylights, stairways, and decorations. There are numerous cafés and restaurants. Angelina's in the Galeries Lafayette is a great stop for high tea, a sweet snack, or gifts. And the store's

Vue sur Coupole café offers light fare with a striking view of the inside of the store. Or you can opt for the Vogue Café in the atrium of the Le Printemps store, where you will feel like you've stepped right into the pages of the famous fashion magazine.

In terms of shopping, you'll find fantastic toy sections, gourmet foods, souvenirs, and of course, plenty of clothing, perfumes, and cosmetics.

If your child is a natural

Opera Area Highlights

- Take a peek into the grand entrance of the Opera House
- Go to the ballet
- Shop in the Grands Magasins
- Have lunch on top of the Galeries Lafayette
- See a real fashion show
- Discover Paris' shopping galleries and passageways
- Visit the Musée Grévin wax museum

fashion critic or future clothing designer, you can catch a live 1-hour **fashion show** at the Galeries Lafayette Store. The shows take place on Friday afternoons at 3pm in the Salon Opera on the 7th floor. Professional models present the store's fashion collection. The shows are free, but you have to to book in advance. *Call: +33 0142 823025 or send an email to: fashionshow@galerieslafayette.com.*

In late summer, you can check out the "Back to School" section of the Grands Magasins. It's fun to compare the French version of school sup-

plies with those back home, and you might find a good gift for friends or teachers back home.

PARIS STORY. *11 Bis, Rue du Scribe. Métro: Opera. Open daily. Shows on the hour, 10am-6pm. Adults: €11; Kids 6-18: €7; Kids under 6: free; 2 Adults and 2 Kids: €29.*

A good rainy-day activity, this 50-minute panoramic film tells the story of Paris' history, legends, and monuments. Headphones are available in 12 different languages, including English.

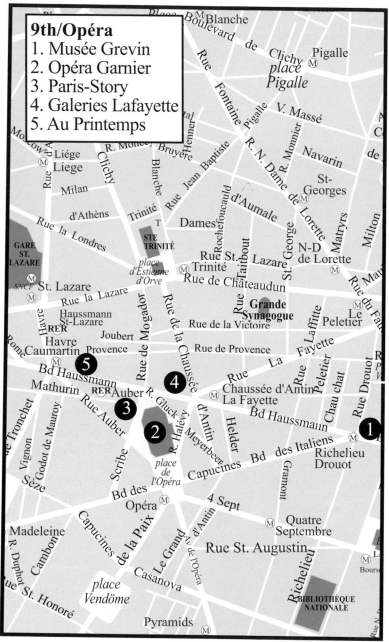

9th/Opéra
1. Musée Grevin
2. Opéra Garnier
3. Paris-Story
4. Galeries Lafayette
5. Au Printemps

GARE SAINT LAZARE (TRAIN STATION). *Place du Hâvre. Métro: Saint Lazare.*
This is the oldest of Paris' train stations. It was built in 1837. The Gare Saint Lazare is where you come if you need to catch a train for Giverny and other parts of Normandy. There are also trains for England (through Dieppe, other British-bound trains go from the Gare du Nord). The station has a hotel called Le Terminus. It was built for the Paris Exposition of 1889.

The Gare Saint-Lazare is featured in Impressionist paintings by **Edouard Manet**, whose art studio was nearby at #58, Rue de Rome, and **Claude Monet**, who used to catch the train here to reach his house at Giverny.

Outside, in front of the station are two funny modern sculptures. One is called *l'Heure de Tous* (Everyone's Time). It is composed of pile of clocks. The other, called *Consigne à Vie* (Baggage Check for Life) is a pile of suitcases. Both were created by an artist named Arman.

GRANDS BOULEVARDS. *East of the Opera, including Boulevard des Capucines, Boulevard des Italiens, Boulevard Montmartre, Boulevard Poissonière, and Boulevard Bonne Nouvelle. Métro: Richelieu Drouot, Grands Boulevards, and Bonne Nouvelle.*
These boulevards were once the sight of a protective wall built to defend the city from its enemies. Later they were lined with classy cafés and theaters. In the 19th century, the Grands Boulevards became more bohemian and home to a lively theater and music hall scene. They were are the setting for Impressionist paintings by Maurice Utrillo and Edouard Manet.

Today, the Grands Boulevards feature theaters, cinemas, shops, and American-style eateries. In fact, if you are homesick for American food, this is where you can find some familiar names and menus such as Subways at 110, rue de Richelieu and Chipotle, Indiana Café, Hard Rock Café, MacDonalds, and even Haagen Daz on the Boulevard Montmartre near the Richelieu Drouot métro.

SHOPPING GALLERIES AND PASSAGES. *Running perpendicular to the Grands Boulevards with entrances on Boulevard des Italiens and Boulevard Montmartre. Métro: Richelieu Drouot.*
These are the best feature of the Grands Boulevards. Long before there were shopping malls, Paris had its indoor shopping galleries and passages. They were built in the second half of the 19th century to offer Parisians a chance to go shopping sheltered from the elements and street traffic. There were over 100 of them across the city. Many were elaborately

decorated with fancy skylights, tile floors, columns, and statues. Some had motifs from Egypt or Ancient Rome. Today, there are over 20 galleries and passages that are still open to the public, many of them renovated in recent years. They remain one of the city's best shopping treats. The ones near the Grands Boulevards have much to please kids of all ages. There are stores featuring comic book characters, dollhouse furniture, teddy bears, and hip clothing. There are also nice cafés and irresistible pastry shops. So make like a 19th century Parisian and stroll through the shopping galleries away from the traffic, inclement weather, and general bustle of the big city.

The first set of passages you will come to if you are arriving from the Avenue de l'Opéra is at #5 Boulevard des Italiens. It is called the **Passage des Princes**, and sure to please kids. The whole place has been transformed into a "Village of Toys."

As you reach the Boulevard Montmartre, you will encounter two sets of passages, facing each other across the boulevard. At #10 Boulevard Montmartre, on the north side of the street, you can enter the **Passage Verdeau** (see photo below). It is filled with fun shops, including the biggest collection of dollhouse furniture and other miniatures in the city. It has an excellent pastry place, a shop that sells rocks and minerals, and one of the oldest cane stores still in existence. This passage also contains a charming hotel (Hotel Chopin) and has Paris' wax museum (see below). Once you reach the end of the Passage Verdeau, cross the small side street to enter the **Passage Jouffroy**. Here there are excellent tearooms, used

bookstores, and shops. It then leads to the Rue Cadet, which has a very nice outdoor market.

On the south side of the Boulevard Montmartre, across the street from the Passage Verdeau, is the **Passage des Panoramas**. This one was developed by an American businessman. It was originally decorated with giant circular paintings called panoramas. It was also the first passageway to be lit with gas lamps. The Passage des Panoramas has several criss-crossing galleries, like a tic-tac-toe board. It eventually leads to the Rue Vivienne. If you follow the Rue Vivienne several blocks south to #6, you will come to the **Galerie Vivienne**. In here don't miss the wonderful toy shop called **Si Tu Veux**, featuring games, toys, teddy bears, and costumes. The Galerie Vivienne leads right into the **Galerie Colbert**. Both of these galleries have undergone facelifts and are very pretty. The Galerie Colbert has a wine shop with a remarkable array of corkscrews.

MUSÉE GRÉVIN (WAX MUSEUM). *10, Boulevard Montmartre. Also opens onto the Passage Verdeau. Métro: Grands Boulevards. Open daily 10am-6:30pm. Adults: €23.50; Kids 6-14: €16.40; Kids under 6: free. Lower prices often available if you buy tickets on line: www.digitick.com/index-css5-grevin-lgen-pg1.html.*

This museum opened in 1888 with figures designed by a sculptor and costume designer named Alfred Grévin. The wax museum's figures include famous actors, sports figures, politicians, historical figures, and even French chefs arranged in scenes depicting their life or times. There is also a section on fictional cartoon characters. The visit opens with a tour through the Hall of Mirrors, which was built for the Paris Universal Exhibition of 1900. At the end of the visit is a part where they explain how the figures are made.

Most of the Grévin museum's wax figures are dressed in clothes that actually belonged to the people they represent. In fact, the designers start with the clothes and model the wax figures to fit into them. The hairpieces are made of real hair and placed in softened wax one strand at a time. Some of the wax figures (mostly politicians) have been stuck with pins and needles by people who believe in voodoo magic. See photo on next page.

LE GRAND REX. *1, Boulevard Poissonière. Métro: Bonne Nouvelle or Grands Boulevards. Rates for movies vary. Self-guided, 50-minute tours (Les Etoiles du Rex)are offered every 5 minutes, 10am-7pm, Wed-Sun during the school year and daily during the summer (though only from 2pm-7pm on Mon). Ask for an English version. Adults: €11; Kids 6-12: €9. Note: the visit includes dark hallways and special effects that may scare smaller children.*

The Grand Rex is a beautiful art-deco style movie theater built in 1932, said to be the biggest in Europe. It has welcomed many movie stars over the years and still has twinkling stars that shine from the ceiling of the main theater. You can go for a movie (note: English language films are likely to be dubbed in French) or opt for a self-guided, backstage tour (ask for an English headset). This is a great rainy day activity.

The tour, called Les Etoiles du Rex (Stars of the Rex), takes you up a glass elevator behind the giant screen. If there is a movie playing, you will catch a glimpse of it from the back. The tour introduces you to cartoon and real movie legends, shows you special effects, lets you feel and hear surround sound at its fullest, and shows films clips of the Rex's history. You even take part in a mini-movie production. At the exit, you can purchase photos or a DVD or USB of your visit. Giggles guaranteed.

CHOCO-STORY (MUSEUM OF CHOCOLATE), *28, Boulevard Bonne-Nouvelle, 75010. Métro: Bonne Nouvelle or Strasbourg Saint Denis. Open daily, 10am-6pm. Adults: €9.50; Students: €8.50; Kids 6-12 years: €6.50; Kids under 6 are free.*

It's hard to resist a museum dedicated to chocolate! This one has exhibits describing the 4,000-year love affair between humans and cocoa, demonstrations of how chocolates are made, and plenty of opportunities for your own taste tests. For kids there are special tours and playmobile displays. And of course, there's a chocolate-filled gift shop.

LE MANOIR DE PARIS (HAUNTED HOUSE), *18, rue du Paradis, 75010 Paris. Métro: Gare de l'Est, Poissonière, or Bonne Nouvelle. Website in English: lemanoirdeparis.com/home. Opening hours vary, but generally run Fri, 6pm-10pm and Sat-Sun, 3pm-7pm. The visit lasts about an hour, but there can be a long wait to get in. Adults: €25; Kids under 16: €20.*

If you like haunted houses, you will love this place, which is really very well done and worth the somewhat pricey entrance fee. Monsters and other creepy characters greet you as soon as you line up the entrance, keeping everyone entertained even before you begin a visit through three floors of dark corridors and scary scenes from different stories and legends. The actors jump out, whisper in your ear, and do a great job of balancing fear and humor. The whole place was designed by an American, now living in Paris, who previously helped create two haunted houses in Texas. They offer both English and French tours (English-speakers get a special glowstick that tells the actors to switch languages). It's a good idea to visit the website ahead of time for a short explanation of the different scenarios. Best for teenagers and not recommended for epileptics (too many strobe lights) or children under 12.

17. TROCADERO

If you want a photo of your family in front of the Eiffel Tower, the Trocadéro terrace is a must stop for you. It is on a hill, directly across the river from the Eiffel Tower, flanked by two rows of golden statues.

The **Place du Trocadéro** is named for a Spanish Fort that was captured by the French in 1823. A magnificent museum was built on the Trocadéro hill for the Paris International Exhibition of 1878. It looked like the Taj Mahal in India. It was torn down and replaced with the current Palais de Chaillot (the two curved buildings surrounding the Trocadéro) for the Paris Exhibition of 1937.

MUSEE DE LA MARINE. *Palais de Chaillot. 17, Place du Trocadéro. On the right as you face the Eiffel Tower. Open Mon, Wed, Thurs, Fri, 11am-6pm; Sat, Sun, 11am-7pm. Closed Tues. Ticket office shuts down 45 minutes before closing time. Adults: €8.50 or €10 for the museum+special exhibits. Kids: Free (though there is a charge for special exhibits). Audioguide: free for adults as part of their entry ticket; Kids: €2. Kids' guide with games and images to help discover the museum collection: €1.50.*

This is a must-see for anyone big or small who likes boats of any kind. The museum has a remarkable collection of large ship models designed for King Louis XIV. There are also models of Columbus' Santa Maria, famous cruise ships, submarines, and many others. You can see a full-size replica of Napoleon's imperial boat. There are live demonstrations by people who make or repair ship models. Special exhibits cater to kids' tastes, with topics such as pirates or ships featured in the *Adventures of Tintin*.

MUSEUM OF MONUMENTS AND ARCHITECTURE. *Palais de Chaillot, 1 Place du Trocadéro et du 11 Novembre, on the left as you face the Eiffel Tower. Métro: Trocadéro. Open 11am-7pm, every day except Tues. Open til 9pm on Thurs. Closed Tues. Adults: €8; Kids: free.*
The museum's permanent collection is divided into three parts. One focuses on historical architecture, with details from cathedrals and civic buildings. A second presents stained glass windows and murals. Upstairs is the contemporary architecture section, with a full-scale model of an apartment by the famous French architect Le Corbusier. It's not for everyone, but it is really well presented and worthwhile for kids who like buildings and models. The café has great views of the Eiffel Tower, especially from the outdoor terrace.

PARIS AQUARIUM. *5, Avenue Albert de Mun. Métro: Trocadéro. Located in the Trocadéro Gardens, below the big esplanade with the golden statues, on the left as you face the Eiffel Tower. Open daily, 10am-7pm. Adults: €20.50; Kids 13-17yrs: €16; Kids 3-12yrs: €13; Kids under 3: free.*
Would you have thought to find sharks this close to the Eiffel Tower? You'll find at least 40 of them here, along with 500 other species of fish and invertebrates. They range from those you could find in the Seine River to ones hailing from tropical waters. The aquarium, originally built in 1867 and renovated in the early 2000s, is housed in former rock quarries.

The **TROCADERO GARDENS** were created for the 1937 Paris Exhibition. The statues lining the fountains celebrate joy and youth. The fountains are very impressive when the water canons (big jets) are turned on. These gardens have become a favorite rendez-vous spot for roller-bladers. You can watch them perform their stunts, framed by the majestic view of the Eiffel Tower. The gardens contain playgrounds and plenty of space for active

Trocadero Highlights

- Have your photo taken with the Eiffel Tower in the background
- Check out Napoleon's golden boat and other amazing ships at the Musée de la Marine
- Watch the roller-bladers and fountains in the Trocadéro Gardens
- Visit the aquarium
- Play in Trocadéro Gardens, including the double-decker carrousel
- Admire the haute couture at the Fashion Museum
- Go window shopping along the Rue de Passy
- See Monet's Impressionist paintings at the Musée Marmottan

kids to run around. Don't miss the **double-decker carrousel** at the bottom of the hill.

MUSEE DE LA MODE DE LA VILLE DE PARIS – PALAIS GALLIERA (FASHION MUSEUM). *10, Avenue Pierre 1er de Serbie. Métro: Alma Marceau. Open 10am-6pm (until 9pm Thurs). Closed Mon. Adults: €8; Youths 14-26: €6; Kids under 14: free.*

This small museum presents revolving exhibits based on its rich collection of costumes, high fashion, and fashion prints and photographs. Highlights include Audrey Hepburn's little black dress from the film *Breakfast at Tiffany's*, clothes worn by King Louis XVI and Queen Marie Antoinette, and gloves worn by actress Sarah Berhardt. There are clothes, accessories, and undergarment with famous labels, such as Elsa Schiaparelli, YSL, Dior, Pierre Balmain, Jean Paul Gautier, and more. The building was restored in 2013.

PASSY NEIGHBORHOOD. *Southwest from the Place du Trocadéro, down the Rue Franklin to the Place de Costa Rica, and Rue de Passy. Métro: Passy.*

This is a very chic neighborhood. The Rue de Passy is a great street for window-shopping, particularly if you favor classic fashions (known in French as Bon Chic, Bon Genre). Think preppy with a French flair. The nearby Rue de l'Annonciation has a lovely outdoor market. It is a nice place to pick up a picnic lunch or some delicious pastries for a snack.

Also in this neighborhood is a statue of **Benjamin Franklin** and a street that bears his name. This statue commemorates the fact that Franklin lived in the nearby Rue Raynouard when he was America's Ambassador to France. In 1776, Franklin successfully persuaded the French King Louis XVI to help support the American War of Independence. It was a good move – without the support of the French navy, French troops, and French General Lafayette, the Americans would not have won the Revolutionary War. Franklin returned to Paris to negotiate the peace treaty recognizing America's independence from Britain.

MUSÉE MARMOTTAN - MUSÉE MONET. *2, Rue Louis Boilly. Métro: La Muette. Open Tues-Sun, 10am-6pm (until 8pm on Thurs). Closed Mon. Adults: €10; Kids ages 7-25: €5; Kids under 7: free. Audioguides: €3. (Note: If you plan on going to Monet's house in Giverny, you can buy a combined ticket for both, here. Adults: €18.50; Kids ages 7-25: €9.)*

This is another fun stop for any child who enjoyed the book, Linnea in Monet's Garden. It is an excellent place to see some of the most important examples of Impressionist art. It is rarely crowded and a good alternative if you are not up to facing the throngs at the Musée d'Orsay. The permanent collection includes many paintings by Claude Monet, including the one called Impression, Soleil Levant (Impression, Sunrise) that gave Impressionism its name. The museum also features works by Monet's friends, Renoir, Sisley, Berthe Morisot, Pissarro, Gauguin, and others. The museum's upper floors contain medieval art objects and furniture from the time of Napoleon I.

Parent Tip: After a tour of the Musée Marmottan head for a break in the **Jardin du Ranelagh**. It is located behind the museum, across the street. There are playgrounds, roller-bladers, pony rides, a puppet theater, and an antique merry-go-round. See photo on left. ❖

MONA BISMARK AMERICAN CULTURAL CENTER, *34, Avenue de New York, 75016. Métro: Alma-Marceau, Iéna, or Trocadéro; Open Wed-Sun, 11am-6pm, Adults: €7; Kids under 12: free.*

This center is located in the former mansion of a wealthy American socialite. It presents temporary exhibits showcasing American art and culture. Recent examples include an exhibit on superhero comic book art, quilt art, and the history of the little black dress in fashion.

PONT DE L'ALMA. *Between Place de l'Alma and Place de la Résistance, Métro: Alma Marceau*

This bridge was built by Napoleon III and named for one of his successful battles in the Crimea in 1854. It is famous for its statue of a **Zouave soldier** on one of the arches by the river, used to measure high water points. Boatmen know that if the Seine's water rises as high as the Zouave's waist during periods of flooding, it is not safe to navigate under the bridges. During the Great Flood of 1910, the Seine's waters rose all the way up to the Zouave's chin.

Who is the Zouave? In 1830, a group of Zouaoua tribesmen from the hills of Algeria and Morocco joined the French army as an auxiliary battalion. Their uniform was based on their brightly colored traditional clothes, including a red sash, blue vest, baggy pants, and red fez (a brimless cap with a tassel). Brave and well trained, the Zouaves developed a reputation as dashing daredevils. They remained an important part of the French military until the early 20th century.

On the Place de l'Alma side of the bridge, there is a full-size replica of the golden torch that sits atop the Statue of Liberty in New York Harbor. This torch sculpture was a given to Paris by a consortium of American companies to celebrate the bicentennial of the French Revolution in 1989. It was briefly used as an informal memorial to Britain's Princess Diana, who was killed as a result of a car crash near this spot.

BATEAUX MOUCHES – TOUR BOAT RIDES. *Pont de l'Alma. Right Bank. Métro: Alma Marceau. Daily departures at 11am, 11:30am, 12:15pm, 1pm, 2pm, 3:15pm, and every 30 minutes from 4-10pm. Adults: €13.50; Kids 4-12: €5.50; Under 4: free. Lunch cruises at 12:30pm. Adults: €55; Kids under 12: €29.*

Always a welcome treat, the Bâteaux Mouches boat rides offer a unique view of many of the city's major monuments and bridges. Regular tours last just over an hour. There are commentaries in French and English. The lunch tour lasts 1.5 hours, and they will supply a birthday cake and candles if needed. Either is a great way to rest weary feet or recover from jet lag. It is also the best vantage point from which to admire the Zouave statue on the Pont de l'Alma and the small replica of the Statue of Liberty on the Ile Aux Cignes.

18. MONTMARTRE

The name **Montmartre** conjures up images of Bohemian artists, accordion players, and Amélie Poulain. Perched atop one of the tallest hills in Paris, this village-like neighborhood has preserved its cobbled streets, little houses, even a vineyard and two windmills. There is much to enchant both adults and children here. So climb to the top of the hill and enjoy the wonderful views and secrets hidden among the winding streets of this village on a hill.

MONTMARTRETRAIN. *Pick it up at the Place Blanche (métro: Blanche) or Place du Tertre. Runs from 10am-6pm every 45 minutes (winter), and 10am-11pm every 30 minutes (summer). Adults: €6.50; Kids: €4.50.*

If you are pressed for time or not up to walking up and down the cobbled streets of Montmartre, you can hop on this little white tourist train for a 35-minute tour of the neighborhood. It winds past the churches, squares, museums, windmills, Montmartre vineyard and cemetery, Lapin Agile restaurant, and more. Explanations are in French and English.

MONTMARTREBUS. *The bus runs a full circuit through the Montmartre neighborhood from Place Pigalle (métro: Pigalle), past Place des Abesses (métro: Abesses), up the Montmartre hill through the historic neighborhood, past the Sacre Coeur Basilica, down the back side of the hill with the vineyards, and loops its way back again. Adults and kids pay 1 métro ticket; Kids under 4 are free.*

This bus is part of the public transit system. You can get on or off anywhere along the circuit.

Montmartre Highlights

- Ride the funicular up the Montmartre hill
- Check out the view from the Sacré Coeur
- Ride the little white train through the neighborhood
- Have your portrait done at the Place du Tertre
- Find the Montmartre vineyards
- Look for the man who could walk through walls
- See Montmartre's two remaining windmills
- Admire the Art Nouveau subway entrance and church on the Place des Abesses
- Find the Wall of Love
- Retrace the footsteps of the saint who carried his chopped off head up the hill

Montmartre
(18th Arrondissement)

1. place des Abbesses
2. Basilique du Sacré Coeur
3. Eglise St-Pierre
4. place du Tertre
5. Espace Salvador-Dali
6. Musée du Vieux Montmartre vineyard
7. Au Lapin Agile
8. Musée d'Art Juif
9. Square S. Buisson
10. Moulin de la Galette
11. Windmill
12. Deux Moulins
13. Moulin Rouge
14. Cimetière de Montmartre
15. Musée d'Art Max Fourny/Halle St-Pierre

Ⓜ Métro Stop

(though you will have to pay again if you get back on). Or stay for the whole circuit and enjoy an unguided tour of the whole neighborhood.

GOING UP TO THE SACRÉ COEUR CHURCH. If you are at the bottom of the Montmartre hill, looking up at the Sacré Coeur Basilica, you have several choices for reaching the top. You can opt for the lovely staircases that wind their way up on either side of the central gardens. You can choose the slightly straighter stairs that run up the hill on both the right and left sides. Or you can head to the left and take a ride on the **funicular**. For the price of a regular métro ticket, you can glide up the hill on this diagonal train track. The ride is fairly short, and some parts take place in tunnels. However, the view when you are out in the open is fun, and kids love it.

BASILIQUE DU SACRÉ COEUR (BASILICA OF THE SA-CRED HEART). *Place du Parvis Sacré Coeur. Métro: Anvers or Château Rouge. Open daily: 6am-10:30pm. Stairs for climbing to the top of the dome are on the left, and open 9am-5pm (winter), 8:30am-8pm (summer).*

One of the most recognizable sights on top of the Montmartre hill is the giant white Basilique du Sacré Coeur. The church is made of a special type of limestone that bleaches itself every time it rains. This explains why the Sacré Coeur looks so white and bright. In contrast, the inside of the church is quite dark. You can climb up the 300 stairs to the top of the dome for a magnificent view of Paris and the surrounding area. There is also an excellent view from the terraces in front of the church. The belfry

contains the largest bell in the world. It weighs 20,000 kilos (19 tons) and is 8 feet in diameter.

The small cobbled streets west of the Sacré Coeur take you into the heart of old Montmartre.

PLACE DU TERTRE. *One block west of the Sacré Coeur Basilica. Métro: Abesses or Lamarck Caulaincourt.*

In the 1880s, many of the old buildings in the center of Paris were torn down as part of the period's great urban renewal projects. Low-income Parisians fled to the outskirts of the city, including to the Montmartre neighborhood. At the time, Montmartre was like a small village with narrow streets, fields, vineyards, and windmills. There were also cafés and dance halls, such as the famous Moulin Rouge. Until World War I, the area attracted many starving artists, musicians, and writers who flocked here to live the bohemian life. Some of their names included painters Henri Toulouse-Lautrec, Paul Cézanne, Auguste Renoir, and Pablo Picasso; composers Hector Berlioz and Jacques Offenbach; and poets Henrich Heine and Guillaume Apollinaire.

The Place du Tertre does its best to keep alive the spirit of Montmartre's artistic heyday. Though quite touristy, it still resembles a village square surrounded by shade trees, shops, and small houses. Here you can purchase reproductions of the works of Montmartre's famous painters as well as other souvenirs. You can also support today's generation of starving artists who display their works in the Place or may offer to do your portrait. It is a fun place to grab a bite in a café and soak in the artistic atmosphere.

If you have budding artists in the family, they may want to pull out the paper and drawing supplies for some artistic inspiration of their own. The nearby **Place du Calvaire** offers a great view of the city, and has a small museum dedicated to the surrealist paintings of Salvador Dali that some kids really enjoy.

EXPLORING SIDE STREETS. *The area by the Sacré Coeur and Place du Tertre can get quite crowded during high tourist season. Luckily, you don't have to go very far into the side streets of Montmartre to escape the crowd and enjoy the quieter charm of the neighborhood.*

If you take the Rue des Saules from the Rue Norvins, Rue Saint Rustique, or Rue Cortot you will run into several Montmartre landmarks. Three restaurants were famous hangouts for artists such as Cezanne, Toulouse-Lautrec, and Renoir. They include the **Auberge de la Bonne Franquette**, **La Maison Rose**, and the **Lapin Agile**. To the right, as you go down the Rue des Saules is the famous **Montmartre vineyard**. Each year on the first Saturday in October, the grapes are picked, then taken to the basement of the district's town hall to be pressed, aged, and bottled. The total wine production is about 700 bottles. The wine is called Clos Montmartre. Profits from the wine's sale pay for neighborhood events and festivities.

Along Rue Lepic, you'll come across Montmartre's two windmills, the **Moulin Radet** and the 600-year old **Moulin de la Galette**. They are all that remain of the 30 or more that used to dot the Montmartre hillside.

At the Place Marcel Aymé you will come across an odd **statue of a man walking through a wall**. It depicts a character from a novel by Aymé. The novel is a story about a man named Dutilleul who discovers he can walk through walls, and uses this skill to become a burglar.

The **Place Emile Goudot** features a building called the **Bâteau Lavoir**, which is full of art studios. This is where artists Pablo Picasso, George Braque, and Juan Gris lived when they were experimenting with a new style of art called cubism.

Further down the hill still is the pretty **Place des Abesses**. This square is notable for its beautiful métro entrance. The glass awning is one of only two left that were designed in the Art Nouveau style by Hector Guimard. There is also an Art Nouveau style church across the street called Eglise Saint Jean de Montmartre.

WALL OF LOVE. *Place des Abbesses, behind the entrance to the Abbesses métro station.*

This wall was created by an artist named Frédéric Baron, who collected over 1,000 written samples of the words "I love you" in all sorts of different languages – even exotic ones like Amaric, Navajo, Catalan, and Yiddish. He picked out 311 of them and had them transcribed on to glazed tiles and placed in this small park. It's a sweet place to take a break and photos of those you love.

FOLLOWING THE TRACES OF SAINT DENIS. *This path takes you through Montmartre, from the Pigalle Métro, up the Rue des Martyrs, Rue Yvonne Le Tac, past the Place Emile Goudeau, Moulin Radet to the Square Suzanne Buisson.*

Saint Denis was the first Bishop of Paris. He is also the patron saint of France. There are different stories about who he really was. Some versions say he was Greek, others that he was from Rome. In either case, he was sent to Paris to spread the word of Christianity around 250 AD, during the Roman occupation of Gaul. He was evidently very good at his work. Along with his two companions, Rustique and Eleuthère, Denis converted many people to Christianity. This made the Roman Emperor furious. He wanted his subjects to worship the Roman gods. The Emperor sent troops to Paris to stop the Christians. Roman soldiers arrested Denis, Rustique and Eleuthere, and many other Christians throughout the city. Denis and his companions were tortured and sentenced to death. According to the legend, the night before the execution was scheduled to take place, Christ (or in some versions a group of angels) appeared to Denis in his jail cell to give him Holy Communion.

The next day Denis, Rustique, and Eleuthère were marched up Mount Mercury (now known as the Montmartre hill) to be executed in front of the temple of Mercury. However, the impatient Roman guards took matters into their own hands and beheaded the three prisoners well before they reached the top. According to the legend, while Rustique and Eleuthère fell to the ground, Denis picked up his head and continued walking up the hill. He washed his head off in a fountain, then walked another six kilometers (4 miles) until he reached the house of a holy woman named Catulla. Denis handed her his head and then collapsed. Catulla had him buried near her house. Today it marks the spot of the great Saint Denis Cathedral, located north of Paris in a suburb called Saint Denis.

You can retrace the footsteps of Saint Denis as a way to enjoy some of the sights of Montmartre. Start at Métro: Pigalle. Walk one block east to the Rue des Martyrs and take it north, up the Montmartre Hill. This is supposedly the path that was taken by Denis and his companions on their way to the execution. When you reach the end of the street, take a right into the Rue Yvonne Le Tac. At #11, you will come to the **Chapel of the Martyrs**. This supposedly marks the spot where Denis, Rustique, and

Eleutère were beheaded. In the 7th century, this chapel was considered to be a place of asylum. Any criminal who made it inside the building could seek refuge and pardon.

Next, go back down the Rue Yvonne Le Tac the way you came, until you reach the Place des Abbesses (described above). Climb up the Rue de Ravignan, admiring the Place Emile Goudeau and Bâteau Lavoir along the way. Turn left into the Rue Norvins, past the Place Marcel Aymé (described above) with its sculpture of the man who could walk through walls. Take the Rue Girardon to the **Square Suzanne Buisson**. This pretty garden features a fountain and a statue of Saint Denis with his head in his hands. It is supposed to mark the spot where Denis rinsed off his head before continuing his journey north. It is also a nice place to play or relax in the shade, if you need a break from walking uphill.

To follow the rest of Saint Denis' path, you would need to go another four miles north and east. This would take you beyond Paris and into the suburb of Saint Denis to the great Saint Denis Basilica. This magnificent, gothic cathedral is well worth a visit. It contains the tombs of the French kings. You don't actually have to walk the whole way. There is an excellent subway station, called Basilique de Saint Denis that you can get to from the Pigalle or Anvers métro, by changing and heading north at the Place de Clichy métro stop.

To continue your tour of Montmartre, meanwhile, go past the Place Dalida and up the Rue de l'Abreuvoir to the Rue de Saules, where you can admire the Montmartre vineyard, Maison Rose, and Lapin Agile. A hike back up the Rue de Saules gets you to the Rue Cortot and to the Place du Tertre. Then head for the Sacré Coeur. You can ride the funicular down the hill or opt for the stairs. At the bottom, kids will enjoy the fancy merry-go-round.

GARE DU NORD TRAIN STATION. *Located south and east of Montmartre, on the Rue Dunkerque. Métro: Gare du Nord.*

This station serves trains going to and from northern France as well as Belgium, the Netherlands, Scandinavia, and trains bound for Britain through Lille (including the Eurostar that goes through the Chunnel).

GARE DE L'EST TRAIN STATION. *Located just a few blocks south and east of the Gare du Nord, on the Place du 8 Mai 1945. Métro: Gare de l'Est.*

This is where you come to catch trains bound for eastern France, Germany, Switzerland, and Austria.

PERE LACHAISE CEMETERY. *Entrances at 8, boulevard de Menilmontant and 16, rue du Repos. Métro: Philippe Auguste or Père Lachaise. Open 8am-6pm. Entrance is free, but it is worth it to buy a map for €3.*

Père Lachaise (see photo below) is like a big park filled with statues, albeit funerary ones, and stray cats. It is the final resting place for scores of famous people. Fans of classic rock will go just to see the tomb of Jim Morrison (lead singer for the Doors, who died of a drug overdose in Paris). Other notable residents include the composers Frédéric Chopin, Francis Poulenc, and Georges Bizet; ill-fated lovers Héloise and Abélard; writers Oscar Wilde, Honoré de Balzac, Marcel Proust, Gertrude Stein, Colette, Molière, and Guillaume Appolinaire; painters Jacques-Louis David, Dominic Ingres, Théodore Géricault, Eugène Delacroix, Camille Pissaro, Georges Seurat, Jean Baptiste Corot, Amedeo Modigliani, and Max Ernst; actors Simone Signoret and Yves Montand; singer Edith Piaf; dancers Isadora Duncan and Jane Avril (depicted in famous paintings of Toulouse Lautrec); urban planner Baron Haussmann and Richard Wallace, the man who gave Paris its characteristic green water fountains. There are numerous monuments to victims of nazi concentration camps, and a memorial wall to the fighters of the Paris Commune uprising in 1871.

19. LA VILLETTE

It's a little hard to imagine that this massive urban park with its modern museums and structures used to be just a little village. But that is where the name, Villette (small village) comes from. Originally a Roman hamlet on the road to Belgium, **La Villette** took on greater importance in the 1800s, when it became the home of Paris' main slaughterhouse. When that work was moved to the suburbs in the 1970s, a massive new plan was devised to transform the site into a series of public parks, museums, and entertainment halls.

The result is a huge green space, dotted with gardens, waterways, playgrounds, and architectural "follies." There is much to spark the interests and joys of children here, starting with the magnificent science museum, leading through a slide shaped like a dragon, across a canal, all the way to an excellent Museum of Music.

CITÉ DES SCIENCES ET DES INDUSTRIES (SCIENCE MUSEUM). *Parc de la Villette, 30, Avenue Corentin Cariou. Métro: Porte de la Villette. Open Tues-Sun, 10am-6pm (Sun, until 7pm). Closed Mon. Adults: €12; Kids 6-12 yr: €9. Kids under 6: free. Additional fees are charged for the planetarium, IMAX theater, or submarine visit. Audioguide rental: €1.50.*

This "Science City" is made to spur your child's curiosity and natural urge to touch and experiment. To get the most out of it and avoid language barrier frustrations rent the audioguide, available in English.

The museum is very interactive with sections on sound, optical illusions, health, the ocean, geology, stars and galaxies, plants, volcanoes, and virtual reality. There are plenty of computer opportunities as well as activities like trying out a helicopter engine, seeing how the gears of a car work, checking out a racing bike prototype, or designing their own puzzle which they then learn how to mass produce.

The Cité des Sciences also contains a **planetarium** and a lower level cafeteria that features its own aquarium. Outside, you can take a self-guided tour (with free audioguide) through the Argonaute submarine. It will give kids an appreciation for the claustrophobia of life on board.

LA GÉODE IMAX MOVIE THEATER. *Next to the Argonaute submarine and Cité des Sciences et des Industries. Open Tues-Sun. Closed Mon. Shows projected every hour from 10 am to 9 pm. Adults: €12; Kids and Students under age 25: €9. Ask for English-language headphones.*

This theater is already cool just from the outside, where its mirrored spherical surfaces reflect the sky and passers-by. Inside it shows 3-D IMAX movies. You are literally surrounded by images that transport you under the sea, into outer space, back to the dinosaurs, etc. Opt for the top rows if you want to avoid a stiff neck. It's so realistic that it is not recommended for children under age 3 or women who are more than 6 months pregnant.

JARDIN DU DRAGON (PLAYGROUND). *Near the Cité des Sciences et des Technologies, on the south side.*

> ## La Villette Highlights
>
> • Explore the human body, the ocean, the solar system, or virtual reality at the Cité des Sciences
> • See an IMAX movie at La Géode
> • Visit a real submarine
> • Play on a giant dragon slide
> • Bounce, pedal, get sprayed with water, and play in the delightful gardens of the Park
> • Go on a canal boat ride
> • Check out the ancient instruments and many musical sounds

This dragon is irresistible if you are a kid. It contains a giant slide plus several smaller ones that offer plenty of opportunities to climb and squeal.

BIG PLAYGROUNDS. *Near the Grande Halle, along the path called Galérie de la Villette. If you are coming from the dragon or science museum, you will need to take the bridge across the Canal de l'Ourcq.*

Technically, this area is known as the Jardin des Vents (Garden of Winds), Jardin des Dunes (Garden of Dunes), and Jardin des Miroirs (Garden of Mirrors). To a kid, and anyone who is young at heart, it is really just a giant playground. These gardens are filled with clever and delightful activities. Large sections (divided by age groups) are covered with moon-bounce type surfaces where kids can jump to their hearts' content. They are connected by wobbly sidewalks. Watching you try to negotiate these will be guaranteed to make the rest of the family laugh. Kids also love trying out the pedal-powered windmills that they can manipulate with their hands or feet. There are mini-mountains to climb and a garden filled with mirrors.

OTHER GARDENS. *In the Parc de la Villette.*

In the vast 3-kilometer stretch – about 2 miles – between the Porte de la Villette side of the park and its Porte de Pantin entrance, you will find several interesting little gardens. They are full of charm and surprises. The Jardin des Equilibres features games where kids try out their skills of balance. The Jardin de Bambous is like walking through a bamboo forest.

The Jardin de la Treille (Trellis Garden) has 90 small fountains decorated with trellises of climbing vines and plants. The Jardin des Frâyeurs Enfantines (Garden of Childhood Fears) takes you through dark paths filled with strange music and sounds of the forest. The Jardin des Brouillards (Garden of Fog) sprays you with jets of mist on warm days.

There are also two wide fields, called Prairies, where kids can run, kick a ball, and generally let loose. The benches, lampposts, trash cans, and other park furniture were designed by architect Philippe Starck. During July and August, the Triangle Prairie is transformed into a free, outdoor movie theater.

Once you are near the canals at La Villette, keep a sharp eye on active toddlers. There are no railings along the water's edge.

PARIS CANAL BOAT RIDE. *19, Quai de la Loire, Dock near the end of the Grande Halle. Métro: Porte de Pantin. Tel. 01 42 40 96 97. A 3-hour ride departs at 2:30 pm and arrives at the Musée d'Orsay at 5:30 pm. Adults: €19; Kids 12-25: €16; Kids 4-11: €12; Under 4: free.*

Enjoy a ride through Paris' canals and locks from the Canal de l'Ourcq to the Seine River and over to the Musée d'Orsay. For kids who love boating, it's a great thrill. You go through locks and tunnels, and see some of Paris' most famous sights. Reserve in advance during high tourist season. The tours sell out quickly.

CANAUXRAMA CANAL BOAT RIDES. *Depart from 13, Quai de la Loire on the Bassin de la Villette. Métro: Jaurés. Website: www.canauxrama.com/en/cruise/cruise-of-the-old-paris_117.html This is 4 métro stops down from Porte de Pantin, past the Canal de l'Ourq and at the southern end of the Bassin de la Villette. Phone: 01 42 39 15 00. Departures at 9:45 am or 2:45 pm. Tours last 3 hours. Adults: €17; Students and Seniors: €13; Kids 4-12: €9; Kids under 4: free.*

These boats take you down through the Saint Martin canal and locks from the Bassin de la Villette to the Arsenal Marina, just before the canal joins with the Seine River. The ride is long for short attention spans, but for those who enjoy boats, the passages through tunnels and locks are fascinating. The sites along the way take you through some truly Parisian neighborhoods and under picturesque footbridges. You'll feel like you've stepped onto the set of Amélie Poulain or any other charming Parisian film. Bring along a picnic. Reserve in advance, during high tourist season.

MUSÉE DE LA MUSIQUE. *In the Cité de la Musique building, 221, Avenue Jean Jaures. Métro: Porte de Pantin. Open Tues-Sun, 12pm-6pm. Closed Mon. Adults: €7; Students and kids under 26: free.*

This is a very interesting museum for any child who plays a musical instrument or enjoys music. It offers not only lots to see, but also many sounds. The exhibits are easy to follow and enjoy thanks to the free headsets (available in English) supplied at the entrance. There are also live presentations by musicians demonstrating all types of different instruments from around the world.

Outside the museum, you can refuel at the **Café de la Musique**. It is conveniently situated facing the Place de la Fountaine aux Lions, which offers plenty of car-free space to run while kids wait for their food.

20. BOIS DE BOULOGNE

This huge park fills most of the western edge of Paris. There are gardens, playgrounds, lakes, and museums. It is here that you can find Paris' only campgrounds, two equestrian centers, two hippodromes, and the Roland Garros stadium which hosts the French Open Tennis competition each year in May.

JARDIN D'ACCLIMATATION. *Entrance at intersection of Boulevard des Sablons and Avenue du Mahatma Gandhi on the N edge of the park. Walk from Métro: Sablons or take the free train from Métro: Porte Maillot. Open daily, 10am-6pm (until 7pm, Jun-Sep). Adults and Kids 3-18: €3; Kids under 3: free. Tickets for rides and attractions are €2.90 each or €35 for a pack of 10. Ask for a free map at the entrance.*

This garden is full of rides and activities for kids of all ages. It's a little old-fashioned but that's part of the charm. For example, the bouncing horse course will remind you of Mary Poppins. There's also a petting zoo and farm, a hall of funny mirrors, and a free puppet show. On summer afternoons, you can go on a camel ride. There are several large playgrounds, organized by age group. The park also has a bowling alley, equestrian center, and poney rides. See photo on next page.

BIKE RENTALS. *These are located across from the main entrance to the Jardin d'Acclimatation. There are special bike lanes and paths throughout the Bois de Boulogne. It's a great way to enjoy the park.*

PRÉ CATALAN. *In the middle of the Bois de Boulogne, off the Allée de la Reine Marguerite, at the same level as the Lac Inférieur.*

This area features big grassy fields and some ancient trees.

There is also a lovely **Shakespearean garden** with plants and herbs that are mentioned in the Bard's plays. From May to October the garden becomes an open-air theater, featuring works by Shakespeare. These are often performed in English by British theater companies.

LAC INFERIEUR AND LAC SUPERIEUR. *Towards the middle of the Bois de Boulogne on its eastern side. Near the Porte de la Muêtte. Métro: Avenue Henri Martin.*

The Lac Supérieur is the smaller of these two lakes. Its most interesting feature is that fact that on warm afternoons, you can rent a remote-controlled toy powerboat to play with on the lake. On the Lac Inférieur you can rent full-sized rowboats. For a nominal fee, you can also take the ferry to the lake's main island.

The Bois de Boulogne has two horse-racing tracks. The **Hippodrôme de Longchamp**, which features thoroughbred races and poney rides for little tikes, is located on the SW side of the Bois, along the Route des Tribunes. Free buses run from Métro: Porte d'Auteuil. Races start at 2pm. The **Hippodrôme d'Auteuil**, located on the SE side of the Bois, along the Route des Lacs features steeple-chase races. There are pony rides and a kids play area. Métro: Porte d'Auteuil.

There is a public swimming pool, with both indoor and outdoor pools, called Piscine d'Auteuil, on the Rue des Lacs de Passy and Allée des Fortifications. Métro: Ranelagh.

ROLAND GARROS TENNIS STADIUM. *2, Avenue Gordon Bennett. On the southern edge of the Bois de Boulogne. Métro: Porte d'Auteuil. You can purchase tickets for the French Open: Tel. 01 47 43 48 00 or www. frenchopen.org.*

This red-clay tennis stadium is named for a French pilot who was the first aviator to fly solo across the Mediterranean Sea. It hosts the annual French Open Tennis Tournament in May. This is a real treat for tennis fans, old and young.

21. DAY TRIPS

Versailles

A fancy palace, spectacular gardens, musical fountains, and fireworks: this is Louis XIV's Château de Versailles. Come taste of the luxury and splendor that was life at court during the reign of the France's Sun King.

VERSAILLES PALACE. *4, Boulevard de la Reine, in Versailles, 20 kilometers southwest of Paris. By car take highway A13 towards Rouen to exit Versailles-Château. By public transportation take RER line C to Versailles Rive Gauche station (this station is only a few blocks from the Palace). The Palace is open Tues-Sun, 9am-6:30pm (May-Sep), 9am-5:30pm (Oct-Apr). Closed Mon. The pricing system in the palace is complicated and confusing. It varies depending on which parts you want to see. The king's apartments are a separate visit from the rest of the palace. If you go to Entrance A, you can opt for a combined ticket, including the king's rooms, queen's rooms, and Hall of Mirrors (Galerie des Glaces). Adults: €15 (includes an audioguide); Kids: free. Entrance to the gardens is free, except during the Grandes Eaux Musicales (Musical Fountains show) – see below.*

Parent tip: To avoid summer crowds, you may want to do the visit backwards. Start with the park and gardens. Have lunch by the Grand Canal. Go for a boat or bike ride. Save the palace for the late afternoon. The western light will be filling the Hall of Mirrors and the crowds will be thinner. ❖

History of the Palace

The palace of Versailles was originally built by King Louis XIII as a small hunting lodge. Louis XIV had already planned to expand Versailles when he saw Nicholas

Fouquet's palace at Vaux-le-Vicomte. Fouquet's palace was so splendid that the king had him arrested. Officially, Fouquet was imprisoned for using state funds for his own luxurious life style. Unofficially, his main crime was to have dared to outshine the Sun King. Louis XIV immediately hired Fouquet's architect Le Vau, painter Le Brun, and landscape designer Le Nôtre to make him an even grander palace at Versailles.

The builders and designers had their work cut out for them at Versailles. The land was marshy and unstable. Workmen had to bring in mountains of earth to build up the land. Fully grown trees were uprooted and replanted to make a forest, many of them dying along the way. A long and complicated system of pipes, pumps, and windmills was installed to drain the swamps and bring water for a grand canal and the multitude of fountains set up to decorate the gardens.

Versailles Highlights

- Visit the king's chambers, queen's chambers, and count the mirrors in the Galerie des Glaces
- See the Grandes Eaux Musicales when all the fountains dance to Baroque music
- Take the little train to the Grand and Petit Trianon
- Go for a bike ride through the park
- Try a Segway tour of the gardens
- Rent a rowboat on the Grand Canal
- Make like kings and queens and ride in a horse-drawn carriage

Louis XIV moved into the new palace in 1682. He made his whole court move from Paris to Versailles with him. It was a good way for the king to show his absolute power and keep an eye on members of his court. He loved to organize elaborate parties and festivities. Louis XIV filled his palace and gardens with musicians, writers, painters, acrobats, and other entertainers. Even the canals were filled with elaborately decorated boats for the amusement of the king and his court. The gardens were decorated with statues and fountains. In spite of all the installations, there was never enough water to run all of the fountains at one time. So when the king took a stroll through the gardens, workmen would whistle back and forth to signal which fountains to turn on and off along the king's path.

The new palace was built to be large, imposing, and extravagantly decorated. It included 700 rooms and 67 staircases. There were over 2,000 windows and 6,000 paintings. The chandeliers, throne, and some of the furniture were made of solid silver. Gold gilding (a thin layer of solid gold paint) covered much of the wall and ceiling decorations. Gold thread was woven into the wall coverings. There were 5,000 pieces of furniture and decorative objects.

Versailles was one of the first royal palaces to be permanently furnished. Prior to that, most furniture was moved along with the king each time the royal court went from one palace to another. After the French Revolution of 1789, all the furniture was sold to the highest bidder. The paintings and antiquities were sent to the Louvre. The silver and metal pieces were melted down. The books were transferred to the national library. The palace was turned into a museum and never again served as a royal residence.

VERSAILLES GARDENS. *Open daily from sunrise to sunset, except during stormy or extreme weather. Entrance to the gardens is free except during special events like the Grandes Eaux Musicales (see below).*

There are over 50 fountains decorating the gardens around the Versailles Palace. Many refer to Greek and Roman mythology:

The **Bassin de Latone** is named after a character in mythology who was seduced by the god Zeus and gave birth to Apollo and his twin sister Diana, goddess of the hunt. One day Latone took her children to have a drink from a spring in a land called Lycia. The locals teased and insulted her. Latone called for Zeus' help. He exacted revenge on the Lycians by turning them into frogs and lizards, which now decorate this fountain.

The **Bassin d'Apollon** is a huge fountain featuring Apollo driving his magnificent golden chariot, pulled by four horses, across the sky. The figure of Apollo was meant to remind his subjects of Louis XIV's power and splendor.

On the north side of the palace is another spectacular fountain, the **Bassin de Neptune**. This is where the Nuits d'Eté shows are held (see below). You can recognize Neptune, god of the seas, by his trident (three-pronged spear).

Hidden among the plants and alleyways is another great fountain. It represents **Enceladus**, a mythical Greek giant who tried to climb Mount Olympus and overthrow Zeus, king of the gods. Zeus sent down a barrage of stones to hold him back. In this fountain you can see the golden figure of Enceladus partially buried under the huge rocks.

The **Bassin du Dragon** at the end of the Allée de l'Eau is not based on Greek or Roman mythology but is still a delight. Here you will see statues of little children riding on swans and fighting off a big dragon. The jet coming from the dragon's mouth can shoot up nearly 30 meters (over 90 feet).

GRAND CANAL. *In the Versailles Gardens.*

In the days of Louis XIV, this canal was filled with golden boats – even a special gondola from Venice. Some of the boats carried musicians who entertained the king and his guests as they ambled round the water. Today, you can rent a more modest rowboat. Though less fancy than the king's, it will still offer nice views of the Palace and gardens.

BICYCLE RENTALS. *Two locations: 1) at the vehicle entrance to the park, on the Boulevard dela Reine; and 2) in the park, by the Grand Canal. Open daily 10am-6:30pm. Closed in December and January.*

These bike rental spots offer a large supply of bicycles, including kid-sized ones and child carriers. It is a great way to explore the vast park around the palace and make your way to the Trianons or Hameau de la Reine. There are plenty of car-free lanes, so you won't have to worry about traffic. Just watch out for the little tourist train that makes the rounds between the palace, Grand Canal, and Trianons.

GRAND TRIANON, PETIT TRIANON, HAMEAU DE LA RE-INE. *On the Versailles grounds, north and west of the Palace. Access from the Avenue du Trianon, Petit Canal, Allée de la Reine, or Allée des Deux Trianons. Open daily 9am-6:30 pm (May-Sep), 9am-5:30 pm (Oct-Apr). Adults: €10; Kids under 26: free.*

These three outbuildings were built as royal residences. The Grand and Petit Trianon were designed as retreats where the king could escape from the royal court from time to time. The Grand Trianon is still used today to house visiting dignitaries. The Hameau de la Reine was built for Marie Antoinette, the wife of Louis XVI. She would go there dressed up as a milk maid and pretend to be in a small country village. There is still a small working farm here.

GRANDES EAUX MUSICALES. *Sat-Sun during the summer from 10 am to 6:30 pm, with different fountains in use at various times. Evening shows take place from 8:30 pm to 11:30 pm. Adults: €10; Kids: 10-18: €6; Kids under 10: free.*

This show emulates the festivities at Versailles during Louis XIV's reign when the fountains would dance to the concerts by Lully and other baroque composers. The king would invite his guests to stroll among the gardens as different fountains became animated to the music. Today, the music is piped in, but the effect is still lovely.

LITTLE TRAIN FOR VERSAILLES GARDENS. *Starts from the Palace (N-side terrace), with stops at the Grand Canal, Petit Trianon, and Grand Trianon. Adults: €7.50; Kids 11-18: €5.80; Kids under 11: free.*

The little train is always a favorite with kids, especially if they are tired of being on their feet. It takes you from the palace to the royal residences and on to the Grand Canal. Hang on to your tickets and you will be able to get on and off all day. Note: another little train leaves from the front of the palace for 45-minute tours of the town of Versailles.

CARRIAGE RIDES and **SEGWAY TOURS** *are also offered starting from the north side terrace.*

If you are in the mood for a royal treat, hop on board one of the horse-drawn carriages for a charming tour of the grounds and park. Your kids will be delighted. Or you can try your hand at a family Segway tour.

Giverny – Monet's House

Venture just an hour west of Paris along the Seine River and you come to the lush, green, rolling hills of Normandy. The region is famous for its apples, creamy butter, and Camembert cheese. This is where Claude Monet had a house and wonderful garden so filled with color it will make you feel like you've walked right into an Impressionist painting.

CLAUDE MONET'S HOUSE AND GARDENS. *84, Rue Claude Monet, in Giverny, 80 kilometers (50 miles) west of Paris. By car, follow the directions for the A13 highway toward Rouen (via the Pont de Saint Cloud on the west side of Paris) to the Bonnières exit, then the D201 to Giverny. By train, go from the Gare Saint Lazare to Vernon, 45 minutes away. From the Vernon train station you can catch a bus, take a taxi, or rent bikes for the 5 kilometer (3 mile) ride to Giverny. There are also tour bus trips to Giverny from Paris. Contact Paris-Vision (Tel. 01 42 60 30 01) or Cityrama (Tel. 01 44 55 61 00). Claude Monet's house and gardens are open daily, Apr-Oct, Tues-Sun, 9:30am-6pm. Closed Mon and Nov-Mar. Adults: €7 (house and* *gardens), €4 (gardens only); Kids 12-18: €5, Kids 7-11: €3 (house and garden); Kids under 7: free.*

"It's just like in the book!," exclaimed a 6-year-old friend on one of our trips to Claude Monet's house in Giverny. Sure enough, if you've seen the book *Linnea in Monet's Garden* by Christina Bjock and Lena Anderson, you'll recognize Monet's pink house, his art studio, the big garden filled with flowers and alleyways, the Japanese footbridge, and the pond full of water lilies. Children love this place, even if they have never heard of Linnea, Monet, or Impressionism. They can't resist the urge to explore the garden paths, hide behind gigantic flowerbeds, and listen to the gobble gobble of the white turkeys. See if they can find the underground passageway to the water lily pond. Do they recognize the Japanese Bridge from his paintings? How about the little green rowboat?

Monet's house offers a glimpse of daily life in the home of a great painter. You'll see the original furniture, decorations, and dishes. There's also one of Monet's art studios, his reading room, and his bedroom. There are lots of Japanese prints on the walls from which he drew inspiration. You can also see how Monet's love of color extended to the inside of his house. Bright blues and yellows dominate throughout the entire house. Don't forget to look out the windows for nice views of the gardens.

At the end of your visit, you'll find Linnea, copies of water lily paintings, and other souvenirs in the gift shop. This was formerly Monet's big studio. Today it is an excellent place to pick up gifts for folks back home.

MUSEE DES IMPRESSIONNISMES (formerly known as The Museum of American Impressionists). *99, Rue Claude Monet, in Giverny. Open daily, Apr-Oct, Tues-Sun, 10am-6pm. Closed Nov-Mar. Adults: €7; Students, Seniors, and Teachers: €4.50; Kids 7-18: €3; Kids under 7: free. Free to all on the first Sun of the month. Audioguide: €3. Special kids activity guide is available free of charge.*

In the 1890s, as Monet's fame and that of other French Impressionist painters spread, other painters came to Giverny to join him, including many Americans. This museum showcases their work. The permanent collection features paintings from 1870 to 1920. Temporary exhibits embrace themes such as depictions of trains in Impressionist paintings or views of the Seine. The museum is bright, airy, and not terribly big – excellent qualities for a kid-friendly visit. Special activities and areas are set up just for kids. There is a café and gift shop featuring a good kids' section.

Theme Parks

If you or your child's idea of a real vacation isn't complete without life size cartoon characters or thrill rides don't worry.

PARC DISNEYLAND AND WALT DISNEY STUDIOS. *Located 32 kilometers E of Paris in the town of Marne-la-Vallée. By car, take highway A4 towards Nancy-Metz to exit 14. The parking lots are huge. Don't forget where you've left your car, and be prepared to hike 10-15 minutes to Marne la Vallée and the park entrance. By public transportation, take the RER line A4 commuter train to the Marne la Valée-Chessy stop. You can also take a special shuttle bus to the park from either Orly or Charles-de-Gaulle airports. Buses leave every 45 minutes. High-speed TGV trains also service the Marne-la-Vallee station from many major French cities. Open year-round, 9am-11pm (July-Sept) 9am-8pm (Fall, Spring), 10am-8pm (Nov-Dec). Entrance costs vary depending on time of year, and whether you purchase a one or several-day pass. Passes can be purchased at many Métro/RER stations, FNAC stores, and Galeries Lafayette department stores. Further information and special discounts are available online at www.disneylandparis.com*

If you've never had a chance to go to the American Disney theme parks or want to compare the French and American ones, here's your chance. Parc Disneyland and Walt Disney Studios are hugely popular with Europeans, including French families. They look on it as a way to get a big dose of American culture without having to cross the Atlantic or give up drinking red wine with lunch.

Just like in the American parks, Parc Disneyland features a Main Street with its afternoon parade of Disney characters and Sleeping Beauty's castle. There are sections (Fantasyland) designed for younger kids and others (Adventureland, Discoveryland, Frontierland) that feature rides for older kids.

Walt Disney Studies offers five production zones that explain how animated movies are made by way of rides and attractions like Stitch Live! and the Twilight Zone of Terror.

Not surprisingly, the parks get very crowded during the summer tourist season. Your best bet during this time is to arrive early and head straight for the most popular rides. Another strategy is to wait until the end of the day to try the favorite sections, when many people are leaving or watching the Main Street Parade. You can also obtain a Fast-Pass for the most crowded rides. These are available by the entrance and give you a specific time when you can go to a particular ride. You will then get to bypass the long line and go through the much shorter Fast-Pass line.

Disney Village livens up as the rest of the parks and attractions close down. There are restaurants, shops, and entertainment to spread the Disney magic well into the evening.

PARC ASTERIX. *Located 35 kilometers N of Paris, near Charles de Gaulle Airport. By car, take highway A1 north to the Parc Asterix exit, located between exits 7 and 8. By public transportation, take RER line B3 from Paris to the Charles de Gaulle/Roissy station where you can catch the Parc Asterix shuttle bus that leaves every 30 minutes. You can purchase a combined RER-Park Entrance tickets for a discount at RER stations in Paris. High-speed TGV trains from across France also stop at the Charles de Gaulle/ Roissy Station, where you can catch the Parc Asterix shuttle. There's also a shuttle bus from Paris that you can catch in front of the Louvre, by the Palais Royal métro at 9 am. Open daily, April-August and every weekend in Sept-Oct, 10am-6pm (Mon-Fri), 9:30am-7pm (Sat-Sun and daily in August). Adults: €46; Kids 3-12: €37; Kids under 3: free. The nearby hotels offer special family rates for lodging plus park entrance. Strollers and wheelchairs are available in the park free of charge. Baby changing station and place to warm up bottles located under the big rock with Asterix on top.*

Parent tip: Due to its proximity to the Charles de Gaulle/Roissy Airport, you may want to save a visit to Parc Asterix for the end of your trip. You can visit the park on the day before your flight home (there are places to check your bags at the park entrance). Spend the night at a hotel near the park or near the airport, and catch your flight out the next day. It's a great way to combine fun and convenience. ❖

If you want to see a truly French theme park, this is the one for you! Parc Asterix is based on the popular French comic book characters **Asterix** and **Obelix**. Their (very funny) adventures are set in the 1st century BC, during the Roman Occupation of Gaul (France). If you've seen any of the comic books, you'll really enjoy recognizing the characters and buildings from the stories. If you haven't seen the books, you'll want to after this visit (Note: they are available in French, English, and numerous other languages). We love this park not only because we are big Asterix fans, but also because it is a more manageable size than Parc Disneyland, yet still offers plenty of fun.

Parc Asterix is divided into several sections, starting with Gaul, Classical Rome, and Ancient Greece. Then you pass through time to Medieval France, the Renaissance, and on to 19th century Paris. There are plenty of activities for kids and adults of all ages. There are some great thrill rides, including a huge wooden roller coaster (see photo below), plenty of loop de loops, and a bobsled ride. There are several different boat rides, ranging from a steep roller coaster one to a hilarious bumper boat ride on the River Styx. There are also lots of funny rides, playgrounds, merry-go-rounds, automates, and shops. You can also take in any number of shows. Examples include a dolphin show in Ancient Greece, a Three Musketeer sword fight in Medieval Paris, a mystery about thieves stealing the Mona Lisa, a magic show in Gaul, and acrobats in the Roman Amphitheater.

Since this is France after all, there are plenty of eateries throughout the park, ranging from a little crêpe hut in the Gaul village to full restaurants by the Medieval and Renaissance sections. There are family-friendly hotels near the park with shuttle service to the park and to the Charles de Gaulle/Roissy airport.

22. BEST SLEEPS & EATS

Paris has many fine hotels. You can generally count on their being clean and well kept. However, be warned that the rooms are often much smaller than the ones you find in hotel chains in the U.S. The ones listed here have been chosen for their location, charm, and family-friendliness. The price ranges noted here reflect official listings – you can often get a better bargain by looking for deals on line.

In terms of restaurants, you will find that most are very happy to cater to kids and families (provided they are reasonably well behaved). If you want something simple, you may want to opt for a café, fast food, or sandwich shop. The selection listed here reflects a variety of options and palates to help each member of your group enjoy French food.

Note: restaurants and other places to eat in this chapter will be highlighted in **blue**, hotels in **red**.

Ile de la Cité & Ile Saint Louis

LES FOUS DE L'ILE, *33, Rue des Deux Ponts, 75004 Paris. Métro: Pont Marie. Tel. 01 43 25 76 67; Open Tues-Fri for lunch and dinner, Sat for dinner only, Sun for lunch. Closed Mon.*

This restaurant has an artsy décor and offers delicious daily specials and pastries. You can also go for afternoon tea and snacks or for Sunday brunch.

LE FLORE EN L'ILE, *42 Quai d'Orleans, 75004 Paris. Métro: Pont Marie. Tel. 01 43 29 88 27. Open daily, breakfast, lunch, and dinner.*

This is a good spot to stop for Berthillon ice cream (see below), hot chocolate, a snack, or a full meal. The outdoor tables offer a great view of the back of Notre Dame Cathedral and the Seine River.

GLACES BERTHILLON, *Main store: 31, Rue Saint Louis en l'Isle, 75004 Paris. Métro: Pont Marie; Open Wed-Sun, 10am-8pm. Other stands open more regularly throughout the Ile Saint Louis.*

This is some of the best ice cream in Paris. Although the scoops are small, they are bursting with flavor. The tough part is picking among the wide selection, including flavors such as vineyard peach, black currant, mirabelle (yellow plum), pain d'epice (spice cake), poire william (pear liquour), and wild strawberries.

Latin Quarter (5th Arrondissement)

HÔTEL DES GRANDES ECOLES***, *75, Rue du Cardinal Lemoine, 75005 Paris; Tel. (0)1 43 26 79 23; Métro: Cardinal Lemoine or Place Monge. Email: Hôtel.Grandes.Ecoles@orange.fr; Website: www.hôtelgrandes-ecoles.com; Rates: €130-€160 for doubles, €20 for extra bed.*

This is one of our all-time favorite Parisian hotels. It offers the best of both worlds: the atmosphere of a quiet country lane, nestled in the heart of the lively Rue Mouffetard neighborhood and Latin Quarter. The hotel is just off the Place de la Contrescarpe, but set back with its own garden and cobbled drive. You are close to major sites, with easy public transportation access to the rest of the city. The rooms are cozy, and a bit old-fashioned. They are distributed among several 3-story buildings. Five of the double rooms are large enough to fit 1-2 extra beds comfortably, and in some there is even a large curtain to separate the adult bed from the kids. When the weather is nice you can eat breakfast or have an afternoon drink on the terrace.

HÔTEL DU LEVANT***, *18, Rue de la Harpe, 75005 Paris. Métro: Saint Michel; Tel. (0)1 46 34 1100; Website: peprso.club-internet.fr/hlevant; Email: hlevant@club-internet.fr; Rates range from €85 for a single to €430 for connecting rooms that accommodate 5 people.*

This hotel is a real gem, especially considering its location in such a central, touristy spot. It is very family-friendly and has been run by the same family for four generations. They take great pride in keeping it clean, tastefully decorated, and up to date. It is situated on one of the pedestrian side streets near the Place Saint Michel, where college students and professors mingle with visitors from all over the world. This means it can get loud and busy outside, though the rooms are sound proofed.

The rooms are quite pretty and several are well designed to accommodate a family of four or five in large or two connecting rooms. Most of the rooms are air-conditioned. The ones on the top floor are especially charming, but beware the elevator is small, so you may have to take turns if you have a large group. A copious breakfast is included in the room rate.

HÔTEL RÉSIDENCE HENRI IV*, *50, Rue des Bernardins, 75005 Paris. Métro: Maubert Mutualité; Tel. (0)1 44 41 31 81; Email: reservation@résidencehenri4.com; Website: www.residencehenri4.com/fr; Rates range from €120 for a standard to €395 for a quadruple superior.*

This handsome hotel combines old-world elegance with modern amenities, including AC and free wifi. The location is both quiet and convenient. It is a great option for families. The hotel is set back from the main road on a little square, with a small playground aross the lane. It feels intimate, because there are only 8 rooms and 5 apartments. Each room or apartment features high ceilings, with decorated friezes and moldings that give the place a feeling of grandeur, as well as a kitchenette with fridge, microwave, stove, utensils, and marble bathrooms. Extra touches like a balcony, 4-post bed, fireplace, or fancy bath products help give you the feel of sleeping in style. The service is extremely friendly and helpful. You can borrow a laptop or Shiatsu massage machine at the front desk. They also will arrange a shuttle or limo to get you to the airport.

HÔTEL LE JARDIN DE CLUNY (BEST WESTERN)*, *9, Rue du Sommérard, 75005 Paris. Métro: Maubert Mutualité or Cluny-La Sorbonne; Tel. 01 43 54 22 66; Website: www.bw-paris-hôtels.com/jardin/; Email: hôtel.decluny@wanadoo.fr; Rates range from €200 to €300 per room (if reserved online) including buffet breakfast and free wifi.*

This hotel has both old features and modern comforts. Although you are in a very central location, the hotel is on a small side street and away from the noise of the main avenues. The rooms are well appointed, air-conditioned, and efficient. There are only 2 rooms on each floor, so you can comfortably rent two adjacent doubles to accommodate a family of four. Some rooms are reserved for non-smokers. There is a pretty garden courtyard in the middle of the hotel. For breakfast you can eat in your room or head downstairs to the Louis XIII style dining room. It features vaulted stone ceilings and copies of the *Woman with a Unicorn* tapestries that you can see in the nearby Cluny Museum.

HÔTEL MERCURE PARIS LA SORBONNE***, *14, Rue de la Sorbonne, 75005 Paris. Métro: Cluny-La Sorbonne; Tel. 01 56 24 34 34 or US central reservations. 1 800 221 4542; Email: H2897@accor-hôtels.com, Website: www.accorhotels.com/gb/hotel-2897-mercure-paris-la-sorbonne/index. shtml; Rates start at €120 per room. Wifi is free.*

Tucked away in the heart of the Latin Quarter, across the street from the historic Sorbonne University, this hotel welcomes families with bright, cheery rooms. It's also more affordable than many in the area. But be aware that some rooms are on the small side, as is typically for central Paris. The best is #503, which is a duplex large enough for a family of 4, with a double bed on the lower level and two singles upstairs. Each room features air-conditioning and the usual amenities of satellite TV, hairdryer, safe, and minibar. You are a stone's throw from the Cluny Museum and Luxembourg Gardens. At the end of a day of touring you can sit back and relax with a cold drink in the cafés of the charming Place de la Sorbonne around the corner from this hotel.

HÔTEL DES TROIS COLLEGES**, *16, Rue Cujas, 75005 Paris. Métro: Luxembourg or Cluny; Tel. 01 43 54 67 30; Email: hôtel@3colleges. com; Website: www.3colleges.fr/en/; Rates range from €125 to €185. Wifi is free.*

This is a really charming hotel, conveniently located near the Luxembourg Gardens and Cluny Museum. It's remarkably quiet and discreet, considering you are in the heart of Paris' Latin Quarter. The welcome is very warm, and the rooms are bright and cozy. The largest ones are on the top floor. They are under the rafters and offer great views of the rooftops of Paris. On the lower floors, you can opt for two double rooms across from each other at the end of the corridor.

EXCELSIOR LATIN HÔTEL***, *20, Rue Cujas, 75005 Paris.Métro: Luxembourg or Cluny. Tel. (0)1 46 34 79 50; Email: excelsior5@orange. com; Website: www.excelsior-Paris-hotel.com; Rates range from €120 for a double to €240 for a family suite, though check for special deals on the website.*

This hotel, located in the heart of the Saint Michel neighborhood of the Latin Quarter has comfort, luxury, and family suites that can easily accommodate 4-5 people. Each has two separate rooms (or rooms separated by a low wall) with combinations of large beds, single beds, and sofa beds, as well as full bathrooms with separate toilets. The décor is clean, modern, and tasteful. The staff is very friendly and helpful. The hotel offers good value for money along with special deals if you book online, including free buffet breakfast and special bath accessories.

VILLA DAUBENTON***, *34 rue de l'Arbalète, 75005 Paris. Métro: Censier Daubenton, Port Royal, or Luxembourg; tel: (0)1 55 43 25 50; Email: contact@villa-daubenton.com; Website: www.villa-daubenton.com; Rates start at €120 for 2 people and 240 for a 4-6 person apartment. Look for special deals on the website.*

Tucked away in a quiet side street of the Latin Quarter, this hotel offers 16 apartments with fully-equipped kitchens. The best for families are the 1 and 2-bedroom apartments on the top floors, which also have a pull-out couch in the living room. The rooms are not fancy, but they offer lots of amenities, such as a clothes washing machine, flat-screen TV, free wifi, full fridge, microwave, range, toaster, hair drying, iron/ironing board, and clothes drying rack. You are just a few blocks from the Rue Mouffetard market street with its food shops and vendors, so will have no trouble gathering food to enjoy in your home away from home. Or, if you don't want to prepare your own meals, there are countless small cafés, restaurants, and eateries in the neighborhood from which to choose. The hotel has a garage.

HÔTEL SAINT JACQUES**, *35, Rue Des Ecoles, 75005 Paris. Métro: Maubert-Mutualité. Tel: 01 44 07 45 45; Website: www.paris-hotel-stjacques.com; Rates range from €105 for a single to €130 for a double and €206 for a triple.*

This is a very friendly hotel in a great Latin Quarter location. The building is in a former mansion, and the owners have taken pride in restoring many of the original details, including ceiling paintings and door details. The rooms

have high ceilings and big windows. The upper floors offer terrific views of the rooftops of Paris, Nôtre Dame Cathedral, and the Panthéon.

HÔTEL ESMERALDA*, *4, Rue Saint Julien Le Pauvre, 75005 Paris. Métro: Saint Michel or Cluny/La Sorbonne; Tel. 01 43 54 19 20; Email: hotel.esmeralda@orange.fr; Website: www.hotel-esmeralda.fr/; Rates: €101-135 for doubles, €140 for triple with view of Nôtre Dame Cathedral.*

This is the same Hôtel Esmeralda as the one featured in the book *Linnea in Monet's Garden*. It's old, funky, and full of charm if you don't mind a bit of shabby gentility and a small staircase. You get exposed beams and old stones. The rooms are small, but the price is hard to beat in such a wonderful location. You are across the river from Nôtre Dame Cathedral, around the corner from Shakespeare and Company English Language Bookshop, and in the heart of the Latin Quarter. Some of the rooms have a view of Nôtre Dame. There is a park across the street with space for kids to play.

HÔTEL RÉSIDENCE LE VERT GALANT*, *41-43, Rue Croulebarbe, 75013 Paris. Métro: Place d'Italie or Les Gobelins; Tel. 01 44 08 83 50; Website: www.vertgalant.com; Rates range from €90 to €150.*

This is a very good find, more affordable than most hotels, as it is a little off the beaten track. However, you still have excellent bus and métro access to all the major sites. What's more, there is a large public park across the street with excellent playground facilities. The rooms are not luxurious, but they are cheery and tastefully decorated. One is equipped for individuals with disabilities. Ground floor rooms open on to the garden. The larger rooms feature fully equipped kitchenettes, which are a great bonus if you are traveling with small children or fussy eaters. If you specify that you are traveling as a family, they can arrange to give you connecting rooms. The owners also run an excellent restaurant, located next door. Called l'Auberge Etchegorry it features delicious Basque specialties from southwestern France. It is located in a building that used to house a popular cabaret, frequented by author Victor Hugo (famous for books like Les Misérables and The Hunchback of Nôtre Dame).

BRASSERIE BALZAR, *49, Rue des Ecoles, 75005 Paris. Métro: Cluny – La Sorbonne; Tel. 01 44 07 14 91; Open daily.*

This is a classic, Parisian institution that has been welcoming French intellectuals from the nearby Sorbonne University for ages. There are tall ceilings, big mirrors, and a 1930s style feel. Underneath their somewhat cold, professional exterior, the waiters are actually quite friendly to kids. The food is traditional and reliable, and it changes to suit the seasons. There is a big aquarium to distract bored children. There are daily specials and several fixed menus, including a kids' menu offering quality choices just like for the grown ups.

LOULOU, *90, Boulevard Saint Germain, 75005, Métro: Cluny-La Sorbonne. Open daily, 9:30am-11pm.*

The motto here is "quality food and friendly people." Though it looks like an American diner, Loulou's takes pride in offering organic eggs, vegetarian dishes, and foods that are gluten-free, not to mention wine and fresh French bread delivered daily. It's a great place for breakfast. There is standard American fare, such as eggs benedict, bagels, and bacon or French touches, like croissants and "pain perdu" (French toast). For other meals, there is a large choice of burgers, and everything from Caesar salad to salmon tartare. And, of course, there are French fries. Just make sure to save room for the cheesecake.

WATT, *3, rue de Cluny, 75005 Paris. Métro: La Sorbonne. Open daily except Sun.*

There's a wide choice of large and small dishes at Watt, from burgers to brunch, and from small appetizers from around the world to full courses of traditional French fare. There's a special pasta menu, salad menu, and a kids' menu offering a choice of burger and fries or pasta, with chocolate mousse for dessert.

LE ZYRIAB, *9th floor, Institut du Monde Arabe, 1, Rue de Fossés Saint Bernard, 75005. Métro: Jussieu. Open daily except Mon. Lunch: 12pm-3pm; Tea: 3pm-6pm; Dinner: 7:30pm-midnight.*

Situated on the top floor and rooftop terrace of the building, the Zyriab offers a fabulous view of Notre Dame Cathedral and the Seine. The food is also worth the visit, featuring many Lebanese and Middle Eastern specialties. You can opt for mezzes, small plates of hot or cold appetizers, or more traditional dishes and menus. It's also a great place to stop for a snack.

LA MOSQUÉE, *39, Rue Geoffroy Saint Hilaire, 75005 (across from entrance to Jardin des Plantes); Métro: Place Monge.*

Walk through the entrance of this restaurant and you'll feel like you've been transported to a Moorish Palace. It is decorated with white walls, carved wood, and beautiful blue and green tiles. The seats are covered with plush pillows and the  tables composed of enormous brass platters. The menu offers North African specialties such as couscous, brochettes (shish kabobs), tajines (stews), and brick (ground meat and egg fried inside a turnover made of phyllo pastry).

For a snack, you can visit the tearoom and garden, where they offer sweet mint tea and North African pastries.

LES DÉLICES D'APHRODITE, *4, Rue de Candolle; Métro: Censier Daubenton, Tel. 01 43 31 40 39. Open Mon-Sat.*
There are plenty of mediocre Greek restaurants in the Latin Quarter. This is one of the good ones. The ingredients are fresh and carefully chosen, including classics such as tzatziki, tarama, and moussaka. You can eat in or opt for take out foods.

JARDIN DES PÂTES, *4, Rue Lacépéde; Métro: Place Monge. Tel: 01 43 31 50 71. Open Mon-Sat, 11am-10:30 pm.*
Located right by one of the entrances to the Jardin des Plantes, this small, hole-in-the-wall restaurant offers a wide variety of types of pasta and pasta dishes. It's all organic, and many of the choices are vegetarian.

Light Fare
CAFÉ DESCARTES, *1, Rue Thouin, 75005. Tel. 01 43 26 17 70. Métro: Place Monge.*
This place offers a daily special, steak and fries, good salads, sandwiches, and other typical café fare at the top of the Ste. Genevieve hill. It is around the corner from where Ernest Hemingway lived when he wrote his classic autobiographical story of living in Paris, An Immoveable Feast. You are in walking distance of the Rue Mouffetard, Institut du Monde Arabe, and Arenes de Lutèce.

MAVROMMATIS, *47, Rue Censier, 75005; Métro: Censier Daubenton. Open Mon-Sat, 11am-8pm.*
Located just around the corner from the Rue Mouffetard market street, this is a great place to pick up take-out Greek food. There are creamy dips and spreads, freshly stuffed grape leaves, grilled shish kabobs, and other Greek delights.

TEA CADDY, *14, Rue Saint Julien le Pauvre, 75005 Paris. Métro: Maubert Mutualité, Cluny/La Sorbonne, or Saint Michel; Tel. 01 43 54 15 56; Open noon-7pm, Closed Tuesdays.*
This little restaurant offers light fare, including breakfast, at affordable prices. There are salads and scrambled eggs; hot dogs and grilled sandwiches; salmon torte and eggs Florentine. For a snack, you can try the scones, muffins, toast, and pastries.

LA FOURMI AILEE, *8, rue du Fouarre, 75005 Paris. Métro: Saint Michel, Cluny-La Sorbonne, or Maubert Mutualité. Tel. 01 43 29 40 99. Open daily for lunch and dinner.*
Located just a stone's throw from Shakespeare and Company Bookshop and Nôtre Dame Cathedral, this small restaurant is filled with books

and a true Left Bank literary atmosphere. It offers quiches, sandwiches, salads, and other light fare, along with pastries and drinks for afternoon tea.

ANGELINA'S, *19, Rue de Vaugirard, 75005 Paris, In the Luxembourg Gardens, near the museum entrance. Open daily 10am- 7:30pm.* This famous Paris institution is a favorite stop for the gourmet hot chocolate and amazing pastries. You can also get brunch, sandwiches, quiche, omelets, salads, pasta dishes, and gourmet plates to  make a full meal (along with wine, if you desire). The deserts, including fancy ice cream dishes, are to die for.

SUGARPLUM, *68 Rue du Cardinal Lemoine, 75005 Paris. Métro: Cardinal Lemoine or Place Monge. www.sugarplumcakeshop.com Open daily except Mon, noon to 7 pm.*

This cake shop sells cakes, muffins, bagels, and other sweets. They also offer tea, coffee, and other beverages. You can eat in or order take out. The shop is run by English speakers, and it is located just down the street from the apartment where Ernest Hemingway lived and wrote his novel, A Moveable Feast.

JADIS ET GOURMANDE, *88, Boulevard Port Royal, 75005 Paris. Métro: Port Royal. Open daily.*

This shop is filled with chocolates that not only taste wonderful but also look beautiful. There are chocolate pianos, chocolate coins, and chocolate letters that you can pick to spell out the names of your loved ones. There are also creatively attractive gift boxes that are bound to be a hit with folks back home.

Saint Germain des Près & Musée d'Orsay (6th Arrondissement)

RÉSIDENCE LE PRINCE RÉGENT**, *28, Rue Monsieur le Prince, 75006 Paris. Métro: Luxembourg; Tel: +33 (0)1 56 24 19 21; Website: www. leprinceregent.com. Rates vary, but range between €260 for a studio to €680 for the 3-bedroom duplex. Book in advance on the website to save money.*

This hotel offers lovely apartments ranging in size from studios to a 3-bedroom duplex that can fit up to 8 people. The rooms are large by Paris standards, and the rates can be a real deal if you are traveling as a large group. The building dates from the 18th century, and it has been luxuriously updated with quality services and details. The apartments have fully equipped kitchens, including both dishwasher and clothes washer. Wifi is free. The staff is very friendly and helpful. There's also a spa on site, and they will offer you an hour of free swimming in the pool each day. The location is excellent, very near the Luxemburg Gardens and Saint Michel shopping. The Polidor restaurant, an old Paris standby, is just across the street.

HÔTEL D'AUBUSSON********, *33 Rue Dauphine, 75006 Paris. Métro: Pont Neuf or Odeon; Tel. (0)1 43 29 43 43; Website: www.hoteldaubusson.com; Rates range from €250 to €370 for the duplex, but check the website for special deals.*

This luxury hotel is expensive but also very pretty, with large rooms and high-end touches, such as marble bathrooms, Hermes bath products, and plush robes. They are quite family friendly, with adjoining rooms that can be connected and duplex rooms with a loft. All rooms are equipped with wifi, tea/coffee making equipment, and AC. The staff is very helpful and the location is in the heart of the Saint Germain neighborhood. It is convenient to major sites, such as the Louvre, Musée d'Orsay, and Luxembourg Gardens, not to mention plenty of shopping opportunities for all tastes and pocket books.

CITADINES SAINT-GERMAIN DES PRES, *53 Quai des Grands Augustins, 75006 Paris. Métro: Saint Michel. Tel. 01 44 07 70 00 or +33 1 41 05 79 05 for worldwide reservations. Website: www.citadines.com/en/france/paris/saint_germain_des_pres/location.html; Rates vary, but range around €500 for a 1-bedroom that can sleep 4.*

The best thing about this apartment-hotel is its location, right on the Seine River in the heart of the Saint-Germain neighborhood. You can easily walk to the Musee d'Orsay, Louvre, Saint Michel and Saint Germain neighborhoods. The apartments are simple and modern, and they come with AC and a fully equipped kitchen area, a living room with a sofa bed, and a bedroom with a queen size bed. There's a small fitness center.

HÔTEL LEFT BANK – SAINT GERMAIN (BEST WESTERN)***, *9, Rue de l'Ancienne Comédie, 75006 Paris. Métro: Odeon; Tel. 01 43 54 01 70; Fax 01 43 26 17 14; Email: lb@paris-hôtels-charm.com; Website: www.secure-hotel-booking.com/smart/hotel-left-bank/2Z99/en/; Rates vary from €200 to €400, but you can get good deals as much as half off by booking early and online at the website.*

This hotel offers charm and a great location. It is situated in the heart of Saint Germain des Près. It is around the corner from the Rue de Buci street market, not far from the Luxembourg Gardens and Cluny Museum. You can walk to Nôtre Dame Cathedral, the Musée d'Orsay, or the Louvre. The rooms feature exposed wooden beams and antique furniture. From the upper floors there are beautiful views of the rooftops and church towers of Paris. Some of the adjacent double rooms can be set up as a 2-room suite. There are doubles, triples, and quadruples with a double bed and two singles. There is also an apartment suite on the top floor that can accommodate up to 5 people.

POLIDOR, *41, Rue Monsieur le Prince, 75006; Métro: Cluny – la Sorbonne or RER: Luxembourg; Tel. 01 43 26 95 34. Open daily for lunch and dinner.*

This restaurant has been around for over 150 years and continues to provide good food at a reasonable price in a friendly atmosphere. You sit at big, family-style tables covered with red-checkered table clothes. The food is traditional French fare, paté, hâchis parmentier (ground beef with mashed potatoes), boeuf bourguignon (beef stew), ham and lentils, stuffed cabbage, salmon steak, and more. There are two down sides. They do not accept credit cards, and the restroom is the old-fashioned hole in the ground style.

CHEZ CLEMENT, *9, Place Saint Andre des Arts, 75006 Paris. Métro: Odeon or Saint Michel. Open for breakfast, lunch, and dinner.*

This chain of restaurants prides itself on fresh ingredients and its special welcome for kids. The adult menu changes with the seasons and ranges from oysters and "escargots" to simpler choices like steak-frites or salad nicoise. For kids, there are actually three different menus, ranging from basic to gourmet. They also offer special activities for kids, such as entertainment, cooking classes, egg hunts, and more.

LA TABLE D'AUDE, *8, Rue de Vaugirard, 75006 Paris. Métro: Odeon or RER: Luxembourg. Open Tues-Fri, Closed in August.*

This jolly restaurant caters to every age group. It offers specialties from southwestern France, and is most famous for its cassoulet – a casserole composed of white beans, sausages and pork meats, and vegetables.

LE BOUILLON RACINE, *3, Rue Racine, 75006 Paris. Métro: Odeon or Cluny-La Sorbonne. Tel. 01 44 32 15 60. Open daily noon to 11 pm.*
If you are in the mood for a fancy family dinner in a beautiful décor, head for this restaurant, just off a side street from the Boulevard Saint Michel. It is situated in a historically-listed Art Nouveau building, and offers a wide range of gourmet delights, such as duck, suckling pig, rib steak, along with vegetarian options. The food is very fresh and refined, and the service is friendly. There are a variety of menus, including one for kids that offers a choice of burger and fries or fish with mashed potatoes, followed by ice cream for dessert.

RESTAURANT DU MUSÉE D'ORSAY, *Level 2 of the Musée d'Orsay; Métro: Solférino; Open Tues-Sun, for lunch, 11:30am-2:30 pm. Thurs, open for dinner. Tea and snacks offered from 3pm-5:30pm. Closed Mon.*
If your child has never eaten in a fancy restaurant this might be a good place to start. The soaring ceiling, big mirrors, and golden details recall the days when Orsay was a train station with a luxury hotel and dining room. Yet it is family friendly, so it's a good place for kids to practice their good restaurant behavior. If the restaurant is too much for your group, you can also opt for the Café Campana on level 5 or the Café de l'Ours on the ground floor near the statue of a polar bear.

CAFÉ MINOTTI, *33, Rue de Verneuil, 75007 (Métro: Solférino); Open daily for lunch and dinner.*
This airy, friendly restaurant is a great place to stop after hours of wandering through the Musée d'Orsay or Saint Germain neighborhood. Legend has it that the Three Musketeers lived down the street. If they were around today, they would undoubtedly approve of this restaurant. The food is very fresh and delicious. The secret here is good, basic ingredients that change regularly to reflect the seasons. For example in summer you might choose the chilled ratatouille or melted goat cheese salad. There are simple omelets, sandwiches, and pasta dishes to please kids' tastes. The chef will adapt a selection to your child's tastes, too.

Light Fare
EGGS AND CO, *11, Rue Bernard Palissy, 75006 Paris. Métro: Saint Germain des Pres. Open daily 10am-6pm.*
This place is popular for lunch or brunch. The ingredients are very fresh, including the organic eggs brought in each day and served in any number of different forms.

BAR DE LA CROIX ROUGE, *2, Carrefour de la Croix Rouge, 75006 Paris. Métro: Saint Sulpice or Sevres Babylone. Open daily (closed Sun in August).*

Great for salads, sandwiches on Poilane bread, and yummy desserts. **POILÂNE**, *8, Rue du Chèrche Midi, 75006 Paris. Métro: Saint Sulpice or Saint Germain des Près; Open Mon-Sat.* This may be the most famous bakery in Paris, thanks to its special dark, round bread (see photo at right). You can get open-faced sandwiches on Poilâne bread in many fancy cafés around the city, but here you get it straight from the oven. The pastries and other varieties of bread are also excellent.

GRANDE EPICERIE IN THE AU BON MARCHÉ DEPARTMENT STORE, *22, Rue de Sèvres, 75007 Paris. Métro: Sevres-Babylone; Open Mon-Sat.*

On the ground level of this historic department store (the first in the world) you will find a huge assortment of gourmet foods. There are several deli and bakery counters where you can get prepared foods. There are also plenty of packaged delights for a snack or to take home as gifts.

PIERRE HERMÉ, *72, Rue Bonaparte, 75006 Paris. Métro: Mabillon or Saint Sulpice.*

A good address, with amazing pastries.

CHRISTIAN CONSTANT, *37, Rue d'Assas, 75006 Paris. Métro: Rennes.*

Another great address with irresistible pastries and a wide selection of delicious ice creams.

Montparnasse

HÔTEL DELAMBRE*, *35, Rue Delambre, 75014 Paris. Métro: Vavin or Edgar Quinet; Tel. 01 43 20 66 31; Email: hôtel@hôteldelambre. com; Website: www.hôteldelambre.com; Rates range around €150 for a double to €215 for the family suite, depending on the room and available specials.*

This is a great little hotel. It is located in the heart of the Montparnasse neighborhood, with easy access to métro and buses. There are some wonderful rooms for families. We liked the L-shaped, mini-suite on the top floor, under the gables with lovely views of the rooftops of Paris. There are also some nice adjoining double rooms on the lower floors. They are in short supply, however, so be sure to reserve well in advance of your trip. As an added convenience, there is a Laundromat next door to the hotel.

HÔTEL JARDIN LE BRÉA***, *14, Rue Bréa, 75006 Paris (Métro: Vavin or Nôtre Dame des Champs). Tel. 01 43 25 44 41; Email: brea.hôtel@ wanadoo.fr; Website: www.jardinlebrea-paris-hotel.com; Rates range around €200 to €220 for a double.*

This pretty hotel is located in the heart of Montparnasse and is only a 5-minute walk from the Luxembourg gardens. The lobby and rooms are decorated with taste and warm Provençal colors. The rooms are divided into standard and superior categories, with the superior ones being a bit larger. All of them are air conditioned. The rooms with two twin beds are definitely bigger than the ones with a double bed. There is a nice sunroom and attractive breakfast room. The neighborhood is also full of toy and children's clothing stores.

LA VILLA DES ARTISTES (BEST WESTERN)***, *9, Rue de la Grande Chaumière, 75006 Paris; (Métro: Vavin) near intersection of Boulevard Montparnasse and Boulevard Raspail; Tel. 01 43 26 60 86; Website: www.villa-artistes.com; Rates range around €159 to €220 for doubles or triples.*

This pretty hotel is very popular with American families. Maybe it's because the parents spent their Junior Year Abroad days in Reid Hall, one block away. Perhaps it's the combination of comfort and convenient location: you are in Montparnasse, surrounded by artists' studios, and a

5-minute walk to the Luxembourg Gardens. Yet you are set back from the hustle and noise of the nearby avenues. The hotel takes its name seriously, promoting contemporary painters with exhibits of their works. It is also decorated with reproductions of paintings from many of Montparnasses' great early 20th century painters. The rooms are separated into standard and deluxe categories. The main difference is that the deluxe rooms are air-conditioned and a bit bigger. There is a pretty little outdoor garden with a fountain where you can eat breakfast in warm weather.

CHEZ FERNAND, *127 Boulevard du Montparnasse, 75006. Métro: Vavin, Edgar Quinet, or Port Royal. Tel. 01 43 27 47 11. Closed Sun.*

This is a small, intimate place that gets kudos from locals and visitors alike. The food is traditional French fare, such as boeuf bourguignon and salmon in hollandaise sauce, but with modern twists and subtle flavors.

SUD-OUEST ET COMPAGNIE, *39, Boulevard du Montparnasse, 75006 Paris. Métro: Montparnasse or Duroc. Tel. 01 42 84 35 35. Open daily, noon-11:30 pm.*

Here you get the bright colors and gourmet fare of France's southwest. That means foie gras, cassoulet, and delicious platters of duck in various guises. There's also steak and a vegetarian plate or salads if you want something lighter. A kids' menu offers hamburger or pasta with a choice of ice cream or chocolate mousse for dessert.

LA COUPOLE, *102, boulevard du Montparnasse, 75014 Paris. Métro: Vavin, Tel. 01 43 20 14 20. Open daily 8:30am-midnight.*

This is a historic and quintessential Parisian landmark, decorated in Art Deco style straight out of Paris' roaring twenties. It has hosted legions of artists and writers like Picasso, Man Ray, Matisse, Hemingway, James Joyce, and Henry Miller. Josephine Baker brought her dancing shoes and Patti Smith played guitar on the terrace. Though many of the famous clients are gone, the décor remains, along with good French "brasserie" fare, and a kids' menu, where they can pick their main course and dessert, just like the grown ups. Anyone celebrating a birthday gets a special tribute and song from the waiters.

WADJA, *10, Rue de la Grande Chaumière, 75006 Paris. Métro: Vavin; Tel. 01 46 33 02 02; Closed Sun all day and Mon lunch.*

I used to eat here in my starving student days when the tables were set family style, and the waiters greeted you by tossing a big chunk of bread directly onto the table. Since then, the place has gone more upscale. Now you get things like salad with stingray; roasted chicken with olive polenta; and rhubarb pie. But the secret to its continued popularity is still the same: offer good food at a reasonable price. Each month, the restaurant features specialties from a different region of France.

JUSTINE, *19 Rue du Commandant Rene Mouchotte, 75014 Paris. Métro: Montparnasse; Tel. 01 44 36 44 00. Open daily, 6:30am-10:30am, noon-10:30 pm. Sunday brunch: noon-3pm.*

This restaurant is located in the Pullman Montparnasse hotel and is famous for its family-friendly fare, including the Sunday "baby-brunch" with special kiddie themes.

TY BREIZ, *52, Boulevard de Vaugirard, 75015 Paris. Métro: Montparnasse or Pasteur. Open for lunch and dinner. Closed Sun-Mon, and in August.*

This is reputed to be the best crêpe restaurant in Paris. It's also very family-friendly. There is a huge selection of savory and sweet crepes, or you can order soup, salad, and "big plates" featuring specialties from different regions of France. If you don't want a crepe for dessert, you can opt for Berthillon ice cream (considered to be the best in the city).

Light fare
MAX POILANE, *29, Rue de l'Ouest, 75014. Métro: Gaité. Open Mon-Fri, 10-7.*

The Poilâne family has become famous for its delicious country-style bread. Here you can try it with a variety of hot and cold sandwiches. There are also salads and other snacks.

LES BONBONS, *6, Rue Bréa, 75006 Paris. Métro: Vavin. Closed on Mondays and in August.*

You'll feel like a kid in a candy shop!

Eiffel Tower & Champs de Mars
HÔTEL ARES PARIS***, *7 rue du General de Larminat, 75015 Paris. Métro: La Motte Piquet Grenelle; Tel. 01 47 34 74 04. Email: contact@ areseiffel.fr; Website: www.ares-paris-hotel.com/; Rates range from €230 for a double to €340 for family room with double and two sofa beds.*

This hotel is located very near the Eiffel Tower, on a quiet street in a pleasant, residential area. It offers a combination of old-fashioned and modern elegance. The rooms are relatively spacious for Paris, and decorated with fancy Italian designer touches throughout. Wifi is free, and the service is helpful and friendly.

HÔTEL D'ORSAY****, *93, Rue de Lille, 75007 Paris. Métro: Solferino or Assemblee Nationale, Tel. 01 47 05 85 54. Website: www.paris-hotel-orsay.com/en/; Rates start at €150 for a double and €350 for the suite.*

This hotel has bright,

cheerful rooms and a cozy atmosphere. The top floor suite is large enough for a family of four. The location is quiet but very central, right by the Musée d'Orsay and in the Saint Germain neighborhood. You can walk across the footbridge to the Louvre and Tuileries Gardens on the other side of the Seine.

Invalides

HÔTEL EIFFEL TURENNE**, *20, Avenue de Tourville, 75007 Paris. Métro: Ecole Militaire, Invalides, or La Tour Maubeuge; Tel. 01 47 05 99 92; Email: hôtel.turenne.paris7@wanadoo.fr; Website: www.hoteleiffelturenne.com/en/ ; Rates start at €200 for a double and €360 for adjoining family rooms, but check the website for much lower, special rates.*

This hotel offers a friendly welcome in a cozy atmosphere. The rooms are small and not luxurious, but they are quite pleasant – some even have a view of the Eiffel Tower. The owners are happy to accommodate families, adding a bed to one of their larger rooms, or offering adjoining rooms with a common door. The hotel is located between the Eiffel Tower (and its large Champs de Mars park) and the Invalides and Rodin Museum in a very pleasant residential area.

LES JARDINS DE VARENNE CAFÉ, *in the Rodin Museum, 77, Rue de Varenne, 75007 Paris. Métro: Varenne; Open daily except Mon, 9:30am-6pm (summer); 9:30am-4pm (winter).*

This is a charming place to have lunch, even if you are not planning to visit the Rodin Museum. You can enjoy the gardens, filled with famous sculptures by Rodin, for €2 per adult; kids are free. The café proposes a large assortment of salads and sandwiches. There is also a daily hot plate special. For dessert there is a nice assortment of tarts and ice cream. When you are done with your food, the kids can frolic among the sculptures.

Les Halles

CHEZ GLADINES, *11 bis, Rue des Halles, 75001 Paris. Métro: Les Halles or Chatelet. Open daily, for lunch and dinner. Sunday brunch, 11am-4pm.*

A fun, family-friendly place with a 1950s décor, including formica table tops and a jukebox. You'll find fresh salads, omelets, and a variety of potato-based comfort food dishes.

Light Fare

STÖHRER, *51, Rue Montorgueil, 75002 Paris. Métro: Etienne Marcel or Les Halles. Open daily 7:30 am-8:30 pm. Closed last two weeks in August.*

The original Mr. Stöhrer was a royal baker who came from Austria to accompany Queen Marie Antoinette in the late 1700s. His pastries were a huge hit, and the shop continues to faithfully produce the same quality that was fit for a queen. You can also get nice sandwiches, quiches, and salads.

Louvre

HÔTEL BRIGHTON********, *218 Rue de Rivoli, 75001 Paris. Métro: Tuileries; Tel: +33 (0)1 47 03 61 61; Website: www.paris-hotel-brighton. com; Rates range from €200 for a classic room to €325-425 for a family suite.*

This luxurious hotel has an amazing, central location. You are right across from the Tuileries Gardens with their playgrounds and room to run. Some of the rooms have fantastic views of the Louvre, Tuileries, and Eiffel Tower. The rooms are spacious and well appointed. The family suites have two rooms and a shared bathroom. The staff is very family-friendly and will go out of their way to ensure you feel welcome and enjoy your time in Paris.

Light Fare

CAFÉ DENON, *On the outdoor terrace of the Denon Wing of the Louvre Museum, Level 1 (around the corner from Géricault's Raft of the Medusa). Métro: Louvre Rivoli or Palais Royal. Open for lunch and tea, 10am-5pm.*

This café offers light sandwiches, hotdogs, and salads. The food is okay, but the main attraction is the location. If the weather is nice, you can sit outside on the terrace, where you can peer through giant statues down onto the Louvre's glass pyramid. The Café Richelieu in the opposite wing of the museum also offers light lunch, tea, and great views.

CAFÉS IN THE TUILERIES GARDENS. *Métro: Tuileries. Open daily, noon-11:30 pm.*

There are four different cafés in the gardens. Each has outdoor seating under the chestnut trees, and some have indoor seating, as well. Offerings include sandwiches, salads, hot dogs, and usually a few hot dishes. The location is ideal. Well away from traffic, plenty of room for kids to run around, and a great place to rest weary feet.

CAFÉ DE LA COMÉDIE, *157, Rue Saint Honoré, 75001 Paris (across from Comédie Française Theater and Palais Royal garden entrance); Métro: Palais Royal.*
We like this café for its great location between the Louvre and Palais Royal. It is on a little square, Place Colette, across a funny modern entrance to the Palais Royal métro station. There is the usual café assortment of salads, sandwiches, omelets, hotdogs, pizza, quiche, steak with fries, and more. What's surprising is the freshness of the ingredients and quality of the desserts. When you're fed and rested you can check out the nice bookstore next door; go across the street to the Palais Royal gardens; head up the Avenue de l'Opéra to tour the Opera House; explore the Louvre; or hop into the métro for a ride to the Champs Elysées.

LE PAIN QUOTIDIEN, *19, Place du Marché Saint-Honoré; 75001 Paris. Métro: Tel: +33 (0)1 42 96 31 70 . Open daily 8am-10pm.*
This chain has restaurants round the world. It offers fresh food that changes with the seasons, including grilled salads, sandwiches, and more. The bread, spreads, and pastries are worth the visit. It's a popular place for families, especially for breakfast, brunch, or a light meal.

LA FERME, *55, Rue Saint Roch, 75001 Paris. Métro: Pyramides; Open Mon-Fri, 8am-7pm; Sat 9am-7pm; Sun 10am-7pm.*
This gourmet take-out place features fresh, organic foods. You pick up a basket and choose from a selection of sandwiches, salads, quiches, yogurt, fruit, fresh-squeezed juices, and more. You can eat there, or enjoy a picnic in the Tuileries or Palais Royal gardens. They also have a location at 28, Boulevard de la Madeleine, 75008, Open daily except Sun, 9am-7pm.

ANGELINA'S, *226, Rue de Rivoli, 75001 Paris. Métro: Tuileries. Open Mon-Fri, 7:30am-7pm, Sat-Sun, 8:30am-7pm.*
This is one of Paris' most classic tearooms, where generations of children have been rewarded for good behavior with a thick cup of hot chocolate and fabulous pastries. The décor is Paris circa 1900. They also offer quiches, salads, and sandwiches. Note that the lines to get in can become long, but it's worth the wait.
There is an alternative location in the Louvre Museum, Richelieu Wing, Open daily except Tues, 10am-5pm (and until 9 pm Wed, Fri).

Marais
HÔTEL LE MAREUIL**, *51 rue de Malte, 75011 Paris. Métro: Oberkampf or Republique; Tel. +33 (0)1 47 00 78 76; Email: contact@hotelmareuil.com; Website: hotelmareuil.com; Rates vary from €160 for a double to €460 for a 2-room suite, but check the web for specials.*

Though located in a trendy neighborhood, this hotel is away from the city buzz and offers large, luxurious rooms in a very peaceful setting. It's a bit off the beaten track, but near the Grands Boulevards and Marais neighborhoods, with métro access to just about every part of the city. The hotel was totally redone in 2012, and they make a point out of welcoming children and families with a deluxe family room on the 6th floor that includes one double bed and a convertible couch, along with a balcony and view of the Paris rooftops. There are also 6 communicating rooms that combine two rooms (double or twin) in a private, family space. Other amenities include AC, premium bedding, bathrobes and slippers, free wifi, nice toiletries, and the possibility of in-room massages. The hotel has a fitness center with sauna and steam room.

HÔTEL DU 7IÈME ART**, *20, Rue Saint Paul, 75004 Paris. Métro: Saint Paul or Sully Morland; Tel. 01 44 54 85 00; Fax 01 42 77 69 10; Email: hôtel7art@wanadoo.fr; Website: www.paris-hotel-7art.com; Rates vary from €85 to €180.*

This is a fun hotel, and one of the few family-friendly establishments we could find in the Marais. The owners are very welcoming to their younger guests. The entire place is decorated with old movie posters and paraphernalia (the 7th art = cinema). The top floor room under the rafters is large enough to accommodate up to four people. There are also double rooms that can be connected with communicating doors. Guests can use the hotel's laundry room: a real plus! There is a large breakfast room that also serves tea and snacks in the afternoon, as well as a small fitness center. The hotel is located in the heart of the Marais. It's a real find, but book your rooms early, because they fill up quickly.

HÔTEL DE LA PLACE DES VÔSGES**, *12, Rue de Birague, 75004 Paris. Métro: St. Paul or Bastille. Tel. 01 42 72 60 46. E-mail: contact@hpdv.net; Website: www.hotelplacedesvosges.com; Rates: starting at €95 for a small double to €160 for a family triple and €200 for a family loft.*

This hotel is right near the lovely Place des Vôsges. In the 1600s the building was a stable. You can still see wooden beams and old stone walls. Today it offers nice clean rooms at a reasonable price, with touches of charm, and a pretty lobby.

LE CITIZEN, *96 Quai de Jemmapes, 75010 Paris. Métro: Jacques Bonsergent; Tel: +33 1 83 62 55 50; Email: cotact@lecitizenhotel.com Website:www.lecitizenhotel.com; Rates: Doubles start at €190, family triple at €300, and a family 2-bedroom apartment at €480.*

This boutique hotel is very popular with families. All of the rooms of the hotel are spacious, modern, and bright with big windows and views overlooking the Saint Martin Canal. The top floor room offers 2 bedrooms and 2 bathrooms. The larger rooms have a bedroom and sitting area with a couch. The room rate includes breakfast, a basket of goodies, and filtered water. Rooms are also stocked with comfy bathrobes and luxurious bath products. They will also lend you an iPad.

RESTAURANT CARUSO, *3, Rue de Turenne, 75004 Paris. Métro: Saint Paul or Filles du Calvaire; Tel. 01 48 87 47 74. Open daily for lunch and dinner.*

This Italian restaurant is a favorite among the neighborhood locals. Kids like the nice selection of pizzas, fresh pasta, and risotto dishes. Adults can enjoy antipasti, and exotic dishes such as pasta cooked in black, squid ink. There are also special lunch and dinner menus that vary with the season.

Light Fare

DAME TARTINE, *2, Rue Brisemiche (across from the Stravinsky Fountain by the Pompidou Center), 75004 Paris. Métro: Hôtel de Ville or Rambuteau.*

This restaurant offers a small selection of cooked platters, interesting salads, and sandwiches made on

wonderful Poilane bread. There's also a kids' menu with a choice of croque monsieur (the wonderful toasted cheese and ham sandwich that is a French specialty; see photo above) salmon, or ham with mashed potatoes, along with a dessert of sweet crèpe or ice cream, and a drink. The prices are very reasonable and the location is excellent. You are on a pedestrian square, next to the Pompidou Center and across from the delightful Stravinsky Fountain. It's a great spot to keep kids entertained.

LE LOIR DANS LA THÉIÈRE, *3, Rue des Rosiers, 75004 Paris; 01 42 72 90 61; Open daily.*

This place is famous for its cushy chairs, light fare, and weekend brunches. You can choose from a selection of salads, pasta dishes, quiches, and omelets. There also are yummy cakes and pastries. It's friendly, affordable and offers a calm haven in the bustling center of the Marais neighborhood.

MI-VA-MI, *23, Rue des Rosiers, 75004 Paris. Métro: Saint Paul or Pont Marie. Open Sun-Thu: 11:30am-12 am, Fri: 11:30am-2pm, Closed Sat.*

In the 1950s and 1960s there was an influx of Jewish immigrants to Paris from North Africa. As a result, you can get excellent kosher food in this traditionally Jewish neighborhood. This shop offers delicious falafel and pita sandwiches of various types. You can sit inside at the few tables or order take-out.

CHEZ H'ANNA, *54, Rue des Rosiers, 75004 Paris; Métro Saint Paul or Pont Marie. Open Tue-Sun: 11:30am-12am. Closed Mon.*

Another great place, famous for its falafel and other kosher fare. You can eat in or order takeout.

Bastille

BRASSERIE BOFINGER, *5 and 7 Rue de la Bastille, 75004 Paris. Métro: Bastille; Tel. 01 42 72 87 82; Open daily, 12pm-3pm, 6:30pm-12am (non-stop in August).*

This is a beautiful restaurant, a Paris classic, and a fun place to take kids who can enjoy a more elegant meal than usual. The food is based around traditional Alsatian dishes such as choucroute royale and plenty of fresh seafood. There's lobster and duck filled with foie gras. But you can also chose among a wide selection of fish, poultry, lamb, and beef steak. Kids have a special menu that also allows them to try some fancy fare. Make sure you show your children the beautiful Tiffany style skylight in one of the dining rooms. Upstairs there are paintings by Hansi, a famous Alsatian artist, depicting scenes of village life in Alsace.

If you or your children are not quite up for the full Bofinger experience, you might want to try the **Petit Bofinger** restaurant across the street. This bistrot offers plenty of excellent food at more moderate prices.

LE GRAND BLEU, *Port de l'Arsenal, across from 46, Boulevard de la Bastille, 75012 Paris. Métro: Bastille; Tel: 01 43 45 19 99. Open daily for lunch and dinner.*

This restaurant specializes in fish and seafood dishes, which is appropriate as it offers a great view of Paris' pleasure harbor and canal boats. There are large terraces, where you can enjoy the open spaces of the Arsenal gardens and Saint Martin canal. There is a kids' menu, and when you are through with the meal, you can enjoy the gardens and playground along the canal.

PENDANT QUE LES ENFANTS JOUENT, *45, Rue Traversière, 75012 Paris. Métro: Gare de Lyon. Open Mon-Fri: 9am-7pm, Sat brunch: 10am-6pm.*

Deliberately kid friendly, they offer light food and snacks with menus that change along with the seasons, but essentially feature quiches, soups, salads, and a daily special. There are two kids' menus for meals, plus an extra for the afternoon snack. There is a small playground, a fun shop, and take out food for purchase. They also organize children's birthday parties.

Light Fare

DALLOYAU, *5, Boulevard Beaumarchais, 75004 Paris. Métro: Bastille. Open 10am-8:30pm. Closed Mon, and August.*

Although you can get wonderful pastries all over Paris, this remains one of the city's best-known addresses for fine pastry. Judge for yourself. The tearoom is upstairs.

RAIMO, *59-61, Boulevard de Reuilly, near the Jardin de Reuilly, 75012 Paris. Métro: Daumesnil.*

Stop here if you are strolling along the Promenade Plantée. There are over 50 flavors of ice cream and sorbet (and you thought Baskin Robbins was tough with 31). Some are very exotic, such as cinnamon, maple syrup, tea, or chestnut. They also have locations at 17, Rue des Archives in the Marais and at 65, Boulevard Saint Germain in the Latin Quarter.

Champs Elysées

HÔTEL LE BRISTOL***, *112 Rue Du Faubourg Saint Honoré, 75008 Paris. Métro: Champs-Elysees; Tel: +33 (1) 5343 4300. Email: reservation@lebristolparis.com; Website: www.lebristolparis.com/eng/welcome; Rates range from $1,000 and up per night, but special deals may reduce those by half or more.*

The Bristol opened as a luxury hotel during the roaring twenties, when it welcomed illustrious fashion designers, like Coco Chanel and Elsa Schiaparelli, along with artists such as Picasso, Mondrian, and Salvador Dali. During WWII, it housed the US embassy, after which it resumed its place as one of Paris' most fashionable hotels, attracting a long list of famous guests ranging from Sofia Loren to Mick Jagger and Princess Grace of Monaco.

Remarkably, for such an illustrious address, the Bristol takes pride in catering to kids and families.

And even without a royal title, you will feel pampered like kings and queens (or princes and princesses). Upon arrival, kids meet the hotel mascot, a rabbit named Hippolyte, and they are given a personalized welcome "passport" with ideas for fun things to do in Paris, a rabbit plush toy, and rabbit-shaped cookies. In the room, kids get their own bathrobes and fancy toiletries. The restaurant and room service have gourmet options for kids. There's a children's activity room and a treasure hunt led by hotel staff for gardening tools, which the kids get to keep. Adults are treated to plenty of luxuries as well, from the plush bedroom and bathroom accessorizes to a spa, fitness center, and lap pool – not to mention gourmet options at the Epicure restaurant, which has 3 Michelin stars. Room choices include a variety of suites and the option to book communicating adjoining rooms. Some have views of the Eiffel Tower.

HÔTEL DE LA TRÉMOILLE *****, *14 rue de la Trémoille, 75008 Paris; Metro Alma-Marceau or Franklin Roosevelt or George V. Tel. 01 56 52 14 00. Email: reservation@hotel-tremoille.com; Website: www.tremoille.com; Rates range from €565-1,260.*

La Trémoille is located not far from the Arc de Triomphe, a few blocks from the Champs-Elysées in what is known as the "Golden Triangle." Originally built in 1883, La Trémoille is now a modern hotel that underwent extensive renovations ten years ago. There are 93 elegant rooms, including 13 suites, decorated in more than 30 color schemes. And here's something you don't see everyday: they have installed a private compartment (a "Hatch," they call it) in each room opening up to the hallway, so that room service can be brought to and from your room without their staff entering your room. Now that's privacy! The rooms are refined, comfortable, spacious and sound-proofed. You will find plush fabrics, Molton Brown bath products, a small terrace or, if you book a suite, you'll be treated to panoramic city views from a private balcony. There is a fitness center (really a workout room), spa, and sauna. The bar and sitting area just off the lobby is a welcome amenity

after a long day of tramping around the city. And the hotel's restaurant, Louis 2, is a good alternative if you wish to stay in for the night (and they offer high-chairs), although there are plenty of restaurants within a five-minute walk. The staff is knowledgable and very kid-friendly.

VILLA SPICY, *8, Avenue Franklin Roosevelt, 75008 Paris. Métro: Franklin Roosevelt. Tel. 01 56 59 62 59. Open daily 8am-11pm.*

This is a good address for fresh and interesting fare, offering a fusion of French and Asian foods. It is close to the Champs Elysées, but somewhat removed from the heavy tourist scene of the avenue. The décor is hip and modern. You get a good assortment of appetizers and main courses, such as pasta with olive tapenade sauce, roasted chicken with chutney, or catch of the day with baby vegetables. There is a kid's menu, and for Sunday brunch they bring in a clown and family-friendly entertainment.

FLAM'S, *16, Rue du Colisée, 75008; Tel. 01 45 62 84 82; Métro: Franklin Roosevelt. Open daily, 12pm-3pm and 6:30pm-11pm, with non-stop service Sat-Sun.*

This restaurant is part of a chain that features Alsacian-style Flammenkeuche, a sort of white pizza with bacon, cheese, and onions. They also have a wide range of variations on the theme, which basically resemble different types of pizzas. There are also large salads and pasta dishes. For dessert you can opt for sweet versions of the pizzas or fancy ice cream parfaits. The food is decent and prices very reasonable.

PAUL, *51, Avenue Franklin Roosevelt (corner Rue de Pontheiu), 75008; Métro: Franklin Roosevelt. Open daily 7am-8pm.*

Part of the ubiquitous Paul chain, this large, bright bakery is just off the Rond Point des Champs Elysées. It features assorted bakery items, pizzas, quiches, sandwiches, fresh fruit juice, and other light fare. It is a great place to stop if you want breakfast, a light meal, or a snack as an alternative to the fast food chains along the Avenue des Champs Elysées. If the weather is good, you can take your food and enjoy a picnic in the gardens between the Rond Point and Place de la Concorde.

Opéra/Grands Boulevards

HÔTEL CHOPIN**, *10, Boulevard Montmartre (in the Passage Jouffroy), 75009 Paris. Métro: Grands Boulevards; Tel. 01 47 70 58 10; Website: http://www.hotelchopin.fr; Rates range from €90 to €150, depending on the rooms, with the more expensive ones being bigger and brighter. Extra bed: free.*

This hotel is utterly charming and located in a wonderful spot. You enter through one of Paris' pretty 19th century shopping galleries. Called the Passage Jouffroy, it features fun shops and tearooms to delight you and your kids. The gallery also contains Paris' wax museum, the Musée Grévin. The hotel has lovely rooms, especially on the top floor (note: smaller rooms on the lower floors can be dark). They have some triples, or you can get several doubles. Some are surprisingly spacious considering the price and class of hotel, and it's worth it to pay for one of the larger ones. On the upper floors you get views over the rooftops and skylights of the Passage Jouffroy. Wifi is available in the lobby, and you can borrow a hairdryer from the front desk, if needed. Staying here is an experience unique to Paris that you will neither regret nor forget. Book in advance, however, because the rooms fill up quickly.

HÔTEL MANSART ****, *5, rue des Capucines. Tel. 01 42 61 50 28. Metro: Opéra or Concorde. Email: Website: www.paris-hotel-mansart.com/ en; Double rooms range from €195-500 depending on the room and season.*

This newly minted 4-star hotel is just around the corner from the glamorous Place Vendome. It is steps away from the Tuileries Gardens and lots of high-end shopping boutiques, including Eric Kayser's excelinclud

bakery and the incomparable Jean-Paul Hevin's chocolate shop. The hotel is named for Louis XIV's renowned architect, Jules Hardouin Mansart, who also designed the Place Vendome, Invalides, and famous chateau at Versailles. Though smaller and cozier than a king's palace, this hotel offers plenty of amenities fit for a king; large rooms and spacious bathrooms, with heated floors and towel racks. A delicious breakfast with all manner of coffee, croissants, bread, cheese, creamy butters and jams, eggs and sausage, and the like. The service here is very courteous, knowledgeable, and above all, extremely good with children.

CAFFÉ BURLOT, *in the Galéries Lafayette Department Store, Rooftop Terrace; 40, Boulevard Haussman, 75009 Paris. Métro: Chaussée d'Antin. Open May-Sept, Mon-Sat, 12pm-6:30pm.*

This café offers Italian-style food, including pizzas, salads, sandwiches, pasta, and other light fare. The food is fine, but what you really come here for is the view. What a panorama it is! You can see most of the city, including a close-up view of the Palais Garnier Opera House roof and straight shot of Sacré Coeur Basilica on top of Montmartre.

DÉLI-CIEUX, *in Le Printemps Department Store, Rooftop (9th floor), 64, Boulevard Haussman, 75009 Paris. Métro: Havre Caumartin. Open Mon-Sat.* The department store is full of tempting eateries, but this one has the most spectacular view of all of Paris. The food is offered as a self-service cafeteria. You can get a burger and fries or Caesar salad, or opt for more traditional French selections like lentil salad, quiche, quenelles, or endives with blue cheese. For dessert there are pastries and Ben & Jerry's ice cream.

Light Fare

LE VALENTIN, *30-32, Passage Jouffroy, 75009 Paris. Métro: Grands Boulevards; Tel. 01 47 70 88 50. Open daily, 8:30am-7:30pm.*

This charming tearoom sells delicious pastries and light meals inside one of Paris' wonderful 19th century shopping galleries. There are salads and sandwiches, as well as a daily hot-plate special. Kids can chose between ham and grilled chicken with mashed potatoes as part of their special menu.

A LA MÈRE DE FAMILLE, *35, Rue Du Faubourg Montmartre, 75009, Métro: Grands Boulevards, Open Tues-Sat, 8:30am-1:30pm, 3pm-7pm.*

This is one of Paris' oldest candy shops. It features not only mouth-watering chocolates, but also many candy specialties from all over France (see photo at right). Pick some up as gifts to bring back home – if you can resist eating them all up yourselves.

Trocadéro & Passy

HÔTEL PASSY EIFFEL***, *10, Rue de Passy, 75016 Paris. Métro: Passy; Tel. 01 45 25 55 66; Email: passyeiffel@wanadoo.fr; Website: www. passyeiffel.com/index-gb.htm; Rates range from €150-180 for a double to €215-240 for a triple. Extra bed or crib provided free of charge.*

This hotel offers a very warm welcome to families. There are family-sized rooms. When those are booked, they will offer to put families in 2 adjoining doubles (with communicating doors). All of the rooms have air-conditioning and some have a view of the Eiffel Tower (ask for one of these in advance). The hotel is located in the lively Rue de Passy, filled with fun shopping, nice cafés, and an open-air market. You are a stone's throw from the Trocadéro Museums, and within easy access to the Eiffel Tower, Ranelagh Gardens, and Musée Marmottan with its collection of Monet paintings.

BÎSTROT DES VIGNES, *1, Rue Jean de Boulogne (between Rue de Passy and Rue de l'Annonciation); Métro: Passy; Open daily, 12pm-2:30pm, 7pm-10:30pm.*

This restaurant offers delicious, traditional French fare at reasonable prices. The menus change with the seasons. But examples of appetizers include choices such as shrimp and grapefruit salad; poached egg with sorrel and smoked salmon; zucchini and eggplant casserole with goat cheese. Main courses may feature such things as grilled fish on a bed of fennel; rabbit in mustard sauce; roasted chicken and potatoes; steak and fries; or their "giant" cheeseburger. Top it all off with a fruit sorbet, chocolate mousse, fresh fruit tart, or cooked pear with ice cream and chocolate sauce. The kids' menu offers a choice of hamburger or fresh fish with a choice of side dish, ice cream, and a drink.

COFFEE PARISIEN, *7, Rue Gustave Courbet, 75016 Paris; Tel. 01 45 53 17 17; Métro: Trocadéro; Open daily, noon-midnight.*

The brainchild of an American guy, who ended up living most of his life in France, this is a French version of an American-style diner. The décor and menu look American, but there is also a French twist. You can get American staples, such as bagels, burgers, and BBQ ribs. Then there's steak tartar, avocado and grapefruit salad, and tarte tatin (French version of apple pie). The menu is extensive, and you're bound to find something for everyone's taste. It's a good Franco-American combination in an easy, relaxed atmosphere. They also have a restaurant at 4, Rue Princesse in Saint Germain.

TARTE JULIE, *14, Rue de l'Annonciation, 75016 Paris. Métro: Passy.*

This little restaurant/takeout place offers a wide array of yummy quiches (lorraine, zucchini, spinach, feta and basil, salmon, etc). There are also salads, gratinées, and fruit pies. A kid's menu proposes a quiche, drink, and ice cream. Budget menus are available for adults, too, offering a slice of quiche or big salad, drink, coffee, and dessert.

Montmartre

RELAIS DE LA BUTTE, *corner of Rue des Trois Frères and Rue Ravignan, on the Place Emile Godeau; 75018 Paris. Métro: Abbesses.*

This is a fun restaurant, especially in the summer when you can eat outside on the pretty terrace. It is just off a quiet square where children can run between courses. On the upper half of the square is the historic Bateau Lavoir building where Picasso, Modigliani, Juan Gris, and many other artists and poets lived for next to nothing. The original building was destroyed in a fire in 1970, but was rebuilt according to the original plans. It still houses starving artists. The restaurant serves up fresh salads, pasta dishes, daily specials, and Italian-style desserts at very reasonable prices. **L'ETOILE DE MONT-MARTRE**, *26, Rue Duhesme, 75018 Paris. Métro: Lamarck-Caulincourt. Open daily, 7:30am-2am, with nonstop meal service from noon to 11pm.*

A favorite among locals, this is a classic little French bistrot type restaurant. It is located on the "back" side of the Montmartre hill, where you end up if you go downhill from the vineyard, past the Lapin Agile, and along the rue de Saule. The choices are quite varied to suit many tastes – from vegetarians to people who only eat burgers, or those who want to try something new like foie gras or croustillant de cochon de lait. They are very kid friendly, offering a children's table for drawing, games, and children's books.

UN ZÈBRE A MONTMARTRE, *38, rue Lepic, 75018 Paris. Métro: Blanche or Abbesses. Open Mon-Sat.*

This lively little place is tucked along the jolly Rue Lepic (see photo on next page). It attracts lots of locals who come to enjoy a light salad, pasta dish, or daily specials such as grilled tuna and onglet de boeuf. Prices are very reasonable. Not to be confused with Le Zebra Restaurant in the nearby Rue des Abesses, which gets mixed reviews.

LA BUTTE GLACÉE. *14, Rue Norvins, 75018 Paris (near Place du Tertre); Métro: Abesses.*

A great place to stop for ice cream or sorbet, with all sorts of tantalizing fruit flavors.

Buttes Chaumont - Belleville
    RESTAURANT LES 400 COUPS, *12, Rue de la Villette, 75019 Paris. Métro: Jourdain. Open Mon-Fri: 12pm-3pm, Sat-Sun, 10:30am-6pm.*
    Specifically designed for kids and families, this place offers an indoor playroom, kids' activities (e.g. lego workshops), high chairs, changing facilities – and good food to boot. They pride themselves on offering locally-produced meats and produce. The prices are very reasonable, and there are two kids' menus, depending on ages and appetites. On weekends, they offer brunch, live music, and other events. The location is near the Buttes Chaumont and Belleville Parks.

PART TWO: PLANNING YOUR TRIP

Traveling with kids, especially very small children, can involve lots of stuff. I used to pride myself on traveling with bags that were so compact I could carry them long distances and never had to check my luggage. That ended when we took our first-born son to Paris as a 7-month old. Suddenly we had a stroller, diaper bag, favorite teddy bear, toys, baby snacks, and full supply of pint-size clothes – not to mention the car seat and porta-crib we borrowed once we got there. Thankfully, as our boys got bigger, the amount of stuff they needed got smaller. They also started pulling their own roller-board suitcases. From ages 3-6 they used kid-size suitcases. Then the graduated to adult-sized bags, though we stuck to the ones that could still fit in the overhead compartment of a plane.

Most children like to pack or help pack their own bags. It is exciting and empowering. Just make sure that you maintain supervision authority (and if needed, veto power). Once they are done, go through a checklist together to ensure they haven't forgotten anything important.

When packing, remember that less is better. No matter how many times you expect to find an elevator or luggage cart, there will moments when you are the ones who will have to lift or carry your own suitcases. You will have a hard time finding a cab if you have lots of gear, and big bags will take up a lot of space in your hotel or apartment room (generally smaller than what you might find in the US).

If your trip includes airplane travel, be sure to bring enough toiletries, medicine, clothing (such as a fresh shirt and set of socks and underwear), and necessities in your carry-on luggage to last you an extra day.

This will see you through if your plane or suitcases are delayed. If you are traveling with a baby or small children pack several sets of clothes, a blanket, snacks, small toys and other entertainment, and a 2-day supply of diapers and wipes in your carry-on luggage to get through the flight and first day.

Note that other than special medications, most things you will need are readily available in Paris.

Parent Tip: Small toys and activities will help make the plane trip and down time more fun. Some suggestions:
• Teenie-beenies and other small stuffed animals
• Micro-machines, Polly Pocket, Legos, beads, and other small toys. Carry them in Ziploc bags.
• Small pads of paper, art supplies, stickers, activity books
• Travel versions of chess, checkers, or other games
• Books and favorite music in electronic format
• Electronic entertainment
• Lightweight, paperback books or e-books. You may want to use this trip as an opportunity to introduce your kids to classic chapter books, such as *Charlotte's Web, From the Mixed Up Files of Mrs. Basil E. Frankweiller, Harry Potter, the Chronicles of Narnia*, or *A Series of Unfortunate Events*. ❖

Other things to pack:

Binoculars: Very useful for looking at gargoyles and other faraway features.

Cameras: If they are old enough, get simple digital cameras for each kid. It's a great way to keep them engaged and looking at the sights around them.

Art supplies: It's amazing how something as simple as a pad of paper and box of colored pencils, markers, or crayons can help while away the hours on a plane ride or waiting for the next course in a restaurant. Fun pad, activity books, and such work well, too.

Travel diaries: Travel diaries are a great way for both parents and kids to record souvenirs and impressions of their trip. They don't need to be fancy, a small spiral notebook works well. You can also purchase special kids' diaries, travel diaries, or even kids' travel diaries at any major bookstore.

WHAT TO KNOW BEFORE YOU GO

Passports: Each member of your family must have a valid passport to enter France. No visa is necessary for stays of less than three months. If you need to obtain or renew a passport for any member of your family, do not put it off until the last minute! It can take as many as 90 days or more to process – even longer if you need to obtain a copy of your birth certificate or other required proofs of citizenship or identity. Passport application forms and instructions are available at your local Passport Agency Office, county courthouse, some post offices, and some travel agencies. They are also accessible online at: *travel.state.gov/*, or you can get them via mail by calling the National Passport Information Center: *Tel. 900/225-5674*.

Adult passports are valid for 10 years, but children's passports are only valid for 5 years.

Be aware that **special rules govern the issuance of children's passports**. Make sure you read the instructions for children's passports carefully, as rules change. Check the website: *travel.state.gov/content/passports/english/passports/under-16.html*.

As of October 2014, the following applied:

• Any child under the age of 16 must have an application signed and presented by BOTH parents (or by one parent with a form and notarized signature from the other).

• Single parents or guardians must submit proof that a sole parent has custody or guardianship of their child.

• Even if you are renewing a child's passport and have the previous one with you, you also will be asked to present the child's birth certificate.

• Children's passport forms must be submitted in person by both parents at a designated post office or Passport Agency Office. If one parent cannot attend, you need to bring an official parental consent form. Your child also must be present.

• Minors ages 16-17 with their own identification can apply for a passport by themselves. However, it is recommended that at least one parent appear in person with the minor to identify him/her and to show parental awareness.

• Note that in some busy cities, you must call in advance for an appointment and may not get one for 2-3 weeks.

• Be sure to **check the website** for the list of required forms, documents, and photos.

Climate: Although Paris is roughly on the same latitude as Fargo, North Dakota, the climate is much milder. Days are short in the winter, but gloriously long in the summer (in June, the sun doesn't set until 10 pm). Winters are chilly, but temperatures do not dip much below freezing. The late fall and early spring can be quite rainy. Early fall and late spring are often sunny and pleasant. Summers are generally warm with occasional showers. Very hot weather is uncommon, which is lucky because it makes the city muggy and uncomfortable, and it raises pollution levels.

Customs & Fashion: French society tends be more formal than American. You will win major points by greeting people with a *Bonjour Monsieur* or *Bonjour Madame*, even if they are the only words of French you ever learn. If you do speak some rudiments of French, be sure to use the formal form "vous" rather than the informal "tu" with anyone other than close friends or children. If you are invited for dinner to someone's home, try not to arrive empty handed. A bouquet of flowers or box of chocolate is appropriate. If you know before you go that you will be visiting French people during your stay, you may want to bring something representing where you live. Examples could include a bottle of the local BBQ sauce, sports memorabilia from your local team, or a book of photographs featuring your hometown or state.

Clothing standards also tend to be a bit more formal in Paris. After all, it's one of the world's fashion capitals. As an adult you won't actually get kicked out of most places for wearing jeans, a t-shirt, and a baseball hat, but you will stand out (and do remember to remove your hat anytime you are indoors). Somehow, even when Parisians dress that way, they seem to look more put together. Maybe it's because they iron everything. If you want to blend in more, simply dress as people do for casual Fridays at work. Standards for children are pretty lenient, although you may want to avoid t-shirts with loud logos. If you want fashionable clothes for your kids, Paris is a great place to buy them. See below for a list of kids' clothing stores.

Regardless of the time of year you visit Paris, it is always a good idea to dress in layers. Even in the summer, the weather can switch from cool to warm and back again. Winters can be damp, and you will glad you packed that extra sweater or layer of fleece to ward off the cold. Be sure to bring a folding umbrella and rain gear for the kids.

Tipping: The tip is usually included (*service compris*) with your bill in a restaurant or café. If the bill says service non compris, then you should leave a 15% tip. The customary tip for taxi rides is 10% as is the usual tip for hairdressers. A small tip of €-1 is customary for washroom or cloakroom attendants. For hotel porters and room service €1.50 is the norm. A €1-2 tip is customary for tour guides and tour bus drivers.

Health insurance: Before you leave home, contact your health insurance company to see if it covers medical expenses abroad. If so, don't forget to bring along your membership card. If not, you may want to purchase supplemental health insurance for travelers.

The US Department of State maintains an extensive list of US-based companies that offer travel health insurance and emergency evacuation services at this website: *travel.state.gov/content/passports/english/go/health/providers.html*.

Safety: Paris is a relatively safe city, particularly compared to American ones. You can walk comfortably in any neighborhood, especially the popular tourist and residential areas. As always, you do need to exercise common street sense and be careful of traffic.

Visitors to Paris do need to be mindful of pickpockets, however, particularly in crowded tourist areas or on public transportation. Stay alert as to the whereabouts of your wallet and valuables.

Our greatest fear as parents has always been of losing track of our children in unfamiliar places. **Here are some tips to reduce the risk and anxiety of a lost child**:

• If your children are old enough, have them learn the name of your hotel, hosts, or street and address where you are staying. Show them where it is on a map. Point out nearby landmarks. Pick up several of your hotel's business cards at the front desk and distribute one to each member of your group.

• If your children are small, secure a label to their clothes, such as the paper luggage labels you get at the airport. Include the child's name, your name, and your address and phone information in Paris. Make sure to show you kids what you are doing and explain why, with words such as, "If you are ever lost, this tag will show a grownup your name and where we are staying, so we can find you".

• When visiting a large museum or site, be sure first to establish an easy-to-find meeting place in case you become separated. We learned this lesson one day when our older son got ahead of us in the Louvre (the world's largest museum) without a rendez-vous plan. When I caught up with him, I asked what he would have done if he had become lost. He answered with perfect 9-year old confidence; "I would have waited for you under the glass pyramid, of course." It was a great plan, except that the rest of us had not been clued in to it.

• Be sure to teach your children the age-old rule of staying in one place if they do get lost. You are more likely to find them if they are not a moving target. We also tell our kids to use the same advice we give at home. If you are lost, tell an official helper (like a police officer or museum guard) or look for another family with children and ask them to help.

• Don't forget to keep track of your adult companions, too. While my husband and I have yet to lose a child in a foreign place, we have lost track of each other. Be sure to have a meeting plan if you are off on separate missions, and throw in a back-up plan just in case, especially if you mobile phones are not working.

BOOKS, VIDEOS, & WEBSITES ON PARIS
Fiction for younger children

Anatole over Paris, and other Anatole adventures by Eve Titus. Whittlesey House Weekly Reader Children's Book Club, 1961. These stories describe the adventures of Anatole, a clever mouse who lives in Paris.

Eloise in Paris, by Kay Thompson, 1957. Six-year old Eloise, who normally lives at the Plaza Hotel in New York, visits Paris with her usual pluck and humor. Although the pictures were drawn in the 1950s, they still give an excellent view of Paris today.

Linnea in Monet's Garden, by Christina Bjork and Lena Anderson, Stockholm, Rabén and Sjögren Publishers, 1985. Young Linnea and her friend Mr. Bloom visit Monet's paintings in Paris and his house and gardens at Giverny. A charming introduction to Impressionist art.

Madeleine, Madeleine and the Gypsies, Madeleine and the Bad Hat, and other Madeleine stories by Ludwig Bemelmans. The classic adventures of a little girl who lives in a boarding school located "in an old house in Paris". Delightful illustrations feature major city sights.

Métro Cat, by Marsha D. Arnold, Golden Books Pub. Co. Inc., 2001. Sophie is a pampered cat who accidentally finds herself in the subway one day, where she discovers a new life of adventures.

The Red Balloon, (adapted from the movie) by Albert Lamorisse, New York, Doubleday & Company Inc, 1956. The adventures of a lonely boy and the balloon that brightens his life in the Belleville neighborhood of Paris.

The Mona Lisa Caper, by Rick Jacobson. Based on a true story that happened in 1911, when Vincenzo Perugia stole the Mona Lisa painting from the Louvre Museum with the intention of taking it to Italy, where he thought it belonged. The book, narrated by Mona Lisa herself, describes how the thief was arrested but became something of a folk hero at home in Italy and how she made her way back to Paris.

Mira's Diary: Lost in Paris by Marissa Moss. This book combines history and mystery, describing the time-traveling adventures of a girl set to find her lost mother. Along the way she runs into adventures, danger, and famous historical figures.

The Invention of Hugo Cabret, by Brian Selznick. This is the book that inspired the movie Hugo, set in Paris of the 1930s. It is about an orphaned boy who lives hidden in a train station taking care of the clocks. He comes across a bookish girl and grumpy old man, who will transport him through various adventures to a new life.

Adèle & Simon, by Barbara McClintock. Designed for young children, this beautifully illustrated story follows a brother and sister as they make their way through Paris landmarks and neighborhoods of the early 20th century. The little brother loses various things along the way, setting the stage for fun games of hide and seek for the reader.

Non-fiction for younger kids

Daily Life in Ancient and Modern Paris (Cities Through Time Series), by Sarah Hoban and Bob Moulder, Lerner Publications Company, 2000. This book brings together glimpses of Paris' history and everyday life.

The Inside-Outside Book of Paris, by Roxie Munro, E.P. Dutton, 1992. This books looks both inside and outside great Parisian sights, such as the Eiffel Tower and Pompidou Center, as well as more mundane places such as a pastry shop or booksellers along the Seine. An interesting and kid-friendly introduction to the city.

Let's Visit the Louvre Museum, by Claude Delafosse, Gallimard Jeunesse, English edition, Moonlight Publishing, London, 1995. A handsome introduction to some of the greatest treasures of the Louvre Museum, highlighted with transparent pages that let you see inside the glass pyramid or Egyptian mummy case.

Look What Came from France, Harvey Miles, New York, Franklin Watts, a division of Grolier Publishing, 1999. From scuba gear to April Fools' Day jokes, a nicely illustrated book outlining common products and customs that have come to us from France.

Monuments That Tell the Story of Paris, by Jean Daly, Editions Parigramme, Paris, 2001. A chronological introduction to some of the great monuments of Paris: from the Roman Arena and Baths, through Medieval and Renaissance splendors, to modern constructions such as the Pompidou Center, Grand Arche de la Défense, and La Villette Science Museum.

Paris (Cities of the World Series), by Conrad R. Stein, Children's Press, A Division of Grolier Publishing Co, Inc. New York, NY. 1996. This is an excellent introduction to the history and culture of Paris, described in broad strokes and illustrated with big, attractive photos.

Paris 1789: A Guide to Paris on the Eve of the Revolution, by Wright, Larousse Kingfisher Chambers, 1999. This book is written as a real travel guide to the Paris of 1789. It is a witty and clever introduction to Paris and the French Revolution.

This is Paris, by Miroslav Sasek, The Macmillan Company, 1959. With 1950s graphics and simple text, this remains one of the most delightful books on Paris for children. Look for it at your public library.

Books for Children About French Artists

Suzette and the Puppy: A Story About Mary Cassatt, by Joan Sweeny and Jennifer Heyd Wharton, Barron's Juveniles, 2000. This is a fictionalized tale about a little girl and a dog based on a painting by Mary Cassatt. It evokes life in Paris in the 1870s among the Impressionists.

Charlotte in Paris, by Joan MacPhail Knight and Melissa Sweet. Charlotte and her family live in 1890s France meeting up with famous Impressionist artists and discovering the fun sites of Paris.

Paris in the Spring with Picasso, by Joan Yolleck. A beautifully illustrated rompt through Paris of the early 20th century with Picasso and other famous artists and literary figures of the era.

Picasso and the Girl with a Ponytail: A Story About Pablo Picasso. By Laurence Anholt, Barron's Educational Series, Inc. 1998. Based on a true story of Picasso and a young girl named Sylvette whose profile and ponytale inspired many of his paintings.

Smart About Art Series, Grosset and Dunlap. This series features fictionalized stories about famous artists. Titles include:

Edgar Degas: Paintings that Dance by Maryann Cocca-Leffler; *Henri Matisse: Drawing with Scissors* by Jane O'Connor; *Claude Monet: Sunshine and Waterlilies* by True Kelley; *Pablo Picasso: Breaking All the Rules* by True Kelley; and *Vincent van Gogh: Sunflowers and Swirly Stars* by Joan Holub.

Katie Meets the Impressionists; Katie and the Mona Lisa; and *Katie and the Sunflowers*, by James Mayhew, Orchard Books. A little girl goes on adventures when she steps into famous paintings and gets to know some of the artists, their subjects, and styles.

Getting to Know the World's Greatest Artists series by Mike Venezia, Grolier Publishing, Children's Press, New York. These books are wonderfully written for children with copies of the artists' works juxtaposed with those of their contemporaries. There are also funny cartoon illustrations by the author to help put each artist's story into a context that kids can understand. Some of the featured artists include: Mary Cassat, Paul Cezanne, Leonardo Da Vinci, Paul Gauguin, Henri Matisse, Claude Monet, Pablo Picasso, Pierre Auguste Renoir, Henri de Toulouse-Lautrec, Vincent Van Gogh.

Fiction for preteens

The Adventures of Asterix the Gaul, and other Asterix comic books by Albert Uderzo and René Goscinny. These delightfully witty comic books feature the Gaul warrior Asterix and his pal Obelix living in 50 BC, who help their little Breton village resist the Roman occupation. Although they do not take place in Paris per se, they are a wonderful introduction to French history and culture.

A Chapel of Thieves, by Bruce Clements, Farrar Straus & Giroux (Juv), 2002. A teen boy adventure story set in 19th century Paris.

The Family Under the Bridge, by Natalie Savage Carlson, Harper Collins Children's Books, 1958. The story of a beggar and a poor family who meet as they live under a bridge in post-WWII Paris.

Mystery of the Métro (My Name is Paris, Book 1), by Elizabeth Howard, Random House, 1987. This is a teen girl mystery adventure set in Paris at the turn of the 20th century.

Rosemary in Paris by Barbara Robertson, Hourglass Adventures #2, Winslow Press, 2001. A 10-year old girl's adventure at the 1889 Paris International Exhibition.

Books for teenagers

The Da Vinci Code, by Dan Brown. This mystery/adventure story has become a best seller and Hollywood movie. It involves great escapes from the Louvre and other Paris spots. True fans can go on entire DaVinci Code tours of Paris, but most teens will enjoy looking for clues from the book in the St. Sulpice Church and Louvre Museum.

The Hunchback of Nôtre Dame, by Victor Hugo. Set in Medieval Paris, this is the tale of the deformed hunchback Quasimodo, his love for the Gypsy girl, Esmeralda, and the public intolerance that leads them both to tragic fates.

An Immovable Feast, by Ernest Hemingway. This largely autobiographical account describes Hemingway's life in Paris as a starving young writer.

Is Paris Burning? by Larry Collins and Dominique Lapierre. A factual account of the Liberation of Paris during WWII, including how close Hitler came to destroying every major monument and bridge in the city.

The Man in the Iron Mask, by Alexandre Dumas. Set during the reign of King Louis XIV, a man is mysteriously imprisoned with his identity hidden behind an iron mask.

Les Miserables, by Victor Hugo. The saga of Jean Valjean, an escaped convict trying to make good but dogged by the relentless police agent,

Javert. His tale criss-crosses those of other characters forced into desperate situations by the trials of war, poverty, and revolution in 19th century Paris.

Père Goriot, by Honore de Balzac. This 19th century novel contrasts the lives of Pere Goriot whose love for his daughters leads to his ruin, with that of Rastignac, an upstart from the country bent on climbing the ladder of fortune and social ambition in Paris.

A Tale of Two Cities, by Charles Dickens. A Dickens classic set in Paris during the French Revolution.

The Three Musketeers, by Alexandre Dumas. This heroic adventures of Athos, Porthos, Aramis, and d'Artagnan, Royal Musketeers in the service of King Louis XIII.

The Bald Soprano, by Eugene Ionesco. A delightful example of French Modern Theater of the Absurd. It has played non-stop at the Théâtre de la Huchette in Paris since its first opening in the 1950s.

Classic Kid Films

The Aristocats. A Walt Disney classic featuring a great jazz party among the rooftops of Paris.

Everafter. A charming version of the Cinderella story, set during the reign of France's king Francois 1st. Though it does not take place in Paris, it gives a nice glimpse of Renaissance France, including a Jeu de Paume match and Leonardo da Vinci, whose masterpieces such as the Mona Lisa still hang in the Louvre.

Madeleine. A delightful romp through Paris based on the books by Ludwig Bemelmans.

The Man in the Iron Mask. A French classic by Alexandre Dumas set during the reign of Louis XIV and filmed at the Vaux le Vicomte Palace outside of Paris.

The Red Balloon. A French classic about a lonely boy named Pascal whose life is brightened by a magical red balloon that follows him everywhere. It is set in the Belleville neighborhood of Paris during the 1950s.

Note: Avoid the Mary Kate and Ashley Olsen movie on Paris. It's terrible and the two twins provide poor role models for making good travelers out of your kids.

FLYING TO PARIS

Generally speaking, you will save money on airfares if you book your tickets several months in advance, especially for travel during the high-seasons (June-August, December 15-January 5). However, discounts vary greatly from year to year, so there is no hard, fast rule. Keep your eye out for special fares on major airline sites and through consolidator websites, such as **Expedia** (*www.expedia.com*); **Travelocity** (*www.travelocity.com*); and **Orbitz** (*www.orbitz.com*).

Here are some tips for planning your plane trip:

• If you are flying to Paris directly from the US, try to book the overnight, trans-Atlantic flight as late in the evening as possible. The later you leave, the more likely you (and your kids) will get some sleep. The later you arrive in Paris, the more likely your body clock will be ready to face a new day.

• The return flight from France to the US is always a daytime trip. Be sure to bring plenty of snacks, (diapers, if needed), small toys, books, activities, and entertainment.

• Take advantage of stopovers and connections. Let kids stretch their legs, get some food, and watch other planes take off and land.

• Bring food (though you will have to purchase liquids after you've passed through security). Waiting for meals on an airplane can be long and disappointing, especially for fussy eaters. Bring your own to play it safe.

GETTING TO & FROM CHARLES DE GAULLE/ROISSY AIRPORT

The **Charles de Gaulle/Roissy Airport** is where all transatlantic flights arrive. It is located 30 kilometers (19 miles) northeast of Paris. It is well linked to the city via public transportation and taxis.

By Taxi

This is the easiest option with suitcases and small children. If there are more than four of you, you may have to wait a bit for a minivan taxi, but it is very doable. Count on €60 or more for fare into the city, plus a charge for luggage and a tip.

By Train

The **Roissy-Rail Suburban B Line (RER B)** connects the Charles de Gaulle Airport train station to the Gare du Nord train station and several other major subway stations in Paris, including Châtelet/Les Halles (a major subway hub), Saint Michel-Nôtre Dame; Luxembourg; Port Royal; Denfert Rochereau; and Cité Universitaire. From the airport you can follow the signs marked Paris par Train or take the free airport shuttle to the RER B Station. Trains run from 5 am to midnight approximately every 15 minutes (more often during rush hour). The fare is about €10 for adults. Kids ages 4-10 are half price. Kids under 4 are free. Tickets are sold at the welcome kiosk in the long corridor leading from the place where you exit the baggage claim area toward the train station. You can also purchase them at the train station from electronic kiosks that take credit cards and coins, or the ticket office (but that option may require a long wait in line).

This is the quickest mode of public transportation into the city, but it requires walking and negotiating escalators to the train station. There are no elevators. It's fairly easy if you are not loaded down with lots of luggage.

By Roissy Bus
The Roissy Bus connects the Charles de Gaulle/Roissy terminals to the Place de l'Opéra in central Paris. Fare: €8.40.

By Air France Bus
There are two Air France buses that will take you from the terminals into the city. One will take you to the Charles de Gaulle/Etoile métro stop, then to the Porte Maillot métro. The other will take you to the Gare de Lyon and Gare Montparnasse train stations. Fare is €15 for adults and €7 for kids ages 2-11. Kids under 2 are free.

GETTING TO & FROM ORLY AIRPORT
The **Orly Airport** is located 18 kilometers (11 miles) south of the city. You may land here if you are arriving from another European city or North Africa. It is also well served by public transportation and taxis.

By Taxi
This is the easiest option with suitcases and small children, although you may have to wait for a minivan taxi if you are traveling with more than 4 people. Count on €50 or more for fare into the city, plus a charge for luggage and a tip.

By Train (option 1)
You can catch an airport shuttle bus to the Suburban C Line train station called Pont de Rungis. This train line connects Orly to several subway stops in the city including the Gare d'Austerlitz train station; St Michel/ Nôtre Dame, Musée d'Orsay; Invalides, Pont de l'Alma; and Champ de Mars/Tour Eiffel. The fare is €8 for adults. Kids ages 4-10 are half price. Kids under 4 are free.

By Train (option 2)

You can catch a shuttle bus to the Suburban B line train station at Antony. This train will take you to numerous major subway stations in the city including Denfert Rochereau; Port Royal; Luxembourg; St Michel Nôtre dame; Châtelet Les Halles (a major subway hub); and the Gare du Nord train station. The fare varies depending which stop you go to in the city. The fare is €8 for adults. Kids ages 4-10 are half price. Kids under 4 are free.

By Orly Bus

The Orly Bus connects the Orly terminals to the Place Denfert Rochereau in Paris. Fare: €6.

By Air France Bus

You can catch an Air France bus from the Orly terminals to the Invalides or the Montparnasse train station in Paris. Fare: €10.

ARRIVING BY TRAIN

If you are traveling to Paris by train, you will arrive in one of Paris' six main train stations. Each of these stations is well connected to the rest of the city by subway and public buses.

The **Gare du Nord** is where you arrive coming from England or northern Europe.

The **Gare de l'Est** services cities in eastern France, Germany, Switzerland, and Austria.

The **Gare de Lyon** is where you go for trains to southern France or Italy.

The **Gare Montparnasse** has trains to Brittany and western France.

The **Gare d'Austerlitz** is where you will arrive from Spain and southwestern France.

The **Gare Saint Lazare** has trains to Giverny and Normandy.

TOURIST WELCOME CENTERS IN PARIS

Website: *www.parisinfo.com*
- **Central Tourist Office**, *25 rue des Pyramides, 75001. Métro: Auber or Pyramides. Tel. 08 92 68 31 12 / 08 92 68 3000. Open Mon-Sat, 10am-7pm; Sun and holidays, 11am-7pm.*
- **Anvers Welcome Center**, *on the median strip facing 72, Boulevard de Rochechouart. Métro: Anvers. Open daily, 10am-6pm.*

- **Gare du Nord Train station**, *kiosk beneath the glass roof in the Ile de France zone. Open daily, 8am-6pm.*
- **Gare de Lyon Train station**, *20, Boulevard Diderot. Open Mon-Sat, 8am-6pm.*
- **Gare de l'Est Train station**, *by platforms 1 and 2. Open Mon-Sat, 8am-7pm.*

GETTING AROUND PARIS

Paris is an easy city to navigate. Most hotels and major department stores offer free street maps. You can also obtain a free bus and subway map in any subway station.

By Walking

Much of Paris' charm is best discovered on foot, so you will want to have comfortable walking shoes. This is an excellent way to explore the parks, shops, museums, markets, and cobbled streets of the city. When you need a rest, there is always a handy café or park bench where you can take a break. When our boys were little, we relied on baby backpacks and sturdy but lightweight umbrella strollers to get around as a family. We found that these were best for negotiating narrow sidewalks, handling cobble-stoned streets, going into shops or museums, descending subway stairs, or climbing on and off of buses. As our children have grown older, they have become good walkers themselves, especially with the promise of an interesting activity and occasional bribe of ice cream or other treats.

By Public Transportation

When you need to cover more distance, you can use Paris' very reliable and user-friendly public transportation system, the **RATP**.

Tickets are good on all buses and subways within the city limit. You can purchase them in any subway station and in many Tabac stores. Individual tickets can also be purchased on a bus. You can buy tickets one at a time, but it is easier and cheaper to buy a *carnet* of 10 or 20 tickets in any subway station. For children ages 6 to 10 years old you can purchase half-price carnets, called *demi-tarif.* Children 5 and under ride for free.

By Métro

Paris has an extensive subway system called the *métro.* There are over 370 métro stations and 15 lines. Trains run daily from approximately 5:30 am to 1 am. The train lines are identified by the name of the last station at each end and by the number of that particular line. An overhead sign on the train platform indicates which direction the train is heading, and often how long the wait is for the next train. Transfers are also well indicated on orange and white overhead signs. The one down-side to using the mé-

tro with small children is that it involves lots of stairs, which can be tricky with toddlers and strollers. On the other hand, older kids love riding the métro, especially if you let them figure out your route on the map.

By RER

Some of the stations within the city will connect you to the suburban train system known as the RER or to the automated Meteor trains. If you take the RER beyond the city limits, you will need to purchase a higher priced ticket from a station ticket agent or automatic machine. Hang on to your ticket for the whole ride. You may need it to exit the train station or be asked to present it during a random ticket control. Be aware that once the RER trains leave the city limits they don't necessarily stop at all the stations along the line. Check the lighted display board on the train platform. Make certain that the light next to the name of your destination is lit. If not, wait for another train.

By Bus

Public buses are a great option, because they allow you to see more of the city. They are also easier than the métro to navigate with a stroller or small children, because they don't involve stairs. Bus maps are available free of charge in any subway station. The bus stops are well marked by either a shelter with glass walls and a big bus map or a pole featuring a yellow and red bus symbol with the name of the stop. Many major streets and avenues have special lanes reserved for buses and taxis, so it is often faster to ride a bus than to try to drive through the city. You can ride on any bus within the city limits for one ticket, but if you transfer from one bus to another you will need to use a new ticket. You use the same tickets as for the métro and can purchase them in any métro station and many Tabac stores. Buses run Mon-Sat from 6:30 am to 8:30 pm. Special routes run until midnight and on Sundays and holidays. These are indicated at the stops.

By Bâtobus

A fun addition to Paris' public transportation options, this is a system of boats that crisscross the Seine River serving 7 stops between the Jardin des Plantes and the Eiffel Tower, including Hôtel de Ville, Nôtre Dame, Saint Germain, Louvre, Musée d'Orsay, and Champs Elysées. The price of each ticket is calculated according to how far you want to go along the route. The Bâtobus is more expensive than other forms of public transportation, but it's fun. The best deal is a one-day or two-day pass that lets you come and go all day. The service runs approximately every 15-25 minutes from 10 am to 11 pm, April through October.

L'Open-Tour Bus

If you have never ridden on a double-decker bus, you may want to explore Paris on the light green Open Tour tourist buses. This is a service that is jointly run by the public transportation system and two private tour companies. There are four routes and 50 stops. You jump on an off when you want at clearly marked stops. Each rider gets a pair of headsets that you can plug in to each bus for a commentary in English or French. The lower deck is like a normal bus and the upper deck is open-air. There are 1,2, and 3-day options. Or you can get a combined bus and boat tour ticket. You can buy the tickets ahead of time on line at: *www.paris. opentour.com/en.*

By Taxi

Taxis are readily available at airports and train stations. There are also many taxi stands scattered throughout the city where you can generally find a cab quickly. The best method is to call for a cab, as it is no longer allowed to just hail one on the street. The front desk person at your hotel should be able to help. The fare is displayed on a meter. Add a 15% tip.

Here are some services you can call:
• **Alpha-Taxi**: *Tel. 01 45 85 85 85*
• **Taxi-Bleu**: *Tel. 01 49 36 10 10*
• **Taxi-Etoile**: *Tel. 01 42 70 41 41*
• **Taxi-G7**: *Tel. 01 47 39 47 39*

By Car

Driving in Paris is not recommended since traffic is very congested and parking is both difficult and expensive. Having said this, we often end up in Paris with a rental car to use for day trips or traveling to other parts of France. One advantage of the traffic congestion is that it gives you time to figure out where you are and need to go. Fortunately, the streets and access to highways are generally well marked. Make sure to stay out of the bus/taxi lanes – generally the one furthest on the right.

Parking in Paris is a headache. Street parking is limited to two hours between 7 am and 7pm, and it's expensive. You will need to locate the parking payment machine along the street and put the receipt on the dashboard of your car, where it is visible. In most residential neighborhoods, parking is free on Saturday and Sunday, from 7 pm to 7 am, and during the month of August, but you should verify this on the parking machine. If you cannot feed the parking machine every two hours, you are better off putting your car in a parking garage. These are indicated by blue signs with a white letter "P." Most garages offer hourly, daily, and weekly rates.

Renting a Car

To drive in France you must be at least 18 years old and have a valid driver's license. If you want to rent a car, you will save money by reserving it in advance through an American consolidator or car rental company. Examples include:
• **AutoEurope**: *Tel. 888/223-5555; www.autoeurope.com*
• **Kemwel**: *Tel. 877/820-0668; www.kemwel.com*
• **Hertz**: *Tel. 800/654-3001; www.hertz.com*
• **Avis**: *Tel. 800/331-1084; www.avis.com*

BASIC INFORMATION
Holidays & Business Hours

Most stores, museums, and public buildings are closed on holidays. Hospitals and police stations remain open, and there are always a few pharmacies on call. Holidays include:
• January 1: New Year's Day
• March or April (date varies): Easter and the Monday after Easter
• May 1: Labor Day
• May 8: Armistice Day (celebrating the end of World War II)
• May (date varies): Ascension
• May (date varies): Pentecost
• July 14: Bastille Day (celebrating the French Revolution)
• August 15: Assumption

• November 1: All Saints' Day
• November 11: Armistice Day (celebrating the end of World War I)
• December 25: Christmas

Business hours vary. Most museums are open 9am-5pm (possibly later one night a week). National museums are closed on Tuesdays. City museums are closed on Mondays. Banks are generally open 9am-4pm, Monday-Friday. Some close for an hour at lunchtime. Post offices are open 8am-7pm, Monday-Friday, and Saturday 8am-12pm. Many food shops are open 9am-7pm, with a several hour break in the afternoon. Open-air markets are generally open 5am-1pm. Restaurants usually serve lunch between 12pm and 2pm, and dinner from 7pm-11pm. Many stores are closed on Sundays, including large department stores and supermarkets.

Money

The **Euro** is the standard currency in France.

Paris is well equipped with automatic teller machines (ATMs) that accept most American bank and credit cards (with a PIN), including the airports and train stations. We have found that this is not only the most convenient way to get cash but also the one that offers the best exchange rate and lowest service charges. You can also change cash or travelers checks at an exchange office, most banks, and fancy hotels – but the fees and exchange rates are less advantageous.

Credit cards, especially VISA, are widely accepted in France, everywhere from restaurants, hotels, and grocery stores to highway toll booths.

Note: Once in a while, credit cards or ATM machines just won't work. This is generally because the electronic lines connecting your transaction to the rest of the world are busy or down. You may have to try several ATMs or wait a few hours to obtain cash. Similarly, if your VISA card is not approved when you are making a store purchase, ask the merchant to try again once or twice. Sometimes, the third try is a charm.

Electricity

Electricity in France runs on **220 volts**, compared to only 110 volts in the US. Most computers and chargers for electronic appliances can function on either current, but it's best to check. Check your hairdryer and other grooming appliances. If they only function on 110 volts, leave them at home. The plugs in France are also different from US or English ones, and similar to the round standard you find across Europe. You can easily find adapters in hardware stores, travel stores, and airports.

Note that electricity is much more expensive in France than in the US. If you are a guest in someone's home, it is best to be mindful of this fact in your use of heating, hot water, lights, and electrical appliances. Note, too, that garbage disposals are non-existent in France. Toss food remains into the trash, not down the sink.

TV Formats

French televisions are set to a different standard of lines per frame, called SECAM, than are American ones which function on the NTSC standard. As a result, you cannot use American-made DVDs or video games in a French machine or vice versa. Similarly, DVDs are set to different standards.

Laundry

While laundry can be just a menial chore at home, it can become a real challenge when traveling, especially with messy kids. We've encountered a variety of strategies for dealing with this issue:

- One family we know simply didn't do laundry during their 3-week trip to Europe. They packed cheap socks and underwear and just threw them away after each use. For the rest, they packed enough to wear for three weeks. This works, of course, but means that you will be carrying a lot of dirty clothes around.
- Our New York City friends were accustomed to taking their family's dirty clothes to the bulk laundry service at home. In Paris, they used the same method, dropping off bulk laundry at the local "Pressing," which also does dry-cleaning.
- Then there is the old globetrotter method of rinsing out your clothes in the hotel sink. Many hotels frown on this, especially if you start stringing drippy clothes all over the room. However, they generally won't balk if you just rinse out a few items and dangle them carefully over the bathtub.
- Some hotels offer laundry and dry-cleaning services.
- One of the advantages of renting an apartment is that it is more likely to have a washing machine. However, few, if any, will have a dryer.
- The other solution is to take an hour out of your day and head to the local Laundromat (Laverie). Ask your hotel to recommend the nearest one.

Health & Medical Tips

- Be sure to fill out the emergency contact information page in the passport of each family member.

- If you or any member of your family uses a prescription medication, bring enough to cover your trip. Ask your health care provider to give you a prescription with the generic name in case you need a refill.
- Know your child's weight in pounds and divide it by 2.2 to convert it to kilos. You may need to know this to find the proper dosage for French medications.
- Bring your own fever thermometer. French ones calculate temperature in Celsius not Fahrenheit.
- Carry fever-reducing medication (kid and adult varieties), a liquid antihistamine/decongestant such as Benadryl, anti-itch cream, antibiotic cream, Band-Aids, a fever thermometer, tablets for indigestion, Bandaids, and eye drops.
- If you don't have what you need, don't fret. France has excellent medical care and services. Pharmacy staff are well trained and can be trusted to give you advice or administer basic first aid. See below for more information.

Emergency Contacts

- **SOS Help English-Speaking hotline** (open daily 3 pm-11 pm): *Tel: 01 46 21 46 46*
- **US Embassy Emergency #**: *Tel. 01-43-12-22-22 and then dial 0 (zero) when you hear the automated greeting*
- **Ambulance**: *Tel. 15 or 01 43 78 26 26*
- **Police**: *Tel. 17*
- **Fire Department**: *Tel. 18*
- **Anti-Poison Center**: *Tel. 01 40 37 04 04*
- **Blood Transfusion Center**: *Tel. 08 00 10 01 09*
- **Burn Center**: *Tel. 01 42 34 17 58*

Doctors & Dentists

The US Embassy in Paris maintains a list of doctors, medical specialists, and dentists who speak English. It is available on their web site at (*www.amb-usa.fr/consul/acs/guide/default.htm*) or at the Embassy's **American Citizen Services**, *open Monday-Friday, located at 2, Rue Saint Florentin by the Place de la Concorde (Métro: Concorde); the embassy phone number is: Tel. 01 43 12 22 22.* For Emergencies during weekends and holidays, call that number and ask for the Embassy Duty Officer.

If you just want to find the nearest doctor, go to your neighborhood pharmacy. Each pharmacy maintains a list of local doctors, dentists, and specialists, including which ones are open during holidays and weekends.

English-Speaking or Bilingual Hospitals

American Hospital of Paris (medical and dental care), *63, Boulevard Victor Hugo, between the Boulevard Victor Hugo, Rue Chauveau, Boulevard du Château, and Boulevard de la Saussaye in the western suburb of Neuilly. Tel: 01 46 41 25 25.* It is two blocks from the Seine (Métro: Pont de Levallois – a good 6 blocks away).

Children's Hospital Emergency Care: *Hopital Necker, 146-151, Rue de Sevres, in Paris at the intersection of the Rue de Sevres and the Boulevard Montparnasse, and Rue de Vaugirard (Métro: Duroc or Falguière). Tel. 01 44 49 40 00.*

Hertford British Hospital, *3, Rue Barbis, between the Rue de Villiers, Rue Chaptal, and Rue Voltaire in the northwestern suburb of Levallois-Perret, (Métro: Anatole France). Tel. 01 46 39 22 22.*

Hopital Foch (many English-speaking staff members), *40, Rue Worth, 92150 (western suburb) Suresnes. Tel. 01 46 25 20 00.*

Emergency burn center, *Tel: 01 58 41 26 49.*

Late-night House Calls

S.O.S. Médecins, a private company that provides after-hours house calls throughout the night. *Tel. 01 47 07 77 77.*

S.O.S. Dentistes will send a dentist to you in the middle of the night if it's urgent. *Tel. 01 42 46 11 20.*

Pharmacies

French pharmacists go through 6 years of specialized university training. They are well qualified to give advice about medications and will administer first aid. Pharmacists also maintain a list of local doctors, dentists, and other health care providers, including those that remain on call during weekends and holidays.

You can recognize a French pharmacy by its **green cross symbol.** English-speaking pharmacies in Paris include:

Anglo-American Pharmacy, *6, Rue de Castiglione, Métro: Tuileries, Tel. 01 42 60 72 96.*

British and American Pharmacy, *1, Rue Auber, Métro: Opéra, Tel. 01 47 42 49 40.*

British Pharmacy, *62, Avenue des Champs-Elysées, Métro:Franklin Roosevelt, Tel. 01 43 59 22 52.*

Anglo-American Pharmacy, *37, Avenue Marceau, Métro: George V or Alma Marceau, Tel. 01 47 20 57 37.*

Late-night or all-night pharmacies in Paris:

Pharmacie des Champs Elysées. *Open 24 hours a day.. 84, avenue des Champs Elysées 75008 Paris. Tel. 01 45 62 02 41.*

Grande Pharmacie Daumesnil. *Open 24 hours a day. 6, place Felix Ebou 75012 Paris. Open 24 hours a day. Tel. 01 43 43 19 03.*

Pharma Presto. Provides 24-hour prescription delivery service. *Tel. 01 42 42 42 50.*

Pharmacie des Halles. *Open until midnight Monday-Saturday and until 10 pm on Sunday. 10, Boulevard de Sébastopol, Métro: Châtelet, Tel. 01 42 72 03 23.*

Dérhy/Pharmacie des Champs. *Open 24 hours/day. 84, Avenue des Champs-Elysées, Métro: George V, Tel. 01 45 62 02 41.*

Matignon. *Near the Champs Elysees, Open until 2 am, daily. 2, Rue Jean-Mermoz, Métro: Franklin Roosevelt, Tel. 01 43 59 86 55.*

Pharmacie de la Place de la Nation. *Open until midnight, daily. 13, Place de la Nation, Métro: Nation, Tel. 01 43 73 24 03.*

Pharmacie d'Italie. *Open until midnight daily. 61, Avenue d'Italie, Métro: Tolbiac, Tel. 01 44 24 19 72.*

Air Quality

Paris can become quite polluted due to the high volume of vehicle traffic, especially if the weather is hot and muggy. The **AirParis** phone service gives updated air quality information (in French) from 9 am to 5:30 pm daily. *Tel. 01 44 59 47 64; Website (English version): www.airparif. asso.fr/en/*

Public Restrooms

Always take advantage of rest rooms (*toilettes*) in public monuments, museums, department stores, cafés, and restaurants. They are generally clean and easy to find. Most large parks also have public rest rooms. Men's rooms may be labeled as Messieurs, Hommes, or a picture of a man. Ladies' rooms may be labeled as Mesdames, Dames, or a picture of a woman. Some public toilets require a small payment to an attendant or in the door handle.

Water Fountains

American-style drinking fountains are rare in Paris, but instead you can use the beautiful Fontaines Wallace, named for the benefactor who installed them on Paris streets in the 1870s. They are dark green sculptures, and feature four female statues holding up a dome that is decorated with dolphins. A steady stream of water flows from under the dome. These are very handy for refilling water bottles as you explore the city.

Many public parks and squares feature another type of public water fountain that is dark green, squat, and sort of resembles a square fire hydrant. Some have a handle on the top that you rotate to get the water flowing. Others have a small spout with a button that you push to get water.

Do not drink from decorative fountains or from a park's garden hose. Their water comes from the Paris canals and is not clean. If you see a sign that says "eau non potable," do not drink the water. "Eau potable" means that it is safe to drink.

Many French people prefer the taste of bottled mineral water to tap water. There are at least 50 brands of mineral water available in France. The French drink an average of 100 liters of bottled water per person each year. That's twice as much as their annual wine consumption. Maybe it's the reason they outlive Americans.

Smoking

Smoking remains far more prevalent in Paris (and throughout Europe) than in the US, though the European Union is increasingly passing laws to limit exposure to second-hand smoke. Restaurants are non-smoking inside, though outdoor terraces are not. Smoking is not allowed on public transportation nor at the airport. Many hotels have floors reserved for non-smokers.

English-language bookshops

WH Smith, *248, Rue de Rivoli, across from the Tuileries Gardens (Métro: Tuileries). Closed Sun.* This is a big bookstore, with a large children's section upstairs.

Galignani Bookseller, *224, rue de Rivoli, across from the Louvre (Métro: Palais Royal/ Musée du Louvre). Closed Sun.* France's oldest English-language bookshop, this store offers an excellent selection of English-language books for both children and adults.

Librairie du Musée du Louvre, *near the glass pyramid entrance of the Louvre. Open daily.* You will find some books in English in both the children's and adult sections of this museum bookstore/gift shop.

Brentano's, *37, Avenue de l'Opéra (Métro: Opéra or Pyramides). Closed Sun.* This store has been around for over 100 years. It offers a huge selection of English-language books on two floors. It also hosts a children's book club.

The Red Wheelbarrow, *13, Rue Charles V (Métro: St. Paul). Closed Sun.* This shop has two locations; this one features children's books in English. The adult books are at their 22, rue Saint Paul location, nearby.

Shakespeare and Company, *37, Rue de la Bucherie, across the river from Nôtre Dame Cathedral (Métro: St. Michel-Nôtre dame). Open daily.* This famous hangout for English and American expatriate writers sells new and used books in English, and still retains its dusty charm and warm atmosphere. The kids' section is upstairs and discounted paperbacks are in racks and boxes outside.

Joseph Gibert, *26-30, Boulevard Saint Michel (Métro: Saint Michel). Closed Sun.* Part of the 100+ year old Gibert bookstore chain, this shop offers new and used books in English both in the sidewalk racks and upstairs.

The Abbey Bookshop, *29, Rue de la Parcheminerie (Métro: Saint Michel or Cluny - La Sorbonne). Closed Sun.* This store offers new and used English, Canadian, and American books.

Nouveau Quartier Latin, *78, Boulevard Saint Michel (Métro: Luxembourg). Closed Sun.* This international bookshop offers books and videos in many languages, including English.

San Francisco Book Co., *17, Rue Monsieur le Prince (Métro: Odeon). Open every afternoon.* This store is chock full of bargain books in English, starting with the outdoor racks and continuing inside.

The Village Voice, *6, Rue Princesse (Métro: Mabillon). Closed Sun.* This shop offers English language books, as well as poetry readings, book signings, and other presentations.

Tea And Tattered Pages, *24, Rue Mayet (Métro: Duroc). Open every afternoon.* This shop offers both used books and a tearoom for a comfortable book browsing and buying experience.

Bouquinistes along the Seine, *especially on the Quai Montebello and Quai Saint Michel. (Métro: Saint Michel). Closed Mon.* These are fun to browse and a great place to pick up small souvenirs. If you're lucky, you can find titles in English.

Telephones & Internet

Making a phone call in Paris can be somewhat confusing. All French phone numbers include 10 digits. The first two are the equivalent of an area code and must be dialed every time whether you are making a local call or phoning another region in France. The codes work as follows:

01: Paris and its suburbs
02: Northwestern France

03: Northeastern France
04: Southeastern France
05: Southwestern France
06: Cell phones
08: toll-free calls

If you are calling from Paris to another town in France: Dial the full ten-digit number. There is no special access code.

If you want to make an international call from France: Dial 00 + country code + area or town code + number.

Country codes are listed in phone booths and phone directories. The US and Canada are 1, except for Hawaii (1808) and Puerto Rico (1809). The UK is 44.

If you are trying to call France from the US: Dial 011 + 33 (Code for France) + drop the "0" and dial only the remaining 9 digits. For example to call the number 01 43 45 46 47 in Paris: Dial 011+33+1+43 45 46 47.

If you want to use a cell phone while you are in Paris: If your American cell phone functions on the GSM (Global System for Mobile communications) standard, you can contact your service provider and ask them to allow you access to international service. Count on spending $2-3/minute for local and long-distance calls. You can get cheaper service for calls within France by purchasing and installing a local SIM card, available at large FNAC stores in Paris.

Internet Access: Wifi access is widely available in hotels, cafés, and designated public parks/spaces.

Post Offices

Post Offices are open Mon-Fri, 8am-7pm, and Sat, 8am-12pm. You can purchase stamps (timbres), buy shipping boxes, and send packages (colis). You can also purchase stamps in a Tabac store.

You can also send packages through **UPS**. For toll-free information: *Tel. 08 00 87 78 77*. There are many UPS sites around Paris, check the website for the one nearest you: *www.ups.com/dropoff?loc=fr_FR&WT. svl=PriNav*

Time

Paris time is 1 hour ahead of London; 6 hours ahead of New York; 7 hours ahead of Chicago; 8 hours ahead of Denver; and 9 hours ahead of San Francisco.

TEMPERATURE CONVERSION CHART						
°F 0	32	41	50	59	68	77
°C -17	0	5	10	15	20	25
°F 86	98.6	100	104			
°C 30	37	38	40			

Most schedules and timetables in France are written in military time, using a 24-hour clock. Thus 6 h is 6 am; 11 h is 11 am; 12 h is noon; 14 h is 2 pm; 20 h is 8pm; and 24 h is midnight.

SHOPPING
Where to Buy Baby Products
Diapers: Known as *couches* (pronounced koosh), they are sold in large supermarkets, some small corner markets, in pharmacies, and at Monoprix and Prisunic stores.

Baby Bottles: You can find both glass and plastic baby bottles (*biberons*) at your local pharmacy. Plastic bottles and sippy cups are also sold at Monoprix or Prisunic stores and in large supermarkets.

Baby Formula: Look for it in the baby food section of the supermarkets or at your local pharmacy.

Baby Food: Known as *petits pots*, you will find a wide range of baby food, including gourmet varieties, in grocery stores, supermarkets, and pharmacies.

Baby Sunscreen, Lotion, Shampoo, Powders, Teething Rings: These are sold in pharmacies and in Prisunic or Monoprix stores.

Strollers, Snuglis, Baby BackPack Carriers, etc: The best place to look for these are large department stores such as the Samaritaine, Galeries Lafayette, Printemps, and Au Bon Marché. Baby specialty stores, such as Natalys (see below) also carry these items.

Baby & Children's Clothing
Any Prisunic or Monoprix store: branches all over the city. These stores offer kids' clothing and gear for all ages at relatively low prices.

Du Pareil au Même: This is a great address for colorful kids' clothing from infancy to age 14. The prices are very reasonable and selection is good, even for boyswear. *Branches located at 1, Rue Saint Denis, 75001, Métro: Châtelet; Forum des Halles, Level –2, 75001, Métro: Les Halles; 7, 14, and 34, Rue Saint Placide, 75006, Métro: Saint Placide; 168, Boulevard*

Saint Germain, 75006, Métro: St. Germain des Pres; 17, Rue Vavin, 75006, Métro: Vavin; 15, 17, and 23, Rue des Mathurins, 75008, Métro: Haver Caumartin; 120-122, Rue du Faubourg Saint Antoine, 75012, Métro: Ledru Rollin; 165, Rue du Chateau des Rentiers, 75013, Métro: Nationale.
Jacadi: What the well-groomed, bon chic bon genre, Paris child is wearing. Excellent quality cotton and wool clothing. Don't miss the sales in early January and late July. *Branches located at 9, Avenue de l'Opéra, 75001; 1, Boulevard des Capucines, 75002; 27, Rue Saint Antoine, 75004; 4, Avenue des Gobelins, 75005; 76, rue d'Assas - Angle 2, rue Vavin, 75006; 73, rue de Sèvres , 75006; 256 Boulevards Saint Germain, 75007; 17, Rue Tronchet, 75008; 54, Boulevard du Temple, 75011; 19 bis Avenue du Général Leclerc, 75014; 331, Rue de Vaugirard, 75015; 114, Rue Lafontaine, 75016; 89, Avenue Paul Doumer, 75016; and 60, Boulevard de Courçelles, 75017; 98, rue Caulincourt, 75018.*
Natalys: Not as highbrow as Jacadi, but a charming assortment of baby clothes and equipment. *Branches located at 74, Rue de Rivoli, 75001, Métro: Châtelet; 74, Rue de Seine, 75006, Métro: Odeon; 47, Rue de Sevres, 75007, Métro: Sevres Babylone; 109 Bis, Rue Saint Dominique, 75007, Métro: Ecole Militaire; 42, Rue Vignon, 75009, Métro: Havre Caumartin; 43, Avenue des Gobelins, 75013, Métro: Gobelins; and 5, Rue Guichard, 75016, Métro: Muette.*
Petit Bateau: Good quality cotton clothing for babies and toddlers. *Branches located at 36, Rue de Sévigné, 75003 Paris, Métro: Saint Paul or Chemin Vert; and 116, Rue Réaumur, 75002 Paris, Métro: Sentier; and 3Bis, Rue de Sèvres, 75006 Paris, Métro: Sevres Babylone.*
Tartine et Chocolat: Cute clothes for children from infancy to age 10. *Branches located at 24, Rue de la Paix, 75002, Métro: Opéra; 266, Boulevard Saint Germain, 75007, Métro: Solférino; 84, Rue du Faubourg Saint Honoré, 75008, Métro: Métro: Saint Phillipe du Roule; 22, Rue Boissy d'Anglas, 75008, Métro: Concorde; and 60, Avenue Paul Doumer, 75016, Métro: Muette.*

Department Stores
If you're the least bit interested in shopping, you'll want to check out one or more of Paris' famous *Grands Magasins* (Department Stores). They are quite spectacular, which is not surprising since Paris invented the first department store. Launched in 1876 by a man named Aristide Boucicaut, it was called the Bon Marché (Good Bargain) and housed in a grand building designed by Gustave Eiffel (of Eiffel Tower fame).
Au Bon Marché, *24, rue de Sèvres (Métro: Sèvres-Babylone), Open Mon-Sat 9:30 am-7 pm.* The world's first department store is still going

strong. Don't miss the gourmet delis in the Grande Epicerie and nice children's sections in the basement.

Au Printemps, *64, boulevard Haussmann, Métro: Havre-Caumartin, RER: Auber or Haussmann-Saint Lazare. Open Mon-Sat. 9:30 am-7 pm (Thurs. until 10pm).* Other branches of this store exist throughout Paris, but this one is by far the best.

Galeries Lafayette, *40, boulevard Haussmann, Métro: Chaussée d'Antin. Open Mon-Sat. 9:30 am-6:45 pm, Thurs until 9 pm.* You will find other branches of this store in town, but this one is definitely the most spectacular. Don't miss the stained glass skylight. The rooftop café is a must stop in the summer for the great view. There is a big souvenir section, excellent toy section, and free fashion shows.

BHV (Bazar de l'Hôtel de Ville), *52-64, rue de Rivoli (Métro: Hôtel de Ville), Open Mon-Sat 9:30 am-7 pm (Wed until 10 pm).* This store features everything for the home from furniture to thumb tacks. You'll find converters and adapters for electrical appliances in the basement.

Toy Stores

Paris has a huge supply of great toy stores, including in the department stores listed above. Here are just a few good addresses:

Le Ciel est à Tout le Monde. *Branches located in the Carrousel du Louvre shopping center, 75001, Métro: Palais Royal or Louvre; at 10, Rue Gay Lussac, 75005, near the Luxembourg Gardens, Métro: Luxembourg; and at 7, Avenue Trudaine, 75009, Métro: Anvers.* This store has lots of wooden toys, models, kites, and sailboats that you can float on the pond.

La Ronde des Jouets, *86, Rue Monge, 75005, Métro: Place Monge.* Another good address for good quality wooden toys, games, dolls, and activities.

Si Tu Veux, *68, Galerie Vivienne, 75001, Métro: Bourse.* A lovely store, with plenty to stimulate your child's imagination including costume and dress-up clothes.

L'Oiseau du Paradis, *211, Boulevard Saint Germain, 75007, Métro: Rue du Bac; 86, rue Monge 75005, Métro: Place Monge; and 96, Avenue Mozart, 75016, Métro: Jasmin.* A classic, classy toy store.

Au Nain Bleu, *5, Boulevard Malesherbes, 75008 Paris, Métro: Madeleine.* An old favorite that features lots of wooden toys and other joys, most of which are made in Europe.

La Boite à Joujoux, *41, Passage Jouffroy, 75009, Métro: Grands Boulevards.* This is paradise for fans of dollhouses and other miniatures.

Pain d'Epices, *29, Passage Jouffroy, 75009, Métro: Grands Boulevards.* This delightful shop, also located in one of Paris' lovely shopping passages, is filled with miniatures, ranging from soldiers and cartoon figures to everything you could want to outfit the dream dollhouse.

Jouet International du Monde, *28, Rue des Trois Bornes, 75011, Métro: Parmentier.* Lots of fun toys from all over the world.

La Grande Recré, *in the Galaxie Shopping Mall, 75013, Métro: Place d'Italie.* A big toy store with a wide variety, including a large section for preschoolers.

Les Cousins d'Alice, *36, Rue Daguerre, 75014, Métro: Denfert Rochereau.* This little shop is full of small, inexpensive treasures as well as books, games, and other toys.

PLAYGROUNDS & SPORTS
Playgrounds

Paris is dotted with fine and sometimes very sophisticated playgrounds – from the smallest tot lot to large, elaborate ones. Here are some favorites:

The **Tuileries garden** has a small, but pleasant playground, *located towards the middle of the gardens, closer to the Rue de Rivoli side, 75001.* In July-August and December-January, you can go to the **Tuileries Fair** and enjoy wild carnival rides and games. Métro: Tuileries. Entrance to the park is free.

The **Jardin des Plantes** has a small playground near the labyrinth and a lovely merry-go-round that features endangered and extinct animals. *It is located near the Rue Geoffroy Saint Hilaire, and Rue Cuvier sides of the garden. Métro: Jussieu or Place Monge, 75005. Entrance is free.*

The **Arènes de Lutèce** park has a playground, plus room to play soccer and other ball games in the old Roman arena. *Located off the Rue Monge, Rue des Arènes, and Rue de Navarre, 75005. Métro: Place Monge or Jussieu. Entrance is free.*

Luxembourg Gardens: These gardens feature a magnificent playground, along with a wooden merry-go-round, puppet show, and wonderful old-fashioned double swings. *They are located on the western side of the park, towards the Rue d'Assas, 75006. Métro: Nôtre Dame des Champs. There is a small fee to enter the playground.*

The **Parc Floral** in the Bois de Vincennes features beautiful playgrounds for children of different ages. There are also fun rides and a delightful mini-golf that features the major monuments of Paris. There are concerts, plays, and a small museum. *Located between Avenue des Minimes* *and Rue de la Pyramide in the Bois. Métro: Château de Vincennes. There is a small fee to enter the park. Rides and minigolf are extra.*

The **Parc André Citroen** has several small playgrounds and lots of wide open spaces. In the summer, don't miss the dancing fountains. They come right out of the pavement at irregular intervals. Kids love trying to run through them in warm weather. This is also where you can ride in a (tethered) hot air balloon above the rooftops of Paris. Located between Quai Andre Citroen and Rue Balard, 75015. Métro: Lourmel. Entrance is free.

The smaller **Parc Georges Brassens** has several playgrounds, including one for kids with disabilities. There is a climbing wall, and in the summer you can rent remote-control boats on the pond. *Located in the Rue des Morillons, 75014, Métro: Convention. Entrance is free.*

The **Jardin d'Acclimatation** in the Bois de Boulogne has wonderful playgrounds divided by age group and skill level. There are also carnival rides and games. *The playgrounds are located on the western side of the Jardin d'Acclimatation. Métro: Les Sablons or take the little train from the Porte Maillot métro station. There is a small fee to enter the park. Rides are extra.*

The **Parc de Belleville** has a big climbing castle with several really long slides built right into the hillside. *Located on the Rue des Courrones and Rue Julien Lacroix side of the park, 75019. Métro: Couronnes. Entrance is free.*

The **Parc de la Villette** has terrific playgrounds. Attractions include a giant dragon slide, numerous moon bounces for different ages, foot-powered windmills, and other fun stuff. *Located near the Cité des Sciences (Science Museum), 75019, Métro: Porte de la Villette. Entrance is free.*

Bicycling

This is a great way to enjoy some of Paris' major sights as a family. There are more than 150 kilometers of bicycle paths and lanes within the city. You can also bicycle in the Tuileries Gardens, by the Seine River, along the Saint Martin Canal, and under the Eiffel Tower free from motorized traffic.

Here are some good addresses for bike tours and rentals. If you need a kid-sized bike or kid carrier, it's a good idea to reserve in advance:

Fat Tire's Bike Tours and Rentals. *Store located at 24, Rue Edgar Faure, Métro: Dupleix (3 blocks south and west of the Eiffel Tower), Tel. 01 56 58 10 54. 24, Rue Edgar Faure, Métro: Dupleix (3 blocks south and west of the Eiffel Tower), Email: info@FatTireBikeToursParis.com Website: www.fattirebiketoursparis.com*

This company organizes bike tours with English-speaking guides. Kids are welcome. Tours last 3-4 hours with plenty of breaks for photos, food, and rest. The groups leave at 11am and 3:30 pm (May-Aug) and 11am (Sept) from under the Eiffle Tower on the south side (look for the company's flag). Note: they also offer Segway tours of the city. Check out details on the Website.

Bike and Roller Blade shops. See section below for shops that rent both bikes and blades.

Park rentals. The Bois de Boulogne, Bois de Vincennes, and gardens at Versailles Palace all offer bike rentals for adults and children.

Vélib. Subscribe on line at: *en.velib.paris.fr.* This is a municipal program with bikes for hire located all over the city. You can buy a 1-day, 1-week, or long term subscription, then pick up and drop off bikes at stands situated in bike stations set up every 300 meters. They are built for city riding, including a large wire basket in front, but only come in one adult size, so feasible if you are traveling with teenagers.

Tour de France Bicycle Race. If you are in Paris in late July, don't miss the last leg of this exciting event. The final stage of the race is traditionally in Paris, with the finish line on the Champs Elysées. The exact route through the city varies each year and is published in one of the local papers on the morning of the race. If you want to avoid the crowds on the Champs Elysées, you can watch the riders from any other spot along the route.

Roller blading

If you like to roller blade, you'll feel right at home in Paris where it's hugely popular. There are plenty of car-free paths through the Luxembourg Gardens, Métro: Nôtre Dame des Champs or Luxembourg; Parc Monceau, Métro: Monceau; Jardin des Tuileries, Métro: Tuileries; on the Champs de Mars, Métro: Bir Hakeim or Ecole Militaire; in the Bois de Vincennes, Métro: Chateau de Vincennes, or Porte Doree or Bois de Boulogne, Métro: Porte d'Auteil or Sablons; and along the Promenade Plantée, Métro: Daumesnil, Gare de Lyon, or Bastille. On Sundays, you can also ride along the parkways next to the Seine where they are closed to motorized vehicles.

Stunt riders gather at the Trocadéro Gardens, Métro: Trocadéro; on the Champs de Mars near the Eiffel Tower, Métro: Champs de Mars; on the esplanade at La Défense, Métro: Esplanade de la Défense, and in front of Nôtre Dame Cathedral, Métro: Cité or Saint Michel.

You can join a group outing with:

Rollers et Coquillages. *Groups meet every Sunday at 2:30 pm at 37, Boulevard Bourdon, 75012, Métro: Bastille.* Ask about special outings for kids and families.

Roller Squad Institute, *7 Rue Jean Giono, 75013 Paris. Métro: Quai de la Gare. Tel. +33 1 56 61 99 61.* They offer group classes and outings for kids on weekends and during school vacations.

Pari-Roller Friday Night Fever. Every Friday night around 10 pm (weather permitting) thousands of experienced roller bladers get together at the Place Raoul Dautry between the Montparnasse Tower and Train Station for a giant group ride. It includes police escorts, first aid workers, and emergency health crews. The tour covers about 20 kilometers through the city and may last until 1 am. The line of rollers can be as long as 1-2 kilometers. Participation is free. If you and your teenage kids are experienced roller-bladers, this can be an amazing experience. Otherwise, it's better just to watch from the sidelines, as it is a very impressive sight.

You can rent roller blades and pads (and also bicycles) from:

- **Bike and Roller**, *6, Rue Saint Julien le Pauvre, 75005, across the Seine from Nôtre dame, Métro: Saint Michel-Nôtre Dame or Maubert Mutualité, Tel. 01 44-07-35-89. Also located at 137, Rue Saint Dominique, 75007, Métro: Pont de l'Alma, Tel. 01 44 18 30 39*
- **Au Vieux Campeur**, *48, Rue des Ecoles, 75005, Métro: Maubert Mutualité, Saint Michel, or Cluny, Tel. 01 53 10 48 48*
- **Roller Pro Shop**, *18, Rue des Ecoles, 75005, Métro: Cluny, Tel. 01 43 25 67 61*
- **Nomades**, *37, Boulevard Bourdon, 75012, Métro: Bastille, Tel. 01 44 54 07 44*
- **Roulez Champions**, *5 rue Humblot 75015, Métro Dupleix. Near the Eiffel Tower. Tel. 01 40 58 12 22*
- **Vertical Line**, *60 bis, Avenue Raymond Poincaré, 75016, Métro: Trocadéro or Victor Hugo, Tel. 01 47 27 21 21*

Skateboarding

Favorite spots for skateboarding include the:

- **Champs de Mars**, *near the southeast side of the Eiffel Tower, Métro: Bir Hakeim or Champs de Mars-Tour Eiffel;*
- **Trocadéro Gardens**, *Métro: Trocadéro;*
- **Esplanade in front of the Montparnasse train station**, *Métro: Montparnasse;*
- **Esplanade at La Défense**, *Métro: Esplanade de la Défense.*

Swimming

Paris has plenty of public swimming pools. Hours of operation vary. Most public pools are open early in the morning and in the afternoon. They tend to be open longer on weekends and during the summer holidays. Most pools are accessible to people with disabilities. Pools generally provide a basket for your clothes that you check into a cloakroom or put in a locker.

Public pools have special **dress codes**. Everyone must wear a swimcap and men must wear "speedo"-style swim suits. Caps and men's/boy's suits are often available for sale at the pool's ticket office or in vending machines near the entrance.

Water Parks & Indoor Pools

Aquaboulevard. *4, Rue Louis Armand, 75015. Métro: Balard or Porte de Versailles.* Kids love this waterpark. It has both indoor and outdoor pools, 10 water slides, fountains, wave pools, hot tubs, a beach, palm trees, and fun for every age. There are also squash courts, food courts, and other sports facilities.

For indoor pools:
- **Piscine des Halles-Suzanne-Berlioux**. *In Les Halles. Level -3. Porte Sainte Eustache, 75001. Métro: Les Halles.*
- **Piscine Saint Mérri**. *16, Rue Renard, 75004. Métro: Hôtel de Ville. Behind the Pompidou Center in the Marais.* Outdoor terrace.
- **Piscine Saint-Germain**. *12, Rue Lobineau, 75006. Métro: Mabillon or Odéon. Under the Saint Germain market.*
- **Piscine Jean Taris**. *16, Rue Thouin, 75005. Métro: Place Monge. Near the Rue Mouffetard and Pantheon.*
- **Piscine Pontoise**. *19, Rue Pontoise, 75005. Métro: Maubert-Mutualité.* Art-deco style architecture. Evening swimming with lights and music. Diving boards and a lap pool with a current.
- **Piscine Beaujon**. *7, Allée Louis de Funès, 75008 Paris. Métro: Courcelles.* Brand new.
- **Piscine Château Landon**. *31, Rue Château Landon, 75010. Métro: Louis Blanc-Stalingrad.* The oldest in Paris.
- **Piscine Jean Boiteux**. *13, Rue Hénard, 75012. Métro: Montgallet.*
- **Piscine de la Butte aux Cailles**. *5, Place Paul Verlaine, 75013. Métro: Place d'Italie.* Charming, old-fashioned, art-deco style. Fed by a natural underground spring. High and low diving boards. (outdoor and indoor pools)

- **Piscine Armand Massard**. *66, Boulevard du Montparnasse, 75014. Métro: Montparnasse.*
- **Piscine Blomet**. *17, Rue Blomet, 75015. Métro : Volontaires or Sèvres-Lecourbe.* Art-deco style with a beautiful stairway.

For Outdoor Pools/Pools with Retractable Roofs:
- **Piscine Josephine Baker**, *Quai Francois Mauriac. Métro: Quai de la Gare. On the Seine River in front of the Grande Bibliotheque.* On a boat, floating on the Seine.
- **Piscine de la Butte aux Cailles**. *5, Place Paul Verlaine, 75013. Métro: Place d'Italie.* Outdoor and indoor pools.
- **Piscine de l'Hôtel Nikko**. *61, Quai de Grenelle, 75015. Métro: Javel or Bir Hakeim.*
- **Piscine Keller**. *14, Rue de l'Ingénieur Robert Keller, 75015. Métro: Charles Michels.* Retractable roof in warm weather.
- **Piscine d'Auteuil**. *1, Route des Lacs de Passy, 75016. Métro: Ranelagh.*
- **Piscine Henry de Montherland**. *32, Boulevard Lannes, 75016. Métro: Rue de la Pompe.*

Tennis

If you want to watch the pros, try to catch the **French Open Tournament**. It takes place in May at the red-clay courts of the **Roland-Garros stadium.** *The stadium is located in the Bois de Boulogne, 2, Avenue Gordon Bennett, 75016, Métro: Porte d'Auteuil.* The final matches are exciting, but if you get tickets for earlier rounds you'll get to see more of the players. *Tickets are available by Tel. 01 47 43 48 00 or www.frenchopen.org.*

The **Paris Open Tennis Championship** takes place in November *at the Bercy Sports Stadium, Palais Omnisport de Bercy, 75012, Métro: Bercy.* It features some of the world's top men's tennis players. For schedules and ticket information you can check the website at: www.atptour.com/en.

You can play tennis at these locations, but may need to reserve in advance:
- **Luxembourg Gardens**, *on the western side of the park. The sign up sheet is in a kiosk near the courts. Tel. 01 43 25 79 18.*
- **La Falguière Sports Center**, *in the Bois de Vincennes, on the Route de la Pyramide, Métro: Chateau de Vincennes. Tel. 01 43 74 40 93.*
- **Henry de Montherland Sports Center** *in the Bois de Boulogne, at 30-32, Boulevard Lannes, 75016. Métro: Porte Dauphine. Tel. 01 45 03 03 64.*
- **Fonds des Princes**, *61, Avenue de la Porte d'Auteuil, 75016. Métro: Porte D'Auteuil. Tel. 01 46 51 82 80).*

• **Quai de Saint-Exupéry** *has courts that are handicap-accessible. 75016. Métro: Porte de Saint Cloud. Tel. 01 45 20 62 59.*
• **Stade Elisabeth**, *7-15, Avenue Paul Appell, 75014. Métro: Porte d'Orleans. Tel. 01 45 40 55 88.*

BON APPETIT!

In France, cooking is an art, and dining is a labor of love. Enjoying good food and companionship are a national pastime – and everyone is welcome to join! Kids, and even dogs, can enjoy a meal in the fanciest of restaurants.

One of the biggest challenges you'll face is choosing among the huge variety of food styles and traditions in Paris. Even if you just stick to French food, you'll face a vast array of regional choices and influences. Remember, this is a country that has more types of cheese than there are days in a year. Broadly speaking, French cooking can be divided into the gourmet "haute cuisine" handed down from royal recipes and practiced in fine restaurants to the everyday-style home cooking that is the joy of many a neighborhood bîstrot.

There are many regional styles. For example Normandy and northern France specialize in dishes featuring creamy sauces, rich butter, apples, and cider. Brittany is famous for fresh seafood, crêpes, and buttery cookies. In Burgundy you find hearty beef stews cooked in red wine. Around Lyon you get sausages and quenelles (a fish or chicken based dumpling). The eastern region of Alsace features sauerkraut with sausages, onion pies, and a form of white pizza with cream, bacon, and onions called a Flammenkeuche. The Dordogne region is famous for black truffles, foie gras, cassoulet (a white bean and meat casserole), and foods cooked in goose or duck fat. Foods from Provence and southwestern France tend to show a Mediterranean influence with lots of olive oil, garlic, tomatoes, sweet peppers, and herbs such as thyme, basil, and rosemary.

Parent Tip: To help keep children distracted between courses in a restaurant, make sure to bring along some entertainment. Drawing supplies work well, as do activity books, small decks of cards, miniature games, small toys, postcards, journals, and story books. ❖

We have included a list of restaurants in this guide that combine good food with a family-friendly atmosphere. Here are some common food terms to help you navigate the menus:

Petit Déjeuner - breakfast

Café – coffee (generally served as a small espresso cup in a café or larger cup if you are ordering breakfast in a hotel); *café noir* – black coffee; *café au lait* – coffee with milk

    Grand café – big cup;

    Café double – double shot

    Café Américain or *alongée* – large cup, not as strong as a double espresso

    Thé – tea

    Sucre – sugar

    Chocolat chaud – hot chocolate

    Lait – milk

    Jus d'orange – orange juice

    Pain – bread

    Tartine – usually a long slice of baguette bread with butter

    Croissant – buttery, flaky, crescent-shaped roll

    Vienneroiseries – breakfast pastries

    Céréales – cereal

    Confiture – jam

    Beurre – butter

    Miel – honey

    Nutella – a spread made of hazelnuts and chocolate

    Oeuf à la coque – soft boiled egg

    Oeufs brouillées – scrambled eggs (rarely offered)

    Oeuf au plat – fried egg

    Oeuf dûr – hardboiled egg

Déjeuner - lunch

    Croque Monsieur – toasted sandwich with melted cheese and ham

    Croque Madame – toasted sandwich with melted cheese, ham, and a fried egg on top

    Crudités – salad (usually a variety of seasonal, cold vegetables and salad)

    Champignon – mushroom

    Cornichon – pickle

    Feuilleté – puff pastry dough generally filled with meat, fish, or vegetable stuffing

    Frites – French fries

    Fromage – cheese

    Jambon – ham

    Pâtes – pasta

    Potage – soup

    Glaçon – ice cube

Legumes - vegetables

Ail – garlic
Aubergine – eggplant
Carottes – carrots; carottes rappées – grated carrot salad
Celerie remoulade – grated celery root salad
Chou – cabbage
Choucroute – sauerkraut
Choufleur – cauliflower
Citrouille – pumpkin
Courgette – zucchini *Courge* – squash
Fenouil – fennel
Haricot vert – green bean; *Haricot blanc* – white bean
Mais – corn
Oignon – onion
Petit pois – peas
Poireau – leek
Poischiche – chickpea
Pomme de terre – potato
Tomate – tomato
Cacauète – peanut

Fruits - fruits

Abricot – apricot
Banane – banana
Cassis – black currant
Cerise – cherry
Citron – lemon; *citron vert* – lime
Fraise – strawberry; *fraise des bois* – wild strawberry
Framboise – raspberry
Groseille – red currant
Melon – cantaloupe
Myrtille – blueberry
Orange – orange
Pêche – peach
Poire – pear
Pomme – apple

Poissons - fish

Anguille – eel
Bar – sea bass

Bouillabaisse – fish stew
Brochet – pike
Cabillaud – cod
Coquilles Saint Jacques – scallops
Crevettes – shrimp
Homard – lobster
Huitres – oysters
Lotte – monkfish
Maquereau – mackerel
Merlan – whiting
Moules – mussels
Raie – skate or sting ray
Rouget – red mullet
Saumon – salmon
Thon – tuna
Truite – trout

Viande - meat

Agneau – lamb
Biftek haché or *steak haché* – hamburger (generally not served with a bun)
Boeuf – beef
Caille – quail
Canard – duck
Cassoulet – meat and white bean casserole
Contrefilet or *filet* – loin steak
Côte de boeuf – T-bone steak
Côtelettes – chops
Dinde – turkey; *dindonneau* – young turkey
Foie – liver
Gigôt d'agneau – leg of lamb
Jambon – ham
Langue – tongue
Lapin – rabbit
Lièvre – hare
Oie – goose
Perdrix – partridge
Pintade – Guinea fowl
Porc – pork
Poulet – chicken

Saucisse – sausage; *Saucisse de Toulouse* – hot dog
Saucisson – salami
Steak tartare – raw ground beef, topped with raw egg
Veau – veal
Bleu – nearly raw
Saignant – very rare
À point – medium rare
Bien cuit – medium

Dessert
Crème Chantilly – whipped cream
Crème Fraiche – cream
Fromage blanc – thick creamy, yogurt-like dessert
Gâteau – cake
Glaçes – ice cream
Orange givrée/citron givrée – frozen orange/lemon filled with orange
or lemon ice
Patisseries – pastries
Petit four – mini pastry
Petit gâteau – cookie
Tarte – pie; *Tarte Tatin* – upside-down apple pie
Yaourt – yogurt

Parent Tip: Do you have a child who functions primarily on peanut
butter? It's not as common in France as in the US, but searching for it
can provide an excuse for a fun treasure hunt through Parisian grocery
stores. **Peanut butter** can be called either *Beurre de Cacaouète* or **Pâte
d'Arachide**. It may come in a jar or a can. It might be located with the
jams and jellies, by the peanuts and other nuts, or in the foreign food section. Occasionally you will have more luck in a small ethnic grocery shop
than at the local supermarket. ❖

WHAT'S THE WORD?
Parlez-vous Français?
     No one expects you to speak fluent French. In fact, increasingly,
you'll find that Parisians want to show off their knowledge of English to
you. However, you will score major points in France if you just try to learn
a few key expressions:

Bonjour Madame – Hello Ma'am
Bonjour Monsieur – Hello Sir

Bonjour Mademoiselle – Hello Miss
S'il Vous Plait – Please
Merci – Thank you
Au-Revoir – Goodbye
Pardon – Excuse me

That's it. The rest is merely icing on the cake.

If you want to be adventurous, here are some more handy words and expressions:

Oui – yes
Non – no
Parlez-vous Anglais? – Do you speak English
Je ne parle pas Français – I do not speak French
Je ne comprends pas – I don't understand
Pourquoi? – Why?
Combien? – How much?
L'addition, s'il vous plait – The (restaurant) bill, please
La note, s'il vous plait – The (hotel) bill, please.
Où est? – Where is?
Où sont les toilettes? – Where are the restrooms?
Qui? – Who?
Qui est la? – Who is there?
Quand? – When?
Qu'est ce que c'est? – What is that?
Quelle heure est il? – What time is it?
Quel etage? – Which floor?
Comment? – How? or What?
Comment allez vous? – How are you?
Avez-vous? – Do you have?
Pouvez-vous? – Could you?
Lequel or Laquelle? – Which?
Donnez-moi – Give me
Je voudrai – I would like
Ca – That
Celui ci – This one
Celui là – That one

Un or *Une* – one
Deux – two
Trois – three

Quatre – four
Cinq – five
Six – six
Sept – seven
Huit – eight
Neuf – nine
Dix – ten
Onze – eleven
Douze – twelve
Treize – thirteen
Quatorze – fourteen
Quinze – fifteen
Seize – sixteen
Dix-sept – seventeen
Dix-huit – eighteen
Dix-neuf – nineteen
Vingt – twenty
Trente – thirty
Quarente – forty
Cinquante – fifty
Soixante – sixty
Soixante-dix – seventy
Quatrevingt – eighty
Quatrevingt-dix – ninety
Cent – 100
Mille – 1,000

Premier – first
Second or *Deuxième* – second
Troisième – third
Quatrième – fourth
Cinquième – fifth
Sixième – sixth
Septième – seventh
Huitième – eighth
Neuvième – ninth
Dixième – tenth

INDEX

Things Change!
Phone numbers, prices, addresses, quality of service – all change. If you come across any new information, let us know. No item is too small! Contact us at:

jopenroad@aol.com

or

www.openroadguides.com

PHOTO CREDITS

The following photos are from wikimedia commons: pp. 9: Benh Lieu Song; p. 37: David Monniaux; p. 50; p. 87: Greudin.

The following images are from Jonathan Stein: p. 36, 105. *The following image is from Betty Borden*: p. 220.

The following images are from flickr.com: p. 1: spacejulien; p. 3 top: photomaggie; p. 3 bottom: Panoramas; p. 8: milena mihaylova; pp. 12: appaloosa; p. 13: sanjanikolic; p. 19: metropol2; p. 23: Andy Hay; pp. 27: morbuto; p. 28: Jeherv; p. 34: La case photo de Got; p. 35: miss karen; pp. 44, 221: ktylerconk; pp. 45: chelseagirl; p. 47: innusa; p. 54: Kimberly Vardeman; p. 55: Tommie Hansen; p. 58: Joe DeSousa; p.63: HarshLight; p. 64: Ludwig Pacifici; p. 67: Tyler Merbler; p. 69: AmitLev; p. 71: chakchouka; p. 77: Rog01; p. 78: Guillaume Baviere; p. 81: Andrea Schaffer; p. 86: Panoramas; p. 90: Luis Irisarri; p. 91: Phillip Capper; p. 94: kimdokhac; p. 96: Cristian Bortes; p. 97: oatsy40; p. 100: dmytrok; p. 102: Marie Thérèse Hébert & Jean Robert Thibault; p. 103: alainlm; p. 108: Fil.Al; p. 110: David Stanley; p. 111: Le blog de Digital Photography; p. 114: Guillaume Baviere; pp. 115, 119: Jack Torcello; p. 118: Diego Albero Román; p. 123: Steve Soper; p. 127: Elena Mazzanti; p. 129: Martin Lewison; p. 130: Panoramas; p. 132: Photogra Fer; p. 135: MJM Photographie; p. 138: Vinicius Pinheiro; p. 149: Timothy Vollmer; p. 159: Kim; p. 165: Julien Menichini; p. 167: John Althouse Cohen; p. 168: Son of Groucho; p. 169: Rosemary Dukelow; p. 209: Ivailo Djilianov; p. 217: palm z; p. 218: Alex Castella; p. 219 top: Ruth L; p. 219 bottom: the_yes_man; p. 222: Naquib Hossain.

223

Visit **www.openroadguides.com** for a list of all
Open Road travel guides, to visit our blog, and to purchase
our books at great discounts!